Funny Cide

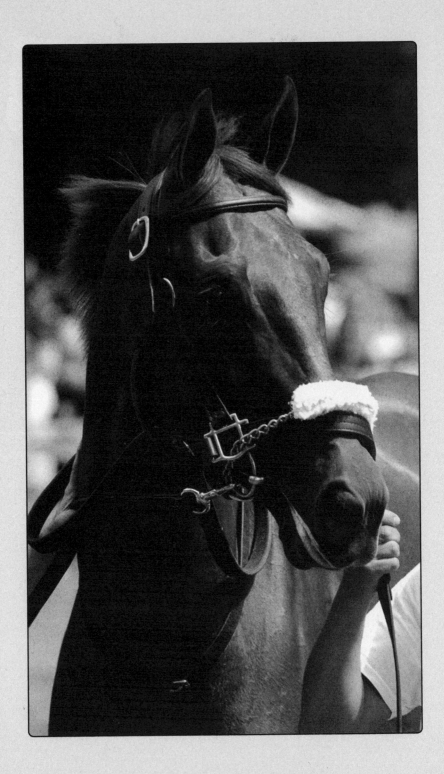

Funny Cide

*How a horse, a trainer, a jockey, and a bunch of high school
buddies took on the sheiks and blue bloods . . . and won*

The Funny Cide Team

with

Sally Jenkins

BERKLEY BOOKS

New York

THE BERKLEY PUBLISHING GROUP
Published by the Penguin Group
Penguin Group (USA) Inc.
375 Hudson Street, New York, New York 10014, USA
Penguin Group (Canada), 10 Alcorn Avenue, Toronto, Ontario M4V 3B2, Canada
(a division of Pearson Penguin Canada Inc.)
Penguin Books Ltd., 80 Strand, London WC2R 0RL, England
Penguin Group Ireland, 25 St. Stephen's Green, Dublin 2, Ireland (a division of Penguin Books Ltd.)
Penguin Group (Australia), 250 Camberwell Road, Camberwell, Victoria 3124, Australia
(a division of Pearson Australia Group Pty. Ltd.)
Penguin Books India Pvt. Ltd., 11 Community Centre, Panchsheel Park, New Delhi—110 017, India
Penguin Group (NZ), Cnr. Airborne and Rosedale Roads, Albany, Auckland 1310, New Zealand
(a division of Pearson New Zealand Ltd.)
Penguin Books (South Africa) (Pty.) Ltd., 24 Sturdee Avenue, Rosebank, Johannesburg 2196, South Africa

Penguin Books Ltd., Registered Offices: 80 Strand, London WC2R 0RL, England

PRINTING HISTORY
G. P. Putnam's Sons hardcover edition / May 2004
Berkley trade paperback edition / March 2005

Berkley trade paperback ISBN: 0-425-20030-2

The Library of Congress has registered the G. P. Putnam's Sons hardcover edition as follows:

Funny Cide : how a horse, a trainer, a jockey, and a bunch of high school buddies took
on the Sheiks and Blue Bloods . . . and won / the Funny Cide Team with Sally Jenkins.
p.   cm.
ISBN 0-399-15179-6 (alk. paper)
1. Funny Cide (Race horse).   2. Race horses—United States—Biography.
3. Horsemen and horsewomen—United States.   I. Jenkins, Sally.   II. Funny Cide Team.
SF355. F86   2004   2004044390
798.4'0092'9—dc22

PRINTED IN THE UNITED STATES OF AMERICA

10 9 8 7 6 5 4 3 2 1

This book is dedicated to all of Funny Cide's handlers, without whom the immense joy he has brought to his owners and fans would never have been realized.

Contents

PART III. A Classic Horse

PART I

Foal

1.

The Odd Stranger

What you know for certain is that you don't know nothing
for certain.

——ALLEN JERKENS, Hall of Fame trainer

Any sorehead disbeliever who
questions the abilities of nature would do well to spend time in a
horse barn. It defies odds that something as carefully aligned and
perfectly timed as a thoroughbred gets born, much less gets to the
Kentucky Derby. Yet things get born all the time, intended and un-
intended, mostly goats and people, but also ponies and donkeys,
and occasionally, through the juncture of chance, and notion, a
thoroughbred horse. A champion horse.

"A million things have to go right to win a race," Barclay Tagg
liked to say. "Only one thing has to go wrong to lose it."

Funny Cide was an improbable horse. The bettors didn't expect him, those backstretch habitués with their curled-up racing forms and their bad loafers, hawkeyeing for a long shot. The breeders didn't expect him, those hands-on gods of the equine universe. The owners didn't expect him, those incurable purchasers of hope. The trainers didn't expect him, either, those closet romantics stamping around in their boots.

We were gamblers, all of us, whether we admit it or not. What other sort of person would stake a dollar bill on an animal that runs on one toe at a time?

In the year 2000, there would be just 33,689 live thoroughbred foals born in North America. Of those, some would not survive infancy and the vast majority would never win a race. Only sixteen of them would run in the 2003 Kentucky Derby.

These were just the starting odds.

For this reason, some people, very rich people, tried to beat the game with their bank accounts. There were a lot of rich people in thoroughbred racing, and they were all rich in different ways. Some of them had "old money" and were named things like Ogden or Penny, and lived on thousand-acre farms that were listed in the National Register of Historic Places. Others were Arab sheiks, or Japanese entrepreneurs, or Houston oilmen, or Hollywood producers. But one thing they had in common was their willingness to spend breathtaking amounts of money on a promising thoroughbred. They traveled by Gulfstream jets and Cadillac Escalades, and they came to the annual thoroughbred sales at Keeneland or Saratoga to purchase exquisitely bred yearlings.

In the millennium spring of 2000, thoroughbred sales would total about $1 billion. Fifty-two yearlings, unraced babies that had never worn a saddle, went at auction for $1 million or more. It was the only sport in the world in which owners were willing to pay athletes seven figures before they ever competed.

As if you could beat luck with a checkbook. As if the weight of all that money could somehow flatten fortune.

If money and pedigree were such sure things, how come they so often failed? If the game was purely about bloodlines and money, the richest owner and the most expensive horse would win every time. But, see, they didn't.

"You always get the odd stranger," said Barclay Tagg's friend Tony Everard.

The odd stranger, the outcast, the overlooked: that was Funny Cide. He wasn't owned by a sultan or a scion. He was the property of ten working-class businessmen and laborers, six of them childhood friends from a tiny nook of New York called Sackets Harbor, who'd each thrown in a few thousand dollars on a dream. They didn't travel by Cadillac, but by yellow school bus. Their trainer wasn't a star but a journeyman of thirty years, and their jockey was a busted-up has-been. Everything about Funny Cide was uncommonly common: his sire was an unspectacular runner and unproven stud named Distorted Humor, who had won just eight races in his career, none of them longer than a mile. His dam, Belle's Good Cide, was an Oklahoma-bred mare who won just two of her twenty-six starts.

Even his name was un-regal. Funny Cide. It sounded like laughing yourself to death.

Funny Cide wasn't the product of money and breeding, but rather, of the vast middle class in horse racing. Had he belonged to a larger stable, or fallen into the hands of a less conscientious trainer, he might not have become what he did. But he was a fortunate horse. Later, everyone involved with him would muse on the word "if." If Joe and Anne McMahon hadn't foaled him . . . if Tony Everard hadn't seen something in the yearling . . . if Robin Smullen hadn't noticed his breathing problem . . . if the right people hadn't found him, bought him, and raced him . . .

You could say that when it came to Funny Cide, things just lined up, like the digits of a combination lock, or the spinning of a roulette wheel and a ball. You could argue long and hard about chance, and luck, and whether it takes skill to hit a long shot. But that doesn't get you anywhere in trying to figure out where Funny Cide came from, and why. What really happened was this: a group of small-time owners and trainers did the right thing by a sweet, unpromising horse.

He was a matter of dumb luck meeting up with hard work. It wouldn't be right to say you earned him—but it wouldn't be wrong, either. Maybe you let yourself in for a little luck after thirty years of labor to make a living for your family, in your boots or your necktie. After all those years of devotion, you make an educated guess and a bold wager. So did you earn it? Maybe, maybe not.

But did you deserve it? Hell, yes.

For five weeks from April to June of 2003, Funny Cide capti-vated the nation as he competed in the three-race classic of Amer-ican thoroughbred racing, the Triple Crown. At the same time, U.S. soldiers were fighting a foreign war, terrorists were lurking, cor-porations downsizing, pension plans collapsing. America needed something to cheer about, and it was Funny Cide. He made the front page of the newspapers in New York, and the network morning shows. By the time he ran in the final event, the Belmont Stakes, a total of 7.4 million households would tune in to see him, making the race the top-rated TV program of any kind for that week in

June. More than six million dollars would be wagered on him at off-track betting parlors. A hundred thousand people would sit in the rain for seven hours to see his stretch run. By then, it almost didn't matter whether he won or not. . . .

Sackets Harbor, New York

A workaday man named J. P. Constance stood on his front porch and blew on a horn. It wasn't a Viking blast, or a long elegant note of jazz, but a staggering, shrill, hilariously warped series of notes. If you listened hard, you could barely distinguish it as an off-key version of that tune from the racetrack—it was the "Call to the Post."

The notes echoed up and down Hounsfield Street, a small lane at the top of a hill in the village of Sackets Harbor. "Village" exactly described the shape and size of the place, because it wasn't big enough to be a town or a burg. It was just a painterly dash of color on the banks of the silver-gray disc of Lake Ontario, a body of water so seemingly horizonless it felt like God's own mirror. Scattered around a tiny crescent harbor was a collection of old Victorian shops and a grand total of 1,386 residents.

Most of the people of Sackets—that's how they referred to it, abbreviated it to just plain "Sackets"—knew each other. They'd known each other from grade school, through high school, and college, or the Army. Once they grew up, they sat next to each other on the planning board, or the school board, or the chamber of commerce board. Some of them married each other—Jack Knowlton, president of the Sackets High class of 1965, met his wife, Dorothy, at an eighth-grade dance. The natives of Sackets could count on two things: the steady wind that blew across Lake Ontario from Canada, and each other.

J. P. Constance was their former mayor. He had been elected, he liked to joke, by bribing his neighbors with fresh baked goods. "It took an awful lot of chocolate chip cookies," he said.

The closeness of the residents was in part a function of the remoteness: Sackets was nearer to the Canadian border than to a major U.S. city. A highway sign proclaimed:

CANADA 31
SYRACUSE 66

For any sign of a building taller than two stories, you had to go ten miles down the road to Watertown, New York, a company town for the U.S. military's Fort Drum, a notoriously tough posting that was the jumping-off point for the 10th Mountain Division. A soldier stationed at Drum was liable to be shipping out for Afghanistan or Iraq, and soon.

The only way to get to Sackets, other than by boat, was by a two-lane highway from Watertown that wove through farmland, most of it less than prosperous; farmhouses with cracked shingles, tin-roofed barns, and rusted silos. A roadside diner advertised, WE DON'T FOOL YA, WE FEED YA. At a **Y** intersection, a sign proclaimed, ENTERING HISTORIC SACKETS HARBOR.

From J. P. and Karen Constance's porch, he could see the homes of his best friends, most of them former schoolmates at Sackets High School. Directly across the street was his old friend and predecessor as mayor, Jean Derouin, and his wife, Jeannie. Next door was the home of Peter Phillips, a retired utility company worker and former head of the school board, and his wife, Bonnie. Just around the corner lived Peter's brother, Mark Phillips, a retired math teacher, with his wife, Gwen. At the far end of the block was the home of Bonnie's brother, Harold Cring, a construction company owner, and his wife, Stephanie.

J.P. himself had lived in Sackets since the third grade, and now he owned an optical shop in Watertown. He was a trim, bespectacled man of fifty-three with a neat wedge of gray-white hair, and he had the *ta-dum* personality of a stand-up comic. His conversation was a constant teasing patter, and his porch was often headquarters for neighborly social gatherings that amounted to block parties.

Hounsfield Street was comprised of a row of single-story, brick and siding ranch houses with good, well-tended gardens. At first glance, nothing set the street apart from any of the other narrow lanes of Sackets. But a second look left a more peculiar impression of incongruous details:

A mailbox with the silhouette of a racehorse emblazoned on it. A lamppost held up by a figurine jockey. A horse flag with a pattern of crimson and gray triangles, emblazoned with the name "Sackatoga."

J. P. Constance, lifelong resident, working man, village comic, and former mayor of Sackets Harbor, blew his horn. The noise was joined by the sound of laughter from the homes of his neighbors. Gradually, one by one, they emerged, and strolled up the street to J.P.'s porch. It was a call they all recognized.

It was the call to cocktail hour.

Belmont Park racetrack, New York

Barclay Tagg was looking for an excuse to quit, but he couldn't find one.

Tagg was tired, not just from working today, or yesterday, but from the last thirty-odd years. To look at him, his age was indeterminate; he was built like a knife blade, his body one long straight edge from his ironed polo shirt to his creased jeans, ending in sharp-toed leather boots with spurs. But there was something stiff and sore in the way he moved, and his chipped-razor of a face told the real story: that he was older than his looks suggested. In fact, he was approaching sixty-five, and a busted-up sixty-five at that. The stiffness was the result of his years as a steeplechaser when he was a young man, and his bones had the fracture lines to prove it—six cracked vertebrae. Now he had a steel rod in his back.

Every morning, Tagg arrived at Belmont's Barn Six in the dark to tend to his modest string of horses. For three decades he had risen at four-thirty A.M., hoisted himself onto and off of horses, fed them, hauled buckets, pried nails, raked hay, cleaned tack. In those thirty years, he'd taken three vacations.

Directly across a narrow asphalt road from Tagg's barn was another barn, emblazoned with the initials "DWL." The letters stood for D. Wayne Lukas, winner of thirteen Triple Crown races and the first trainer to reach $200 million in earnings, thanks to his corporatized approach to horses.

The Belmont barn was just one part of Lukas's massive and extravagant thoroughbred operation; at his peak in the 1990s, he once had as many as 250 horses in his care. Among his wealthy owners were software giants and rappers, and in one five-year stretch they had spent over $100 million on thoroughbred purchases.

On the side of the barn, a series of large painted plaques announced the names and victories of the various superstar horses that Lukas's stalls had housed. Thunder Gulch, winner of the Kentucky Derby and the Belmont. Charismatic, winner of the Derby and the Preakness. Tabasco Cat, winner of the Belmont Stakes.

Barclay had no such plaques on his barn. His Belmont operation consisted of eighteen stalls, and the stalls weren't always full, either. In a year, his owners might buy a few new horses. There had been some hard seasons when his string of horses dwindled down to two, or none. If he didn't have a barn full of contenders, it meant a threadbare winter. Barclay got to the point where he simply expected hard times, because thinking that way was a shortcut. Unlike Lukas, with his multiple strings of horses, each horse more regally bred than the last, and owners with limitless pockets, Barclay had to wait and work for the rare gem.

It wasn't a question of talent. Barclay was as good a trainer as you could find; anyone on the backstretch would tell you that. It was just that Lukas's odds of succeeding were simply better.

Barclay was respected among his peers, known as a horseman of deep knowledge and uncompromising methods who over the years had done more, with less, than just about anybody. He'd taken a lot of castoffs and turned them into nice runners, and he'd had thirty-eight stakes winners in all. But he'd never had the big horse.

The trouble was, he'd never been able to honey-talk an owner. He didn't have the stomach to persuade them to pay a million dollars for a yearling. He didn't know how to chitchat them on the phone. Or slick them over with explanations and excuses if the horse wasn't well and couldn't run.

Barclay didn't brook any interference. The first time an owner questioned him a little too closely, or suggested he should run the horse instead of rest him, Barclay's shoulders rode up around his ears and he got an edge to his voice. "If people are conscious that I'm honest and hardworking and trying to do what's best for them, and they pay their bills on time, I'm grateful to have them as owners," he'd say. "If they're going to second-guess you all the time, I don't want 'em."

For instance, he thought he'd found his big horse in 1985, a colt named Roo Art. The horse won each of his first four races. But the owners kept telling Barclay what to do—they insisted he race against tougher competition in New York, while Barclay wanted an easier race in Maryland. Finally, he opened his mouth and heard himself saying, "Look, I'm not comfortable training for you. I think you need to give this horse to Wayne Lukas. We'll all sleep better." The owners did what he suggested. Lukas won the Suburban Handicap with Roo Art.

But by the spring of 2000, after all the hardscrabble years, Barclay had finally cobbled together a decent, comfortable life. He'd raised two teenaged daughters by himself, put them through college, and now they were safely grown with lives of their own. He'd met the right girl, Robin Smullen, a superb horsewoman twenty years his junior, who'd become his partner. They worked together at the barn every day, and went home together every night.

He owned a cottage in Laurel, Maryland, and a condo in Florida, and thanks to the booming economy, swelling with high-tech and telecommunications stocks, he had a good portfolio of retirement savings. He did the math: as soon as he hit one million dollars in savings, he was done. He could retire.

Then the economic bubble burst. Enron, Adelphi, Tyson, AOL. The money evaporated. In a matter of months, Barclay Tagg's life savings were worth half what they had been. So he had to keep working.

People called Barclay a pessimist and wondered why he always looked for things to go wrong. But actually, he was just a realist. "You have a big, fat, shiny racehorse that's running beautifully," he said. "You leave the barn that night and the horse is fine. You go to the barn the next morning, and he's crippled himself in his stall."

That was how it went, whether you were talking horses, or stocks. There were just too many things that could go wrong. So instead of retiring, Barclay kept trying to find horses, and hoping nothing bad happened to them, and hoping something good might come along.

It was a game of hope, he told himself, and he'd been hoping for thirty years.

Belmont Park racetrack, New York

Jose Santos needed a mount, badly.

He was nearing forty-two years old, and it took two steel plates and a dozen steel pins to hold him together. He had four kids, one ex-wife, and, back home in Chile, seven younger brothers and sisters. He'd fired four different agents.

Santos had once been the nation's leading jockey. But in 1988, as soon as he rose to the top of the jockey list, it was as if the cables got cut, and he plummeted down again. He had suffered catastrophic injuries, a divorce, and debt. He'd been up and down so many times, he needed a seasick remedy.

By the spring of 2000, Jose was in another career stall, struggling simply to get decent mounts, and in an attempt to resuscitate his career, he fired yet another agent. He looked around for a replacement, and his attention settled on Mike Sellito, a laconic ex–New York cop who hung around the backstretch out of love for the horses. Sellito was known around the Belmont track as simply "Mike the Cop."

Sellito's first ambition was to be a police officer, but he was badly injured while tending to a roadside accident one day. A passing motorist struck him, and it tore up his knee. That made it hard to chase bad guys, so Mike decided to make a career out of the track, as a jockey's agent.

Together, Santos and Sellito made a curious and gimpy pair. Santos was a slight but muscled figure with a shock of pitch-black hair brushed back from his face, the bones of which stood out sharply. Sellito was a large, lumbering man with a stolid personality, and a way of quietly watching everything around him, even when he seemed oblivious. But they shared an understanding: they were both determined to make it, and in order to make it, they needed to find a good horse.

They showed up at the track at five A.M. and listened to word of mouth. They talked to backstretch gossips, and to exercise riders in the track kitchen. Jose was willing to gallop anything, long shots and bums. He wasn't cut out for any other kind of work. He just wanted to ride.

"It's my job, and I know how to do it," he told Sellito. "You give me a hammer, and I don't know what to do."

Saratoga Springs, New York

Jackson Knowlton was allergic to horses. He owned them. He bet on them. He handicapped them. Couldn't be around them.

Open any of the drawers in his desk in a whitewashed suite of offices at Empire Health Advisors, and you'd find a stack of magazines about horses. In the den of his Saratoga home, the tables were stacked high with magazines and newspapers and books on the subject: bloodstock, breeding, training, history. Jack spent the better part of six weeks every summer at the Carousel bar in the Saratoga clubhouse, poring over the *Daily Racing Form* with his pals and horse-owning partners Dave Mahan and Gus Williams. But if he got within a few feet of a horse, he started sneezing, and his eyes filled up.

Early in the mornings, you'd see Jack wandering the Saratoga backside, gazing at the panorama: horses galloping on the track, being washed and groomed, or hotwalked. But while other owners grilled their trainers in the shed row, or fed the horses peppermints from the flat palm of their hands, Jack kept his respectful distance. He stood somewhat apart from the barns, hands in the pockets of his slacks. (Consequently, he was the perfect owner for Barclay Tagg.)

To Jack, horses were the thinking man's wager. There were slots, and dice, and a game of blackjack, and who didn't enjoy raking a stack of chips across a felt table? But those were all forms of gambling, and there was a distinct difference between a gambler and a bettor. There were games of luck, and games of skill, and Jack believed that it took skill to bet on horses.

To hear him tell it, playing the horses fell somewhere between bridge and stock-trading. What's more, it was a noble three-hundred-year-old tradition. Even George Washington was a two-dollar bettor, back when one gentleman farmer bet another, "My horse is faster than yours."

Jack was a gamesman, in the old-fashioned sense. In high

school at Sackets Harbor, he was a star athlete, a halfback on the football team, and a shooting guard on the basketball team, and he played baseball and ran track for four years as well. As a sophomore, he'd knocked down a legendary winning shot to send tiny Sackets to the state sectional basketball tournament in Syracuse. But then it all ended; he was too small for an athletic scholarship, and he got to Ithaca College on an academic ride.

He'd spent his life at games, and suddenly, they were over. There was no more playing. In a way, the horses filled the empty place for him. He made his first serious wager in his senior year at Ithaca in 1969, when he was working on a degree in history and political science and sweating out the Vietnam draft lottery.

A lottery was another kind of luck—but in the Vietnam lottery, you hoped for the wrong number, a high number. Your draft number was seared into your brain, and into that of your parents, and of your fiancée. Nearly three decades later, Dorothy could still recite it: No. 289. Jack was lucky; he didn't get called up. Instead he went to a few peace marches, attended graduate school at the State University of New York at Albany, and got married to Dorothy, the girl from the eighth-grade dance, who was now in nursing school.

To Jack, racing was an intellectual puzzle: if you read the numbers smartly, considered the speed of the track and the previous performances of the horse, factored in all the available information, you could make smart bets and win more than you lost. That wasn't dumb luck. That was real *winning*, the ultimate control.

After Jack and Dorothy got married, they moved to Albany, thirty miles from Saratoga, and they'd go to the famous old racecourse, with its unmistakable turreted grandstand and antique clubhouse. It became their favorite way to spend a summer day off:

they would pack a lunch and go to the races. Eventually, they found themselves moving there; it was a beautiful old resort town, an oasis of sophistication in upstate New York. Saratoga's Union Avenue was proclaimed by Henry James to be the most gracious street in America.

Even after the kids came, a daughter in 1970 and a son in 1971, they still went to the track on summer days, wheeling the children in strollers. Jack would take the kids to the paddock and show them the horses. He'd point out the shine in their eyes, or something in their step.

As Jack got older and made a little money, he got into owning. In 1982, he started with standardbred trotters, buying in with some friends and neighbors, five guys who called themselves the Breakfast Club. You didn't have to be a millionaire to own a harness horse, you just had to come up with a few thousand dollars. But you *felt* like a rich man. You were the owner of something. Jack spent a dozen years as an owner in harness racing, running many of his standardbreds in $2,500 claiming races.

Jack had no illusions about the horse game: middle-class owners with moderately priced horses didn't get rich in racing, and sometimes they got poor. The statistics were staggering: a horse owner was likely to pay out two dollars for every dollar he earned.

But owning did something for him. In every other respect, his behavior was thoroughly responsible, even predictable. By the spring of 2000, Jackson Knowlton, the former two-time class president of Sackets High School, was now a diligent health-care consultant on the downside of his fifties. He was majority owner of his own firm, Empire Health Advisors, and had grown children. Jack didn't *seem* like the wagering type—unless you noticed the speculative arch to his eyebrow when it came to the horses.

To the layman, the thirty minutes before a race was a bore, but for Jack it was a time of wondrous workings in the mind. He calculated, evaluated, and searched his own good sense, and even, sometimes, his intuition. "Bet the mortgage on that one," he'd say.

To Jack, a good bettor looked for a value play. If you bet favorites all the time, you'd lose money. The odds were so stingy that even when the favorite won, it didn't pay very much—and not enough to offset the losses. Betting the favorites was a sure way to the poorhouse. If you wanted to stay ahead, you had to bet longer odds. You could bet a horse that had a shot at 5–1, or 6–1, or 7–1, but it was even better to make exotic bets with longer odds, such as exactas and trifectas. Then if you won, the rewards were considerably higher. That was a value play, a bet that made sense. It was all about being a smart risk-taker.

But sometimes, things didn't make any sense at all. Dorothy would pick a horse for the color of the silks, or because the name was cute, or out of superstition. That wasn't betting to Jack—even when she won.

In that summer of 2000, Dorothy decided to place a bet at Saratoga based on the date of her wedding day, August 23. She handed her son Aaron, newly graduated from college and already as much of a track habitué as his father, the sum of six dollars. She told him to make a bet for her when he went to the track that afternoon. She gave him careful instructions. "Play my anniversary," she said, "in a trifecta." She told him exactly which race and which horses to box: she wanted to bet the 8 horse, and the 2, and the 3.

Aaron went into the clubhouse, picked up a racing form, and surveyed the horses his mother had asked him to bet on. The horses

Dorothy had picked were the longest shots. There was no way they could win. He decided not to make the bet. He laid down a handful of smart bets for himself, and left the window.

But then he paused. His mother was bound to ask him if he'd made the bet. *You know what? I'd better put this in,* he thought. He went back to the window and got the bet down just in time, 8-2-3.

Aaron and Jack went to the backstretch to watch the race. Their own horses didn't come in, not one. Aaron tore up his tickets. He reached for his mother's ticket and glanced down at it, and checked the board. "Oh. My. God," he said. The board read: 8-2-3.

The trifecta was worth $2,600. The winning horse paid $100 on a two-dollar bet, and Dorothy had hit all three. It drove Jack crazy. Here he was pondering the odds and the track conditions, and Dorothy hit the big one out of blind superstition.

To Jack, the game was called "I'm smarter than he is." It was about testing his knowledge, and testing it against all the other bettors. With the invention of simulcasting—the system by which bets could be placed offtrack, from all around the country—it meant that a horseplayer was betting against innumerable opponents: against the house, the bookies, and 40,000 or so other bettors.

The game humbled him again and again—sometimes he'd pick five straight losers. But when he picked a winner, he walked on water.

To Jack, it wasn't about the money. It was about being right.

Lexington, Kentucky

A thoroughbred is a contradictory animal, at war with its own nature, a creature of locomotive strength running on legs of champagne-glass delicacy.

The head of a horse is designed less to hold a brain than it is to take in air. It's a large oxygen inhalator, turning vapor into speed. The heart and lungs are oversized knots of tissue placed in a massive chest purely for the purpose of sending blood coursing toward the hooves. Yet the feet and ankles are dainty.

Too often, the physical makeup of a horse isn't quite right: if the horse is fast, it's not strong enough, or if it's strong, it lacks stamina. Its chest might be too big for its legs, or its knees might be crooked. The thing to look for is conformation, a good figure.

But as Tony Everard liked to say, in a lilting Irish accent that made every word he spoke sound like wisdom, "That's just the outside of a horse. You can't look inside." Tony had seen some terrible-looking horses, "Horrible-legged things," as he called them, "but they were real runners."

Breeding a horse was like cracking a code: how to mate the right stallion to the right mare so as to produce a perfectly weighted, formed, and balanced animal. Breeders also tried to eliminate the unpredictable from the bloodlines; the weak, or the ordinary, or the unknown. They bred the best to the best—and hoped for the best.

Sometimes, a coupling between a top stallion and a broodmare produced exactly what a human mind envisioned: a beautiful, balanced racehorse. The greatest, like Secretariat and Affirmed, were bred for greatness, the offspring of other great horses. They began their careers as great horses themselves, and then only further verified their greatness.

But what confused matters was that sometimes poor runners made good sires, while sometimes great runners weren't worth a lick in the breeding shed. You saw it all the time, a mediocre thoroughbred that produced multiple stakes winners, while the greatest racehorse in the world might be a total bust. The nation's leading sire was a horse called Storm Cat, who, though he wasn't a spectacular runner himself, had produced ninety-two stakes winners in his first eleven crops of foals.

Nevertheless, in the spring of 2000, the thoroughbred market was booming. Buyers were paying those ever-soaring prices for yearlings with exquisite breeding, and the stud fees that produced them were skyrocketing, too. Storm Cat commanded a $300,000 stud fee, and with the latest farm technology, he could mate with more than 100 mares a season.

But as Andrew Beyer, the legendary horse-racing commentator for the *Washington Post* and the inventor of the Beyer Figures for judging thoroughbred speed, observed: "The breeding business today is beginning to look like a speculative bubble." People were buying and breeding horses, he remarked, with the same rationale "that once led investors to pay exorbitant prices for stocks in dot-com companies that never made a profit."

Why did people with money want only the best-looking horses, bred down to the smallest technicality in their pedigree? In a way, pedigree was just another attempt to reduce the dauntingly long odds of thoroughbred racing.

One of the top breeding and racing farms in Kentucky was Juddmonte Farms, an immense, rolling bluegrass expanse of 2,500 acres owned by the Saudi prince Khalid Abdullah. Juddmonte was home to more than 500 broodmares, and thousands of horses had jogged its pastures. Of those broodmares, among the most valuable was a fourteen-year-old lady named Toussaud, who was not only a fast runner herself but had produced blazing progeny, and done so consistently. In six attempts to foal, she had produced five stakes winners.

The breeders at Juddmonte thought so highly of her as a brood-mare that when they mated her, they did so with the Kentucky Derby in mind. Juddmonte, for all of its largesse, still had not pro-duced a Derby winner, despite the best efforts of its Hall of Fame trainer, Bobby Frankel, for over a decade. But then, a Kentucky Derby horse had to be bred for size, stamina, and speed all at once, and it didn't hurt to have fast-maturing genes, either. A Derby horse had to be able to run a mile and a quarter on the dirt around two turns by the age of three. It was the horse equivalent of asking a college kid to play in the Super Bowl.

Toussaud was bred to Juddmonte's best: Unbridled, the 1990 Kentucky Derby and Breeders' Cup Classic winner, a broad-shouldered, loping horse. Given Toussaud's record as a dam, and Unbridled's record as a runner, their progeny would surely be a su-perhorse.

By April of 2000, Toussaud was ready to foal. The new colt, the son of Unbridled, came into the world. He was dropped into a deep, comfortable bed in a capacious stall with doors the size of a garage, and with climate control. From the moment he was born, the foal was regarded as a potential superstar. He would be named, appropriately enough, Empire Maker. Three years later, he would in fact run in the Kentucky Derby, as the favorite.

But back in that spring of 2000, another dam was about to give birth. This one was housed in a small clapboard barn on a farm of just 350 acres in Saratoga Springs, New York. The farm was owned by Joe and Anne McMahon, a couple of reliable, self-made horse people to whom money meant a mortgage payment and grocery bills.

Late on the night of April 23, 2000, a night watchman on the McMahons' farm shone his light into a stall, and saw that a less than illustrious foal was about to be born.

"Whoa!" he called.

2.

Desperados and Weanlings

I guess in the end it worked out, because the right guy
bought him, and did a great job with him, and got him in the
next guy's hands, who was also the right guy. And the rest is
history.

—DOUG CAUTHEN, president and CEO of
WinStar Farms, breeder of Funny Cide

Light, and spring, make a horse.
A mare is sent into heat by the lengthening of days, and so each
year at rich, rolling emerald-grassed farms, the increase of daylight
meant that horses would be born. That, in turn, meant that Joe and
Anne McMahon wouldn't sleep much.

It was foaling season, and the McMahons had four barns full of
pregnant mares. Half of them were within a couple of weeks of
their due dates, and from eighty-five to ninety-five foals were expected, all told. Throughout March and April, the babies kept on
coming. They were popping out all over, sometimes two at the same

time, and they came at all hours. For some reason, many of them decided to be born between midnight and four A.M., which didn't just make for sleepless nights. It made for sleepless weeks, and sleepless months.

There was an endless cycle to the breedings, foalings, and weanings, and the work went on through the days and nights, so nothing could ever really be put away. Wheelbarrows, shanks, hoses, buckets, Bobcats, feed troughs, and giant bales of hay were ever at the ready.

Later on, the McMahons would laugh about how unremarkably Funny Cide arrived in their lives. They remembered him about as well as you could remember one of eighty-five foals who dropped into the straw on another long, sleepless night. There were no signs, no thunderbolts or lunar eclipses or flocks of eagles to announce his coming.

The McMahon farm in spring was 350 acres of fecundity. Their barns were neat, green-painted structures with shiny tin roofs, and inside the varnished plank stalls were swollen broodmares ready to foal, in deep beds of clean straw. A chalkboard at each stall detailed the care and feeding instructions of each horse. FABULOUS FANNY 1 SCOOP 2X DAY, KEEP IN FOR VET.

The McMahons' old Colonial brick farmhouse sat at the bottom of a verdant hillside made greener by massive weeping willows, which in the spring volunteered new limbs that swept the grass like brooms. At the foot of the hill, pastures gently flattened and rolled off into the distance, with nothing but occasional fencing and barns interrupting the view of mares and colts in the far fields, grazing.

A breeding farm was alternately the most gratifying and heartbreaking end of the thoroughbred business, and certainly the hardest end of it. You had to love horses, or you could never do it—it was just too much work. You started with an idea of a horse, not yet even a seed that could be planted, and tried to see it to fruition by putting a stallion with a mare. But there was occasionally a sad story. You found a stud, matched him with a broodmare, and nurtured the mare when she was with foal—and then you checked her one day, and what had been growing in her belly was simply gone. Somehow, she'd miscarried. Or, worse, a foal was turned the wrong way, or came to the world weak, and developed some ailment, and died. Or the mother got colic, or the foal hurt himself out in the paddock, an accident.

Even when the foals arrived easily and grew beautifully, with straight legs, in the end the McMahons sold them. Selling horses was their business—if they kept the best horses to themselves, then nobody would want to buy the others.

On the night of April 23, 2000, the McMahons were expecting two foals—or so they thought. Joe and Anne went through the barns at ten o'clock, just before the night watchman came on duty. They toured the stalls to make sure the mares were eating well, that none were colicky or agitated or acting peculiarly. If it wasn't like a mare to lie down, but she was on her side, or warm, or blowing, it meant something was wrong. When you were around horses as much as Joe and Anne were, you got to know when things weren't right. Neither of them noticed anything when they checked Belle's Good Cide. She was nearly two weeks premature, twelve days from her due date, and she didn't seem restless. They concentrated on the two mares that were due to deliver, Rajana's Honor and John's Little Lady.

Joe stayed with one mare, and Anne stayed with the other. If problems arose and a delivery turned difficult, it might take both of them to get a foal out. After checking the horses, they settled down to wait. Now for the next few hours they would carefully monitor the mares in labor. There would be no sleep for anyone; surely there was something they should be doing.

The McMahons' diligent night watchman, Donny Holden, arrived. Donny never missed a night tending to "his" horses. He lived with his wife, Barb, an hour down the road, and he watched over the horses like they were his own children, every single night. Sometimes, he and Barb would ride by the barn to check on them, even on his day off. He had a quiet, gentle rapport with the mares that many veteran handlers would envy. The mares knew and trusted him, and he could settle even the most fractious of thoroughbreds.

Donny paced the plank floors of the barns, double-checking on all of the horses and doing odd chores. Whatever needed to be done, he did: he fixed the water buckets, patched the screens, added extra bedding to the stalls, groomed mares, made friends with shy babies. He walked through the dimness of the barns and peered at each mare. He arrived at the stall of the Oklahoma mare, Belle's Good Cide. She moved in the darkness. Instead of sleeping or standing quietly, she was agitated. Her bags were dripping with milk.

"Whoa," he said, his voice ringing down the shed row. "Belle's foaling, too!"

Donny made Belle comfortable, and then he went to check on Anne and Joe, who had their hands full. Rajana's Honor and John's Little Lady had each just foaled. The wet, wobbly newborns and the mares were doing well, and they could be on their own for a little bit, so Joe and Anne and Donny all returned to Belle's Good Cide.

Two foals were not unusual. But three? It made for a very big night.

The McMahons made their living by ushering new things into the world, mostly foals, but there had been a time when they raised trees, too. Even in the hardscrabble years, they considered themselves lucky in their choice of work: they were in the business of newness.

They first met over horses, at Saratoga Race Course in 1968. She was a Skidmore girl, a doctor's daughter from Rhode Island with a skein of long brown hair, who had grown up loving and dreaming about horses, and riding for pleasure. He was a life-long race fan who had worked at the Saratoga Race Course as a groom, an exercise rider, an ambulance driver, a hot walker, and, in the off-season, a groundskeeper. He would do anything just to be at the track. How did a groundskeeper meet and marry a Skidmore girl? "Well, I was lucky," Joe would say later. "There weren't many pretty young girls who liked to hang around a racetrack out of season and talk to the maintenance crew."

Anne chose Skidmore because she was fascinated by the horse culture of Saratoga and by the antique beauty of the old grandstand and track. On the day that her father drove her to campus for a col-lege interview, they passed by the gracious turrets of the club-house, and she knew, "This is where I want to be." She would never leave Saratoga.

Anne loved to stroll through the grounds of the racecourse in the autumn, when it was closed for the season. She became friendly with an English professor and his wife, and began walking their Airedale, Tess, around the track. She would wander through the deserted paddock and infield, the wide-open spaces ringed by trees changing colors, daydreaming of steeplechase jumpers, or of the starting gates bursting open and horses charging through the apertures and down the dirt track.

She wandered through the dappled light into the paddock area, where she noticed a young man pruning the old maple trees. She paused to talk with him. Joe McMahon was the sort of guy who would still look basically the same thirty years later, thick brown hair curling across his forehead, good chin, and an outdoor build, the kind that came from working, as opposed to working out.

"Isn't it beautiful?" she said. He agreed, and they began chatting about the track's history, and about horses in general.

Joe's family had lived in Saratoga since the 1800s; his grandfather was a grocer and his father was a jeweler, but Joe never wanted to be anything but a horseman. He tried college for a couple of years, in western Nebraska, but he didn't like studying indoors, and he missed the horses, so he quit and came home, and he went to work back at Saratoga.

An arborist had his hands full at Saratoga, because the paddock, backstretch, and infield were studded with elms, maples, and oaks. The head arborist, Chuck Denew, taught Joe how to climb the trees and prune the limbs, and how to plant new trees to replace the ones that were damaged by ice storms or wind, or killed by Dutch elm disease. Joe learned how to trim away the dead wood, take out the dead trees, and plant the new saplings.

Anne began walking the Airedale to the racecourse regularly. She would find Joe and talk with him while the dog capered around the infield or backstretch. After a year of strolling and talking, they began to date, and things quickly turned serious. They both knew what they wanted: to marry and start a horse farm together.

By then he'd already bought his first horses, from a Saratoga sale for thoroughbreds that no one else wanted. You seldom bought a nice horse out of that sale, but Joe bought a two-year-old filly for seven hundred dollars, and another for two hundred dollars as a broodmare. These two would become their first racehorse and their "foundation" broodmare.

Joe and Anne were wed when she was a sophomore at Skidmore, in the summer of 1970. Next, Joe began looking for land on which to start their farm. He supported them by working at the track, and taking extra work as a tree-trimmer; he would drive around the city looking for dead trees, and go knock on the door and say, "Hey, I can take that tree down for you for two hundred dollars." Anne continued in school in the mornings, and she exercised horses on a local farm in the afternoons, including their own seven-hundred-dollar filly. Her name was No She Won't—but she did. She became a winner in her second start, a small success that convinced them more than ever that they wanted their own farm.

Joe was familiar with the old Tippett place. Everyone in town knew, or knew of, a wealthy old socialite named Liz Whitney Tippett. She had been married to Jock Whitney, the urbane sportsman and entrepreneur who had owned the *New York Herald-Tribune* and, for a time, the New York Mets. Liz Whitney had been beautiful once, and she was semi-legendary in Virginia and Saratoga horse circles as an eccentric carouser, as infamous as she was famous. She owned half a dozen estates in Virginia, Florida, Long Island, and Ireland. She summered in Saratoga, where everybody had a Liz Whitney story.

Joe had known her since the mid-1960s, when his uncle Howard Reilly was the caretaker of her property. One afternoon, Liz stopped the teenaged Joe as he worked at the track and asked if he wanted extra work. The race meet was ending, and so was her summer stay, and she needed someone to move her furniture from Saratoga to her home in Westbury, Long Island. He accepted, and she told him to come to her place, a large farm on the outskirts of town, at seven A.M. on a Monday.

Joe showed up at the appointed hour, with a truck ready to load. He rang the doorbell and waited. After a while, Liz Whitney Tippett opened the door in a purple muumuu. She was holding a long-neck bottle of Miller High Life.

"I'm not ready yet," she said, whiskey-voiced. "Come back at ten o'clock or eleven o'clock and we'll load it up then."

Joe had heard she was eccentric. After all, she went to and from Saratoga in a pink-and-purple four-passenger Bell Jet helicopter. He just said okay, and went to get breakfast.

When Joe came back later, she was more presentable, and he loaded the furniture into the truck, as well as her two white Alsatian dogs, and they drove to Westbury. It was the start of a peculiar relationship. He did odd jobs for her and enjoyed her idiosyncrasies, and they got to like each other in a mutually gruff kind of way.

Liz Whitney Tippett's farm was lovely but run-down. She had planted most of the acreage with Christmas trees, nearly a hundred thousand of them, because someone had told her it was a way to put the land to use and make money. But the farm had become overgrown, and it needed better care. Shortly after Anne and Joe had their first son, Michael, in 1971, they moved to the farm to become caretakers.

The McMahons had barely settled in with their new family when, one day in 1972, they heard from a neighbor that Liz was thinking of selling the farm. A well-heeled young couple showed up to look at the house. As Anne showed the prospective buyers around the property, she did whatever she could to discourage the sale. She mentioned that the farm sat outside the Saratoga Springs school district, and therefore it was a bad place to raise children. She mentioned how terrible and sulfurous the well water was. After the couple fled, Joe called Liz and asked if the place was really for sale.

Liz said she wouldn't mind selling it. Joe said, "For how much?" She thought about it and said, "Fifty thousand." But there was a caveat. She insisted on retaining the rights to the Christmas trees for two years. The sale price was $50,000, plus two dollars a tree for any trees they sold in the next two years. Liz had no idea about Christmas trees, how to grow them or cut them, but she wasn't going to give them away. She was going to get her money out of those trees.

It was exactly what Joe and Anne were looking for, a spread big enough for horses, but close to town and affordable. They agreed to buy the farm. Joe and Anne moved with their baby into the run-down house, and they stabled their first horses in five makeshift stalls.

They had a second son, and watched the trees grow, wondering how they would ever get them out of there. Shortly before their second Christmas on the farm, a guy presented himself at the McMahons' front door. He said, "I'm from down in Alexandria, Virginia, and I'm buying these Christmas trees from Liz Tippett." Joe just stared at him and said, "Sure." He took him out and walked him around the farm. The whole place was Christmas trees.

The visitor said, "Well, I only want to buy three thousand of them." They struck a deal. Joe cut about 800 trees and stacked them at the edge of the road, and the visitor loaded them on his tractor trailer and drove away. Joe went back into the fields and cut another 2,200 of those Christmas trees and stacked them up, huge piles of them by the road. But the guy never came back. The trees just sat there.

Exactly two weeks before Christmas, Joe called Liz. "Listen, this guy hasn't come back for these trees," he said. "Has he paid you anything for them?"

"No," she said. "He's supposed to pay me after he sells them."

"Well, I don't think he's coming back."

"What should we do?"

Joe thought for a moment and then said, "Let's sell them ourselves." He suggested they put an ad in the paper, "Christmas trees for sale." So that's what they did: he and Liz Whitney Tippett went into the Christmas-tree business together.

Joe put an ad in the *Albany Times Union,* "Any tree $4, pick your own from 2,000 trees!" People came out to the farm to pick out and buy their fresh-cut Christmas trees on the cheap, and in two weeks, he sold them out.

Christmas morning came. At about seven-thirty, Joe and Anne were opening presents with their little ones when the phone rang. He picked up the receiver and said, "Merry Christmas."

He heard a rough whiskey voice say, "How did we do?"

"Who is this?" he asked.

"It's Liz. How did we do?"

Joe tried not to burst out laughing. He managed to say, "I think we did all right."

"Are you going to send me a check this week?"

"Yeah, I'll send you a check this week."

"How much for?"

It was as if it were the last dollar she was waiting on. Joe said,

"We sold about a thousand of them. Why don't we split the money? I did all the work and you supplied the trees."

She said, "Well, you take whatever you need to out of it, and send the rest to me."

Joe agreed, and she abruptly hung up. She never said "Merry Christmas" or "Thank you." Just "Send me a check this week."

Joe and Anne thought it was hilarious, and they suspected that Liz thought so, too, because she delighted in telling the story. For years afterward, until she finally died, she regaled dinner parties with the tale of how Joe McMahon had made a fortune off of her Christmas trees.

"That son of a bitch McMahon stole my farm from me," she'd say, "and now he's getting rich out there on my trees."

The McMahons weren't getting rich.

They did anything they could to earn extra cash, and they put every penny back into the farm. They took in horses as boarders, broke yearlings, and transported other people's horses. They even repaired tack. And, of course, they raised and sold Christmas trees.

They had no idea what they were doing in the beginning, except that they had to make it work. They cleared pastures, built barns, and put up fences. The two-hundred-dollar mare had her first foals in 1971 and 1972, and both became winners at the track. One was named Cider Hill, because Anne trained him by galloping him up the slope to a neighboring apple orchard. The other they called Ghost Road, because Michael thought he looked like a ghost when he was draped in his white fly sheet after training. When they sold their first yearlings for $6,500 and $7,500 apiece, it was a huge windfall.

Foaling was an around-the-clock job, and so was raising a family. Their own family grew to five children: Mike, John, Jane, Kate, and Tara. Joe and Anne moved through the days, and the months, and the years, constantly on the brink of exhaustion.

Sleep was a catnap after lunch. If they wanted more than that, they had to wait until summer. In the early days of running the farm, Anne would nap on Little League benches. While her boys played ball, and other parents whooped and applauded, or yelled at the umpires, Anne sat with her eyes half-closed, struggling not to doze and fall off the bench. The crack of the bat, or the slap of the ball in a glove, would startle her awake. Joe worked nonstop, rarely getting to the games at all.

Once, Anne fell asleep at a gymnastics meet. While her daughters tumbled on the mats and danced across the bars and beams, Anne found herself leaning her head against a wall, her eyes closing into deep, blank unconsciousness.

As the kids grew up, they worked the farm alongside Joe and Anne, and they became horsemen and -women in their own right. John and his fiancée, Kate, went off to New Zealand to study farming and came back with new ideas for pastures. Jane and her husband, Rodrigo Ubillo, managed the stallions. Kate and Tara worked with yearlings. Their eldest son, Mike, specialized in bloodstock, and he married a Kentucky veterinarian, now Natanya Nieman McMahon, D.V.M.

Each year, Joe and Anne tried to upgrade the farm. They parlayed that first two-hundred-dollar mare into a little more every year: better bloodlines, or more animals. Cash was always short, because every penny had to be put back into the horses, into trying to produce a better-quality thoroughbred.

It was a high-risk business. So many things could go wrong: if you overlooked one small thing, it could turn into a crisis—and you'd pay for it for a year.

First of all, the majority of stallions were busts. The rule of thumb was that nine out of ten stallions failed to produce runners. If a breeder invested in a sire and it failed, within three years your asset had gone from 100 percent valuation down to 5 percent.

Money was everything in the horse-breeding business: you needed money to expand, money to buy better stallions, and money to buy better mares, so you could breed better foals. For which you could charge more money. Without money, you were limited.

For that, though, there was something called the New York State Thoroughbred Breeding and Development Fund. The program was designed to give the state's fledgling thoroughbred business a leg up, and to keep farmers on their land. The McMahons benefited from the fund over the years and used it make crucial improvements, and eventually Joe would become active in promoting it. Slowly and steadily, they built the farm until they could raise and sell enough horses to pay the mortgage.

It took a decade of work to clear all the Christmas trees. Once a tree was gone, they didn't replant. Eventually, field by field, they cleared the land, removing the stumps, bulldozing and smoothing the ground and turning it into pastures. It wasn't until 1980 that Joe was free to work the farm full-time and could get out of the tree-removal business.

By the late 1990s, the McMahons had been making their living on the farm for thirty years, but it had never once been easy. They remained a small farm of a hundred acres with about twenty-five foals a year. They were still struggling to grow. The motivating factor was the same as always: they didn't have enough money.

The McMahons did, however, have something else by now: knowledge and experience. Perhaps they could trade that for better horses. They looked toward the larger Kentucky horse farms with the idea of making a swap. They looked in particular to a large farm in Versailles, Kentucky, called Prestonwood, where they heard there was a problem stallion. The rumor was that the horse was so difficult that Prestonwood wanted to get rid of him. His name was Personal Flag, and he was an absolute desperado of a horse; no one could get near him without feeling his teeth or his hooves.

Practically everyone in the business had stories about Personal Flag. The horse was savage to his handlers; he kicked people, bit them, went after them with his teeth and *tried* to hurt them. He didn't just take a bite. Once he got ahold of you, he didn't want to let go.

But Personal Flag was a valuable horse, too. The fact that he would fight back meant that he had the right stuff to be a racehorse, and to sire racehorses. He was the kind of horse who was not intimidated. But he was wary, and he perceived the procedures of horse care, and most of his handlers, as threatening. His reputation preceded him, and in turn his handling got rougher. When a horse is treated as if he will be dangerous, he becomes even meaner. So far, no one had learned how to work with this horse without causing a fight.

Prestonwood tried different tactics with the horse, but he simply hated humans. The farm even brought in a horse whisperer to try to gentle the horse, one of those semi-mystics who got inside the head of an animal. But the horse whisperer said, "This is a difficult horse. You're not going to re-educate him."

Prestonwood was in a dilemma. The horse was a badass—but he was a very successful stud, and he had good foals. His offspring were talented, and very popular with New York bettors, too.

Any horse farm was a perpetually high-risk investment for its owners, and the larger the farm, like Prestonwood, the higher the stakes. The stallion business was as speculative and high-risk as any endeavor outside a casino. A successful stallion prospect had to balance the books for a lot of losses. Personal Flag was as valuable as he was difficult.

Joe called the manager of Prestonwood, a guy named Rich Decker, and introduced himself, describing his farm and his experience as a breeder. "I've heard of you," Decker said. "I know who you are." Joe explained that he was interested in talking to him about Personal Flag. He was aware that the horse was a management problem: maybe the horse would fare better at a small farm, with consistent hands-on care, than at a big farm where he tried to bite the arm off of a different groom every day.

Joe was in need of a new stallion, he said, and Prestonwood was looking to get rid of a problem horse. He proposed a deal: he would take the horse and see what they could do with him, in exchange for a controlling interest in him. Decker, intrigued, agreed to the deal. He would ship the horse to the McMahons and re-syndicate him in New York. "Do whatever you can to make a profit," Decker said. He all but said, "Take him. Just get him out of here."

It was the McMahons' theory that a small farm was sometimes a better home for a desperado horse. While large breeding farms

were luxurious and beautiful settings, they worked on rigid schedules and insisted on a certain look and behavior from the animals.
Horses were showpieces, very much on view, shiny and spotless at
all times, more like expensive movie stars than regular animals. A
horse at a large, famous Kentucky farm wasn't allowed to stand in
its stall dirty from rolling in the pasture.

When the staff was told to turn the stallions out at four o'clock,
that's what they did, and there were too many horses to deal with
to give each animal a choice in the matter. If Personal Flag didn't
want to be turned out, that was too bad. But when Personal Flag
didn't like his routine, he got nasty. He refused to cooperate, and
then the grooms tried to force him, and then the horse got really
mad, and they ended up in a fight.

Prestonwood sent Personal Flag all over the world as a stud. It
was common practice to ship Northern Hemisphere stallions to the
Southern Hemisphere so they could breed in the off-season, too,
and Prestonwood wasn't sorry to be rid of him. It didn't matter
where he went; his handlers had an awful time. Soon they couldn't
even hire a groom for him. Overseas, word went around as to how
to deal with Personal Flag: you needed two handlers, each of them
with a baseball bat for self-defense. If the horse went after one
handler and started chewing, the other one would threaten him
with the bat.

Prestonwood arranged to ship Personal Flag back to the States
from his stud tour overseas. First, he had to go to a federal quarantine barn, where horses that had been out of the country were observed for seventy-two hours to make sure they had no problems
or illnesses.

Joe arrived to pick up Personal Flag from quarantine on a cold night in December. He stood at a loading bay and watched as stallion after stallion was walked down the shed row and onto a loading ramp. A federal agent would yell out the name of a horse, and a handler would step forward to take possession of him and load him into a van.

At two o'clock in the morning, Personal Flag still hadn't arrived. Now the place was almost deserted. The only people left in the quarantine area were Joe and the vet who was in charge.

"You're here for Personal Flag, aren't you?" the vet said.

"Yeah," Joe said.

"Well, he's kind of tough," the vet said. "We didn't think it would be a good idea to bring him down here with all these people around. We were afraid that he might hurt somebody."

The vet didn't even want to walk Personal Flag out of the barn. Instead, he suggested that Joe load Personal Flag straight from his stall onto the truck. The less walking Personal Flag had to do, the less chance there was that he would lunge at a handler.

The vet said, "You can drop the ramp right here," and pointed to a spot *inside* the barn. "Personal Flag is down in that end stall," he said. With that, the vet backed away.

Joe walked down to Personal Flag's stall. Leaning on the wall outside the stall were two wooden clubs. A handler gave the clubs to Joe. "There he is," he said, and stepped back. Joe realized that the barn crew was still hanging around. Joe got the feeling they wanted to see if Personal Flag was going to draw blood.

But that night, there was no blood spilled. Personal Flag didn't put up a fight; he allowed himself, if warily, to be loaded into the van, and Joe brought him home to Saratoga without incident.

When they arrived at the farm, Joe opened the van to find that his new killer horse had broken his halter and torn his blanket off.

Joe summoned Anne. Together, they would have to put a new halter and blanket on their horse and get him into the stall. Joe
climbed into the trailer and carefully approached the horse, wondering if he was in for a fight, but Personal Flag let him slip the
halter on without a skirmish. Joe said to Anne, "I'll hold him, you
put the blanket on." They led him out of the van without any trouble at all. *Maybe he isn't as bad as his reputation,* Anne thought.

For a couple of days, the horse seemed all right—as long as nobody touched him. He was peaceful and happy out in his paddock,
with a blanket on, despite the fact that Saratoga was enduring a
brutal cold spell; it couldn't have been more than ten degrees even
in the sun, and it dropped to twenty below at night. Personal Flag
just wandered his paddock, and showed no signs of wanting to
come into a barn.

Joe and Anne didn't try to chase him or herd him. They just
opened the gate and asked him if he wanted to come in. Finally,
after a couple of days, he decided to walk through the gate. From
then on, he began to trust them. Progress had been made.

The way Joe and Anne saw it, Personal Flag was an older horse
who was tired of doing the bidding of humans, and of having his
routine pleasures interrupted. You didn't try to bully a horse like
that and say, "You're going to do things our way."

Instead, the McMahons decided to meet Personal Flag halfway.
Since he was basically a breeding horse, not a show horse, they
didn't need to groom him to make him look pretty. His talent as a
stud was well known, and anyone who checked the record book
could see what kind of offspring he'd thrown. That ought to be
good enough. What did it hurt to let him go muddy and uncombed,
if that's what made him happy? "Let's live and let live," Joe said.

There was one last fight coming: the McMahons brought Personal Flag to the breeding shed. Awaiting him was a gray mare. He immediately went after her. He bit her on the neck, and she began gushing blood all over the shed. Joe called a halt. "We can't deal with this," he said. "I'm not going to do this to a mare." He put Personal Flag back in the barn.

"We've got to find a better way," Joe said to his son, John, the stallion's chief handler.

"What do you want to do?" John asked.

"Let's put a muzzle on him."

But everyone who worked with Personal Flag had found it impossible to muzzle him; he fought and reared.

"They said you can't do that."

"Well, we have to do something."

Joe decided to try the horse equivalent of a pacifier on Personal Flag. He unearthed a leather muzzle and handed it to John. "Put that up in front of his mouth, and let him bite on it, and maybe that will calm him," he said. "When he grabs ahold of it, he'll think he's grabbing you. And then maybe we can just snap the muzzle on him."

John was a very fit guy who was used to handling big horses, but just in case, Joe said, "I'll stand by the door here, in case he gets really wild and you start losing the battle."

John nodded, and went into the stall. Very calmly, he took hold of the horse and showed him the muzzle. Personal Flag gave him a long look—and all of a sudden he tried to rear away. Luckily, his stall had a low ceiling, and he couldn't reach his full height, which was a big seventeen hands. Still, he hauled John three feet into the air, whipping his head around and trying to shake him off. John was strong enough to hang on, swaying above the ground. He didn't panic, and just stayed with it until the horse came down again.

Calmer now, Personal Flag began chewing on the muzzle. John quietly snapped it closed. He'd won the battle.

They took Personal Flag to the breeding shed, and he bred his mare. Then they brought him back to his stall and took his muzzle off. And from then on, they bred Personal Flag without problems.

Joe and Anne would always believe that if it hadn't been for Personal Flag, they never would have had Funny Cide. It was the start of a flourishing partnership with Prestonwood. The good relationship between the farms was largely due to the friendship between the McMahons' son Mike, and a young bloodstock agent at Prestonwood, Doug Cauthen.

Eventually, Prestonwood came under new ownership; it had been owned by some Houston oilmen, Art, Jack, and J. R. Preston, but in late 1999, the Prestons sold out to a couple of fellow Texans, Kenny Troutt and Bill Casner, who renamed it WinStar. They bought everything, lock, stock, and barrel, including Personal Flag.

Personal Flag wasn't the only problem WinStar had bought. The farm had also inherited some broodmares that weren't of very exciting quality, and it was costing $20,000 to $30,000 apiece yearly to keep them living in the style to which they were accustomed. The farm couldn't get a good sale price for the mares, and their foals wouldn't bring much, either. WinStar's new CEO, Doug Cauthen, had to figure out what to do with them.

Again the McMahons provided an answer. Mike McMahon hit on the idea of sending the mares in foal to New York. Joe and Anne had been successful in partnering with Prestonwood on stallions, so why not ship the broodmares up north to Saratoga, so they could foal there? That way, the offspring would be eligible for the lucrative, restricted New York racing program.

New York offered year-round racing and healthy purses at showplace tracks such as Belmont, Saratoga, and Aqueduct. But to be eligible for many of the races, a horse had to be born in New York. There were only 3,000 or so mares in the state, and they produced about 2,000 foals every year, which made for a small talent pool. If WinStar made some of its foals eligible to race in New York, they would be big fish in a small pond.

It would be a joint venture: WinStar would supply the mares, and the McMahons would supply the care and feeding, the veterinary tending, and the work. They would be fifty-fifty partners in the mares and offspring.

WinStar sent up nine mares in foal, carrying the first progeny of Distorted Humor, a nice sprinter who had won several graded stakes races. This would be his first crop as a sire. One of the mares he impregnated was Belle's Good Cide, the unremarkable Oklahoma-bred daughter of Slewacide that WinStar had inherited upon purchasing the farm.

No one thought of it as a particularly valuable pairing. Distorted Humor's stud fee was just ten thousand dollars.

It was quiet in the barn, almost peaceful, except for Belle's groans when she pushed. The groans were not unlike the sounds the mare made when she was snoring, a deep, thousand-pound thoroughbred exhalation. There was no screaming or whinnying. The strong muscles of her underbelly would spasm, and she would sigh and push, and a long, low sound would come from deep in her throat.

Every once in a while, Belle got up for a moment, and then she lay back down. Each time she did so, it was nature's way of turning the foal, of ushering it through the pelvis and closer to delivery. Joe and Anne watched carefully for signs of real trouble—if the mare's labor lasted for too long or became violent, it could mean a bad presentation—but there were none. The foal was properly presented, nothing awkward or incorrect about his position.

Belle's foal would be the third of the three born that night, and Joe and Anne were so busy that there really wasn't much time to take note of anything except that he was healthy. A normal foaling, from start to finish, generally took about half an hour once the baby started to come. The mare's labor depended on how hard she pushed, and on how big the foal was: an average-sized colt weighed between 100 and 120 pounds.

It wasn't a hard foaling, because he was a narrow little thing, slimmer than most. He just slipped into the world. At about ten-thirty, the new foal dropped into the straw and broke from the sac clean and wet.

Once he arrived, the McMahons didn't interfere much. Some breeders might rush in with a supply of fresh towels and wipe the foal off, but the McMahons believed the mare needed to bond with the foal, and they didn't want to interrupt nature. She began to nuzzle him and lick him clean. They just watched closely to make sure that everything was all right.

He got to his feet. He looked around brightly, as if to say, "I'm here." He was a leggy, vigorous thing, they noticed. Some foals were born weak, especially premature ones, and you had to work with them for a while to get them going. But this foal got up easily, and he was quick to go to his mother to nurse.

The foal slept, and nursed. The following day, they gave him a routine blood test to be sure he had absorbed immunities from his dam's milk. The test result wasn't quite right, it showed he hadn't gotten enough protection from the mare's colostrum, but this was an easy fix; a transfusion of plasma gave him the antibodies.

As the foal grew, he also grew in the affections of the McMahons. He was a bit small in stature, but he had a broad, muscular back and an unusually shiny, deep-red coat. His disposition was willing, bright, and playful, and he was almost perky in the way he held his head and carried himself. He became one of Anne's favorites to lead in and out of the barn at feeding time.

But when the vet, Annina Lacour, arrived to give him his vaccinations, he fought like hell. He refused to be handled or pushed around. He kicked his legs everywhere, furiously trying to avoid the needle. To the vet, it was a good, healthy sign: it meant he was a competitive horse.

When the foal was only a few days old, the McMahons got a call from WinStar's Rich Decker, asking to buy back Belle's Good Cide and her foal. One of WinStar's owners, Kenny Troutt, had researched Belle's bloodline and decided she had some value, after all; another of her offspring was training well in Florida, so they wanted to keep her. The McMahons agreed. In exchange, they got full ownership in another mare and a foal that they later sold for $105,000. It was a huge profit—but later, it would look like they'd traded away the lottery ticket. "It was a good deal that day," Joe would say.

For the next five and half months, Funny Cide lived at the McMahon farm with his mother. At first, Belle and Funny stayed together in the same stall and were turned out each day into a pasture with other mares and foals. The foals stood next to their mothers, rubbing up against them and staring around curiously, and cautiously exploring. Gradually the foals became playmates, shoving each other, dropping their heads and kicking, and capering around. The McMahons were creating a pack, so that when it was time for the foals to be weaned, it would be less traumatic for them.

Weaning was a stressful time for everyone: for the foals and mares, and for Joe and Anne, too. The foals had to be separated from their mothers so that they could be prepared for the sales. There was no easy way to go about it, but over the years Joe and Anne had learned ways. They weaned them together, in age groups, so that the foals weren't so bereft. Two at a time, the mares were led out of their fields and taken off the farm, leaving two weanlings to buddy up and be friends. As before, Funny Cide was turned out in a pasture alongside the same foals with whom he had grown up— but it was the last time the foals would see their dams. Sometimes, when their mothers didn't return after an hour or so, the foals began to protest. They cried and grew agitated, moving in circles, stamping and exhaling in frustration. But together in a field, the herd mentality took over, and the foals got over the shock of separation.

That spring and summer in the McMahons' pasture, the weanlings tried to outrun one another from one end of the field to the other. They play-raced, shoved each other, tried to knock each other down, and practically wrestled. It was like watching a pack of teenaged boys.

Doug Cauthen of WinStar came to the McMahons' farm to look at the weanling they had partnered. He saw what the McMahons saw in Belle's foal, "a nice, decent horse," but nothing extraordinary. There was nothing to suggest that he would be an especially valuable colt, except that he had an exceptional shoulder and girth, and a nice long stride.

The WinStar execs decided to move the weanling back to Kentucky to raise him and prepare for the sales. Some Kentucky horse people thought that even the grass and the soil of their state were superior—it was supposed to be something about the limestone. The WinStar people wanted to eye the new weanling firsthand and watch how he grew. Depending on how he matured, he might sell in Kentucky rather than New York.

But as Funny Cide matured, his looks did not improve. He wasn't filling out and turning into the kind of colt wealthy buyers at the Kentucky sales were likely to spend a lot of money on. WinStar decided he would be better received in New York and returned him to the McMahon farm. They asked the McMahons to consign him to the Fasig Tipton sale for New York–breds, a less competitive market.

On the evening of August 12, 2001, in Saratoga Springs, New York, the as yet unnamed colt made his first public appearance. He was a rough-looking little chestnut as he stood beside a barn, surveyed by unimpressed buyers. One after another, owners and trainers passed on the horse. Worse than the colt's unproven and somewhat commonplace breeding was his appearance. He was narrow and immature. "Backward" was the way he was viewed by the staff at WinStar.

Joe McMahon was more blunt. He called him "roach-backed and clubfooted." In Joe's opinion, the colt was a little awkward, with his hind end higher than his front. Also, it looked like he might have bad feet. It took years for a thoroughbred's hooves to grow, and when they showed signs of going wrong, it was a bad sign for a racehorse's future. In Funny Cide's case, the angle of his hooves was too steep. You wanted a nice forty-five-degree angle. This colt seemed to be standing on his toes.

Among the buyers at the sale that night was Barclay Tagg. He paused and looked at the horse. He ran his eye over the narrow

form, the shoulders, and the hindquarters. He surveyed the yearling's legs and stopped at his feet. To a veteran trainer, that was a
liability. It meant the horse could be vulnerable to soreness, easily injured. Tagg moved on.

Only one man stopped and took notice of WinStar's chestnut
yearling. He was a sixty-something pinhooker and transplanted
Irishman from Ocala, Florida, named Tony Everard. "Pinhooker"
is racing slang for someone who buys young horses on the cheap,
trains and improves them, and then tries to resell them for a large
profit. It's one of the more difficult ways to earn a living in the thoroughbred world, but Everard was known as a good pinhooker who
routinely sold horses for two and three times more than he paid for
them. He had an eye. He was also regarded as a first-rate trainer
of young horses; owners often sent their yearlings to Everard's New
Episode Training Center to learn to become racehorses.

Everard always looked at the McMahons' weanlings because
they had a long-standing relationship in the horse business. Everard knew they ran a good farm. They raised a strong horse, fed well
and wisely, and were honest about the animal's faults and virtues.
He'd had good luck with the horses he bought from them. He'd purchased a colt named Instant Friendship for only $16,000, and it
went on to win more than $1 million. Also, Joe always showed
Tony the ones he liked the best.

Everard liked the little colt well enough—despite the feet—to
ask a vet to examine him. The vet went over him and found no
problems, save for one. "He's a ridgeling," the vet announced.
"Ridgeling" meant he had one un-descended testicle, and it wasn't
necessarily a problem. Everard wasn't unduly concerned.

Everard was the highest bidder and purchased the horse for
$22,000. It was an extremely moderate price by the Fasig Tipton

standards. The more majestically bred babies at Fasig Tipton sales would go for seven figures. But not this one.

Everard arranged for his new horse to be shipped to his sixty-five-acre farm in Ocala. Also on the shipment to the New Episode Training Center were several other horses from the New York sale that Everard had agreed to break and train for a price. At the New Episode Training Center, the yearling was turned out in a far pasture with a dozen other colts. It would be his home for the next eight months.

Back in Saratoga, Joe and Anne McMahon didn't think much about his departure from their lives. They were too busy building and expanding the farm, getting ready for next winter's new foals, and enjoying their grandchildren.

On fall afternoons when the racing and foaling seasons were over and the barns were quiet, Joe liked to take his grandsons to the deserted Saratoga Race Course, and sometimes he would point out the trees and tell them he used to take care of them. The trees didn't mean much to anybody else, but to Joe and Anne they marked their relationship, their lives and family in Saratoga, and their dream of owning horses. He would stroll in the paddock with the little boys, point to a handsome young oak, and say, "I'm particularly proud of that one." He had helped to plant it, and it had grown, and now it was a good-sized tree.

3.

The Sackets Six

You don't ever win in this game, because you immediately go
out to some expensive place and pay five or six dollars for a
Coors Light.

—J. P. CONSTANCE

Hardly anybody knows any-
body for fifty years anymore. It's not that kind of world; friends de-
tach, families move, and the average American eighteen-year-old
can expect to have had 9.2 jobs by the time he or she reaches thirty-
four, according to the Bureau of Labor Statistics. But in Sackets
Harbor, J. P. Constance or Harold Cring could walk down Main
Street and pass their old grade-school teachers, ladies in their
eighties who were still living there. It was one of the charms, or pe-
culiarities, of dwelling in the same place they grew up: they were
eternally reminded of their childhoods. Even as middle-aged men,
they couldn't always bring themselves to call their old teachers by

their first names, Sally or Thelma. Instead they'd nod and say, "Hi, Mrs. Kimmett," and "Hi, Mrs. Thomas."

The seasons changed in Sackets, but the people didn't. In the summer, the fields were full of fat rolled hay, and dotted by gray tinder-like barns and rusted-out cars. Stands of oaks and beeches waved, and the air was heavy with humidity and sweet with oxygen, and you could buy sunflowers and fresh honey from roadside stands. But in the autumn, the air went cold and dry, and wedges of birds shot across the pewter sky, which was indistinguishable from the gray lake. Everyone put their boats up in their backyards and shut up the barns to wait for the snow that would lie like a quilt on the countryside for months, until spring.

On Memorial Day of 1995, Jean Derouin hosted a spring picnic for his friends and neighbors in his backyard on Hounsfield Street. Most of the people milling around on the lawn had lived in Sackets their entire lives, departing only briefly for college or the service before returning to find professions, buy homes, and raise families. They were such a close group that later J.P. would joke, "If one of us had bought an airplane, all of us would have taken flying lessons."

Sausages and hamburgers smoked on a grill, and guests played volleyball or bocce, or stood under a tent, picking at a buffet of food. Sitting at a picnic table in the tent, drinking beer and eating barbecue, was a group of men who had graduated from Sackets High within five years of each other:

Their host, Jean Derouin ('64), was a ruddy-faced and genial man who had served three terms as the village mayor. J. P. Constance ('67) was the owner of Meade Optical in Watertown and, as Jean's successor as mayor, managed to combine authority with the antic manners of W. C. Fields. Harold Cring ('67) was stolid and solidly built, in black-rimmed glasses, and he owned his own construction company, Bette and Cring. Larry Reinhardt ('65), a trim, V-shaped man with a rich mustache and well-pressed shirt, was a project manager for Harold's construction company. Mark Phillips ('65) was a math teacher, but he could have been mistaken for a sailor, with his creased face and trimmed white beard. His elder brother was Peter Phillips ('62), a small, ebullient man with a compact build from working for a utility company, and bright, fun-seeking eyes beneath his receding hairline.

Their attention was turned on Jack Knowlton. The former president of the class of '65, Jack still looked and dressed like a boy athlete, in polo shirts and khakis and loafers, though his head of floppy hair had now turned salt-and-pepper. Jack lived three hours away in Saratoga, but he came back to Sackets regularly to visit Marian Knowlton, his mother. Marian was one of those Sackets schoolteachers of whom they were all so respectful, a village fixture who evoked memories of maps, Vasco da Gama, Ptolemy, the cotton gin, the spelling of Mississippi, and a thousand other answers to pop-quiz questions. Everyone had passed through Mrs. Knowlton's sixth-grade classroom at the Sackets School at one time or another.

Whenever Jack visited from Saratoga, he came with tales of adventure in the harness-racing business. Horses were the topic as his pals crowded elbow to elbow around the table. It was Peter Phillips who, that day, in the grip of his ebullience and beer, uttered the life-altering sentence.

"Hey, Jack," Pete said. "When are you going to get *us* into the horse-racing business?"

Jack stopped eating, and arched his speculative eyebrow. They all burst out laughing. Once Jack started talking about the horses, you'd better have an exit strategy, or you could find yourself feeling the empty leather at the bottom of your wallet. "Bet the mortgage on that one," Jack liked to say.

Interesting they should bring it up, Jack told them. Actually, he'd gotten out of the harness-racing business, and he had something better in mind. The truth was, he was tired of spending too much money with too little return, and he was looking to do something a little riskier. Harness horses were plodders; not only did they run slow, but they didn't make much. Lately, he'd thought about trying to own a horse that would run on the big track at Saratoga. Thoroughbred racing. That's where the real money and excitement were to be found.

"I'm kind of thinking of doing something with owning a thoroughbred," Jack said.

"Well, what's that all about?" Peter said.

"You know, racehorses."

Anyone with a little disposable income could own a standardbred and put him in a harness race, Jack explained. But thoroughbreds were something altogether different. They were the top of the line, the rarest, purest, and most expensive of creatures, and they were also edgy, fragile, and difficult to develop.

"How much would one cost?" Peter asked.

Jack described the thoroughbred market to his friends: a top Kentucky colt could bring one million dollars or more at a sale like Keeneland. But those were just the most expensive thoroughbreds. If you were willing to be sensible and look outside Kentucky, there was a whole other, more reasonable range of horses available. In New York, for instance, the horses were comparatively cheap: you could buy a New York–bred for maybe fifteen to twenty thousand dollars.

Now J.P. jumped in, animated. "Well, maybe we should talk about it, Jack," he said.

Harold Cring was skeptical. When Harold wasn't balancing the books for his construction company, he was juggling the bills and tuitions for his eight children, who were at that moment running around the lawn. A twenty-to-thirty-thousand-dollar thoroughbred horse meant they'd have to put up at least five thousand dollars each. A five-grand gamble on a racehorse? That was about the dumbest thing he'd ever heard. "No way," he said, shaking his head.

Jack found it hard to argue with Harold. As eager as he was to sell his old friends on the idea of becoming horse owners, the economics were forbidding. Buying a horse was the cheap part; then there was the cost of training, stabling, and caring for the horse, the vet bills, and the feed bills. Even a cheap horse cost $30,000 to $50,000 a year to keep. Yet the average American racehorse earned only about $16,000 in purse money. In other words, it earned only one dollar back for every two spent.

The Sackets guys had to be prepared to lose money, Jack said. The statistics showed they could reasonably expect only fifty cents back on each dollar they put in. Thoroughbred owning had so many financial pitfalls that it had spawned a saying: "Anyone can buy a horse, but hardly anyone can afford to own one."

"There's only one reason to do it," Jack said, "and that's to have fun."

Having discharged his responsibility for full disclosure, Jack now felt free to offer them reasons to consider the plan. In New York racing, the economics were slightly more in the owners' favor, he explained. You had a chance not to go broke. A $20,000 horse, if he was any good, could run for $40,000 purses. If they stayed on the lower end of owning, and purchased lesser-bred horses for moderate prices, they would have a fighting chance to get their money back. "If you break even, that's a pretty good deal," Jack told them. And think of the fun they would have together in the process.

To Jack, the fun of it was the most persuasive argument in favor of owning. There was nothing like seeing your horse in a race. The cheapest claiming race at Saratoga, Jack said, was a fabulous thrill if it was *your* horse running.

The guys looked around the table at one another. For five thousand dollars apiece, they could own a thoroughbred. Kings owned thoroughbreds, and magnates owned thoroughbreds. It was an utterly romantic idea—made even more romantic by the fact that, by now, they had been swilling beer for several hours. They were at least smart enough not to make any decisions while they were drinking. Instead, J.P. took charge. "Well, let's do this," he said. "Tomorrow we'll hold a meeting over on my porch. If you're interested, show up with your checkbook."

Some of them were smoking cigars when they came out of the tent.

To grow up in Sackets was to grow up amid odds and ends of eras. A child digging with a toy shovel and bucket would find grapeshot or musket balls from the War of 1812. Sometimes, people came across cannonballs while working in their gardens.

Sackets was established in the early 1800s by a New York lawyer and land speculator, Augustus Sacket, who bought a parcel of land at auction, sight unseen, and arrived on horseback to discover that he'd purchased a vast acreage of cedar and white oak ringing the silvery Lake Ontario. A natural hook in the peninsula made for a deep-water harbor, sheltered from lake surges and winds that roared across the lake for more than two hundred miles. That, combined with the high limestone bluffs along the lake, made it an ideal site for a military fort.

A frontier town for trappers and traders quickly took shape along the lip of the lake. Sacket put up a sawmill, and he built himself an impressive Federal-style home. It was a prematurely elegant structure. An 1806 town resolution announced, "A bounty of 10 dollars be allowed any inhabitant of town for each wolf or panther destroyed in this town." But within five years, the wolves and panthers had been beaten back, and Sacket's Harbor (the apostrophe would eventually disappear) had become an active port and important military outpost. On the waterfront, shipbuilders raised huge wood skeletons of boats, and wharves and warehouses lined the banks of the lake as if it were a freshwater ocean.

It was impossible to be reared in Sackets and not learn from Bob Brennan, the town's historian, a World War II vet and former telephone repairmen turned scholar, that Sackets was the most neglected historical site in New York State. Brennan had been born in Sackets Harbor when the local babies were delivered by the town midwife, and he was so steeped in Sackets knowledge that it was he who solved the centuries-old disagreement over the spelling of the town name. Some spelled it Sacketts, and some Sackets, and the county historians and the post office even got into the debate, but it was Brennan who settled it. He prowled through the old graveyards until he finally found the founder's headstone, and there it was, S-a-c-k-e-t.

Brennan was a vivid narrator of Sackets' role in the War of

1812: the village was the headquarters for both the Army and the Navy in the northern frontier of the war, and twice repulsed attacks from the British. In 1813, the British landed on a nearby island and waded across the shoals toward the town with the intent of invading, but they were stopped and defeated on a large field just outside the harbor by militia and a quick-thinking officer who wheeled his troops into position. On another occasion, the British Navy tried to shell the town by sending boats across the mouth of the harbor, but the wind died.

Sackets' architecture was not unlike the history of the town itself: faded epochs piled one on another. There was the old sawmill of rough-hewn stone, a heavy granite mason's hall, a few brick and columned Greek-revival mansions once owned by shipbuilders and merchants, some pretty Victorians, and the brick-and-board shops of town. Lastly, there were the newer cement-and-siding homes, and on the outskirts, the farmhouses and barns. This jumble of buildings ran downhill to a marina, and a greensward with grassy mounds that was the old battlefield.

Lowering on the bluffs above the town was an abandoned and decaying military post, the gray-stoned Madison Barracks. For 140 years, Madison Barracks had lent prestige, social life, and prosperity to the village. It was built in 1816 during a postwar boom, when Sackets was still considered an important lake port. Young officers commissioned from West Point often found themselves stationed in Sackets, and from 1848 to 1849, one Lieutenant Ulysses S. Grant occupied a small apartment with a peeling window sash on the backside of the barracks. His new wife, Julia Dent, later recalled the village and reflected on both its charm and the measures they took to break the snowbound boredom of their lives there. "How very pleasant was the memory of our stay," she wrote years later. "We thought nothing of driving ten or twelve miles in our sleigh to a party at Brownsville or Watertown. We would dance or play whist and after a splendid supper drive home with great glee."

From the 1870s through the 1940s, Sackets flourished. It was a mecca for boating and fishing (bass and perch), with steam locomotives and ferry schooners shuttling soldiers and vacationers. Shops and businesses blossomed on Main Street, fifty-three in all lining the boulevard. Villagers enjoyed walking out with young officers and watching polo matches, and in the evenings, they could pay a dime to see the latest film at the Barracks auditorium.

It was an important destination—until it suddenly wasn't anymore. After World War II, the military abruptly left Sackets. It no longer had use for a quaint post on benign Lake Ontario, and so the Army did what it does when it no longer needs a base: it simply left. Without the military, the New York Central Railroad abandoned the village, too. A once active and illustrious military post, a center of command as well as a freshwater shipbuilding port, was left to molder. Watertown, with its proximity to what would become Fort Drum, became the important destination.

Among the things the Army left behind was a large cemetery. Madison Barracks had provided a burying ground for its officers, but at some point in mid-century it was decided to move the graves, in the dead of winter. The men given the job did it hastily and with little reverence, perhaps because it was exhausting work in the cold and the heavy snow. Buried somewhere in the Sackets cemetery was Brigadier General Zebulon Pike, the man who discovered Pike's Peak, but by the time the burial detail was done with their hasty work, his grave was lost. He now lies with other casualties of 1812, in a mass grave, his bones mixed with those of his men.

Long after the cemetery was moved, bones would work their way to the surface of the original site. Bob Brennan was once out strolling by Madison Barracks when he paused to watch a telephone lineman dig a hole for a new pole. As the worker sank the pole, bones began churning up through the dirt—it was an abandoned grave.

By the 1950s, with the barracks closed and the railroad gone, businesses began to fail. All that was left were three small grocery stores, a clothing store, a hardware store, a pharmacy, and a saloon with a swinging door. There was also a diner named Fat Mary's that had greasy fries and pinball machines. With no upkeep, some of the buildings began to sag and collapse. The winters did their damage, too. With every load of snow, boards bent and then rotted and broke. Roofs caved in. Mortar crumbled and bricks fell.

The residents who were left behind looked for ways to scratch out a living. The Phillips boys, Peter and Mark, were the sons of a plumber, George. When George was out of work during one long winter from November until Easter, he sold shoes door-to-door rather than collect unemployment.

Some of the fathers increasingly disappeared into bars. Later, Jack decided that many of the village men drank out of a combination of strain and boredom, pent up in a town with too few job prospects and too many responsibilities. Drinking was as much a part of the culture of Sackets as snow; there was little else to do over the long winters, which were so cold, the local joke went, that the dogs froze to the fire hydrants.

Jack Knowlton's father, Ted, sold candy and cigarettes to stores around the county, and he later became a Ford salesman in Watertown. But when he left the house, it wasn't only to work. He was drinking. Jack's mother, Marian, continued to go about her routine. She did her lesson plans and graded papers, and taught the village kids world history, long division, spelling, and art. Marian told people that Ted spent all his time working; at least, that was the front she put on, but Jack expected she probably knew better. That was just the public story.

Ted was a functional alcoholic, as were many of the fathers of Sackets Harbor. They couldn't afford to be non-functional alcoholics, because they worked too hard and had too many kids to support for that, so they functioned, and they drank, almost reflexively. Some of them eventually weren't functional, like Jean Derouin's dad, a sheet-metal worker who all but disappeared into drunkenness and left Jean's mother to support nine children by waiting on tables.

Ted was pals with J.P.'s father, Forrest Constance, who was a meat-cutter, working six days a week at the Grand Union in Watertown to support his seven children. Forrest was at the store by eight in the morning and didn't get home until after six, and he worked every Saturday. His idea of a day off was to fish, or to throw a picnic at the American Legion hall.

Both Ted Knowlton and Forrest Constance were World War II vets; Ted had served in the infantry in the Phillipines, and Forrest had been a staff sergeant in the European theater. Forrest was in a nasty fight that he'd never talk about; all J.P. knew was that his unit was surrounded by Germans in Alsace-Lorraine. Forrest had a tough time when he came home, suffering so badly from nightmares that sometimes he would crawl out of bed and run into the kitchen, acting like he was shooting.

The Constance home consisted of seven kids in a three-bedroom house with one bath, and the line at the bathroom door was long. On Sunday nights, a full tub had to bathe two people. Then they'd drain it for the next two. There was no dallying in the bathroom; if you didn't do your duty and get out, someone pounded the door down.

The house was heated by a kerosene stove that J.P. filled every day for years, and it was an improvement over the potbellied coal stove that for a while had been their main source of heat. The household finances were so perilous that J.P. started working at ten years old, mowing lawns and washing cars for two bucks. He got a job at the local Laundromat, opening it every evening and closing it up at night, and shoveling the walk, for fifty dollars a month.

While the fathers worked and drank, the mothers and the schoolteachers ran the town and raised the kids. J.P.'s mother worked as a county clerk to supplement the family income. Rita Cring was a teacher's aide. The mothers helped keep an eye on one another's kids. "You boys get home now" was a constant refrain.

There was a nine o'clock curfew for anyone under sixteen. Each night the siren rang at the fire hall, signaling that it was time to be indoors. Sometimes, the eleven Cring kids would test the curfew—Harold and his sister Bonnie liked to see if they could run around the block after dark without getting caught. The penalty was to go before a rather lenient judge, who more often than not sentenced them to wash the fire trucks.

The kids who grew up in Sackets didn't sit in the house and watch TV—mainly because most households couldn't afford a TV in the first place. Sackets got only two channels, and cable wouldn't arrive until the mid-1980s. The Constance family actually had two TVs, both of them broken, but they were broken in different ways: one got sound, and one got a picture. When the Beatles were on

Ed Sullivan, J.P. watched the good screen while he listened to the sound from the other.

The boys' lives revolved around two things, school and sports. There were the games they played at Sackets High, and then there were the ones they played in the streets or empty fields, with dirt spots as the bases. They wore the same pair of sneakers for every sport. Sometimes in the dead of winter they shoveled off an outdoor basketball court, or would sneak into the abandoned gym at Madison Barracks. The gym was drafty—most of the windows had been broken out, and pigeons were living in there—but it was a place to play. Every once in a while, somebody's foot would go through a rotting floorboard.

Their grainy black-and-white yearbook pictures show boys in white button-down shirts and narrow neckties with small knots, with their hair cropped or neatly combed back.

1962
Peter Phillips
Four years of track, basketball and football, plus baseball his senior year.

Quote: "He'd rather make history than study it."

What would happen if?: Pete Phillips lost the wave in his hair?

Last will: I, Pete Phillips, do will and bequeath my ability to have five different history teachers and still flunk, to anyone who likes history.

Ambition: To pass a history regents.

Pet peeve: The Alexandria Bay football team.

Expression: Not me.

Voted most attractive.

1964
Jean Derouin
Four years of football, basketball, baseball and track.

Quote: "Life is a jest, and all things show it; I thought so once, but now I know it."

Pet peeve: To smear GB in football.

Expression: Censored.

Ambition: Physical education teacher.

Voted most popular.

1965
Jackson William Knowlton
Four years of baseball, football, track and basketball.

Class president for two years.

Quote: "A finger in every pie."

Pet peeve: Senior girls.

Expression: Is it necessary?

Ambition: To manage the Yankees.

Voted most athletic.

Mark Joseph Phillips
Four years of football and track; three years of basketball and two years of tennis.

Quote: "All nature wears one universal grin."

Larry Lynn Reinhardt
Quote: "I have hardly ever known a mathematician who was capable of reasoning."

Happiness is: Saturday night.

Voted most likely to succeed.

1967

Jon Phillip Constance

Four years of band and pep band.

Quote: "Thoughts of life he has but one and that for sure is
having fun."

Pet peeve: Girls who think they know everything, but don't
know anything.

Ambition: Hotel manager.

Expression: Come again.

In 10 years: Bellboy at the Sackets Hilton.

Harold Rupert Cring

One year of baseball.

Quote: "My heart is not here; my heart's in the Highlands
a-chasing the deer."

In 10 years: No Thumbs.

On Friday nights in the autumn, they raided a local apple orchard, which they named Happy Jack's, after Jack, who was the
getaway driver. They had a system. They would drive by in a car,
and slow down, and a squad of boys would hop out and sneak over
the fence and start picking apples. Meanwhile, Jack would pull
over and raise the hood, as if he had engine trouble. Law enforce-
ment in Sackets consisted of a lone squad car, and everybody recognized it by the headlights. The slogan was "Double headlights
up and down." That meant the cops were coming, and everybody
would take off running.

If the cop cruiser came by, Jack would busy himself under the
hood. Sometimes the cop would say, "Hey, you need any help?"
Jack would wave and say, "No, I think I got it fixed now." As soon

as the cop drove up the road, the boys would take off running with their apples, and throw them in the back of the car.

The strong winters slowed life. Blizzards came and buried the cars, and school closed for a week. The snow piled higher and higher until it drifted. Sometimes, the banks got so huge that you could stand on top of them and touch the telephone wires.

Once, Jack got so bored that he organized a skating party, four or five miles across Lake Ontario. "It's there, and it's a Sunday," Jack said, so he and Dorothy and Jean and some of their pals set off. They skated over the lake ice, which was frozen several feet thick, with nothing in front of them but the white vastness. They skated until their ankles bruised inside their skates and their calves trembled from the effort.

Sometimes, for fun, they would kick the streetlights out. One bored evening, they discovered that if you kicked a pole hard enough, the light would go out for a moment—and then flicker back on. They would take a running start and give it a high, sharp karate kick, and snuff out the light. Harold Cring was the one who discovered that you could kick a whole block of them out, one by one, in a kind of domino effect, blink, blink, blink. If Harold was really fast, he could momentarily darken an entire street, before the lights would hum and flicker back on in sequence, with a tink-tink-tink of the bulbs.

Between the curfew and the hawk eyes of the schoolteachers, there wasn't much trouble to get into, but they tried. Mark Phillips and some buddies stole the outhouse from a neighbor's home and moved it onto Main Street. They skipped school to watch the World Series, and when they got caught, they had to scrub the urinals with toothbrushes for two hours. One Halloween night, Jack, Jean, and

J.P.'s older brother, Eric, dragged some old telephone poles to an alley that ran behind Main Street and set them on fire. First, they put up barricades up and down the alley so they couldn't be chased by the cops, who fortunately doubled as volunteer firemen. Then the boys doused the logs with kerosene and lit them, and as the flames rose up, they took off running as fast as they could into the dark, tripping over all the barricades they had put up.

They built bonfires by the lake. There was an old abandoned date-packing factory in town, with a huge repository of wooden boxes that used to hold the fruit. The boys would drag the rotting old boxes to the lake, pile them high, and light them. But the boxes burned too quickly. "This is a bunch of bull," Mark Phillips said, and threw a couple of old tires in the fire so it would burn slower. The black smoke covered the town and dirtied all of the windows for days.

Few of the adults in town were willing to help the boys imagine bigger futures. An exception was Marian Knowlton, who insisted that Jack would go to college on an academic scholarship, which he did when he won a New York Regents scholarship. There was no such thing as a guidance counselor or an official college adviser. Almost invariably, discipline in Sackets came with a work assignment. When Harold got caught playing football in the Sackets High hallway, the principal gave him a stick with a nail on one end and told him to pick up the garbage on the street outside. If you got nabbed doing something, it meant washing the fire trucks, or shoveling snow from the walks, or some other piece of civic duty. It was a lesson the Sackets boys wouldn't forget.

Once, Harold got pulled over for speeding. But instead of writing out a ticket, the cop said, "What can you do?" Harold said,

"Well, I'm a carpenter." Harold's dad, Kenneth, supported his eleven kids as a superintendent for a general contractor, and Harold had begun working for him when he was sixteen.

"I don't need any carpentry," the cop said. "But I'll tell you what. Can you rake a lawn?"

"Yeah."

"Be at my house tomorrow morning at eight o'clock."

Harold showed up the next morning at the cop's house, and there was his friend Don Murphy, also holding a rake. "What are you in for?" Harold asked. "Speeding," Don said. Harold said, "I can't believe this." They had to rake the guy's whole lawn to get out of a ticket.

When they got older and closer to graduation, they would ride around in cars drinking beer. They would drive a mile out of town on one of the million back roads to the abundant countryside and find an abandoned house and have a beer party. Or, someone would bring 45-rpm records and they'd have a gym dance, listening to "Blue Velvet," or Pat Boone or Patsy Cline.

Madison Barracks was a forbidden destination, which made it all the more popular. They would sneak into the old officers' club and wander through the ransacked rooms, or find a place to sit and drink beer. In one of the downstairs rooms there was a piano, and sometimes kids would go down there and play it, the tinkling notes floating eerily through the dust motes.

Invariably, someone thought he saw a ghost.

One by one, the letters started to arrive. "Greetings from the President," they began.

It wouldn't be right to say that the Sackets Harbor experience with the war in Vietnam was reflective of the national experience, because there were two distinctly separate Vietnam experiences. There was the upper-middle-class experience of deferments, disinterest, or demonstrations, and then there was the experience of the working-class men who were drafted or enlisted and actually served, and that was the experience the boys of Sackets tended to be familiar with.

Later, the Ford administration's clemency board would cite the statistics: of the 27 million men eligible for conscription during the Vietnam era, only 2.2 million were drafted, and the vast majority came from the working class and minorities. Fifteen million were deferred, exempted, or disqualified. This was what was meant by the phrase "selective service." Avoiding Vietnam was a privilege of the knowledge class.

All the guys who grew up together in Sackets Harbor sweated the draft. Some got called up, and some didn't. Those who got called, served. J. P. Constance spent two years in the Marine Corps. His brother Eric Constance, the former star quarterback for Sackets High and lighter of telephone poles, and Jack's lifelong best friend, enlisted in the Army. He flew helicopters in Vietnam for a year, stationed at Duc Phoh, south of Da Nang, and would spend seven years in the service all told, emerging as a captain.

Jean Derouin also shipped out for Southeast Asia. He would not have the luxury of a student deferment; he might have been one of the best all-around athletes at Sackets High, but no one had told him that there were such things as athletic scholarships, and his mother, feeding nine kids on a waitress's earnings, could hardly afford college. When Jean graduated from high school, the logical thing to do was join up. He enlisted in the Air Force, made sergeant, and spent 1967 and 1968 in Vietnam as an Air Force policeman, serving at Phan Rang, thirty miles south of Cam Ranh Bay. There was no describing the sheer misery of Vietnam—the heat, rain, bugs, snakes, dust, brown water, and overall pestilence. Jean pulled security duty, and the highlight of his stay was when Bob Hope visited and Jean was assigned to be his bodyguard for two weeks. Hope's call sign was Court Jester, and he turned out to be a tiny man. The traveling show included Miss World, Barbara McNair, and Gary Crosby, the son of Bing, who thought it was a big joke to sneak up on the soldiers and laughingly try to grab their weapons.

When Jean came home to Sackets, he got a two-dollar-an-hour job with a company in Watertown that made electric motors for power-driven machines like electric typewriters and projectors. He would stay there for the next twenty years, finally becoming a manufacturer's rep. He always regretted not going to college, and at least once a week he told his four kids, "I will be the only one in this house without a degree." Three of the four got their degrees.

J.P. got drafted. After he graduated from Sackets in '67, he went to Canton, a two-year state college with a program in hotel management, which suited his life's ambition to manage the Holiday Inn in Watertown, and he had to work like a dog to pay the tuition. He pumped gas, delivered sandwiches, and did catering jobs, and in the summer he worked at his grandmother's fish-and-tackle store, getting up at six A.M. to sell bait, seven days a week. When he finished Canton, he got a job selling Chevys, and proposed to his college girlfriend, Karen, and they set the wedding date: October 25.

The week before they were to be married, he went to the post office for his mail, and there was the letter. J.P. opened it. "Greetings from the President," it said.

J.P. had to go home and tell his fiancée that he'd been drafted.

Karen and J.P. sat on a sofa and cried together for hours. "Don't worry," he said, "we'll get married anyway. I'll get a deferment." Over the next few days, J.P. contacted his draft board and asked for the deferment, pleading his engagement and his outstanding college debt. He was turned down—just because you owed money and wanted to get married didn't mean you couldn't go to Vietnam. He was instructed to report for induction on the seventeenth of November.

J.P. had exactly one month of wedded bliss before he got on a bus with lots of other boys from Sackets and Watertown, bound for Syracuse. There, he took another physical and some aptitude tests, and filled out a questionnaire, on which he mentioned his hotel-management ambitions. While J.P. was standing in a line and waiting to be told what to do, a sawed-off little Marine sergeant trolled the room for volunteers. There were few takers. The sergeant examined the aptitude tests, and when he read J.P.'s, he looked up and barked, "Constance! Come here, boy." He escorted J.P. into his office. As soon as the door closed, J.P. said, "I'll tell you right now, I'm not going into the Marine Corps." But the sergeant flipped open a manual and showed J.P. a chapter on military classifications.

"It says here you're qualified to be a manager of a non-commissioned officer's club," the sergeant said.

"That's a bar, right?" J.P. said.

"Booze and food," the sergeant said.

"That's not a bad deal," J.P. said, and he fell for it. Next thing he knew, he was sent to Parris Island for fourteen weeks of training. He spent Christmas on a rifle range. When it came time to learn his posting, he stood in a platoon racked at attention while an officer read off a series of numbers that indicated what his detail would be. "Constance, thirteen hundred," he heard.

J.P. said, "Sir, what's thirteen hundred mean?"

"Truck driver, boy."

J.P. spent the next two years in the Marine Corps driving trucks in the motor pool and never got near an NCO club. Instead, from Parris Island he went to Norfolk, Virginia, where Karen joined him, and they had six months together before he was sent to California and then Southeast Asia.

After two months of training, J.P. and two hundred of his fellow Marines boarded a plane for Okinawa, where they were issued rifles. From there, they flew to Da Nang. Someone yelled at J.P., "We're bunking down here." He was told to report back for formation the next day, when some of the Marines would be assigned other duty.

The next morning, a Marine officer pulled seventeen men out of the two hundred and formed them up to be transferred to Japan. J.P. was relieved to be one of them; it would be his job to put together a line of trucks and make them ready for strike forces in the theater. He spent his last ten months in Japan, and he came home a corporal, proud that he didn't get out one day early.

Curiously, few of the boys from Sackets ever looked toward that sign that said CANADA, 31 MILES. One of them did, though. Jack Colhoun was the golden child of Sackets High, a five-sport star athlete and Eagle Scout, president of the class of '63, and he could trace his ancestors to the *Mayflower*. Everyone idolized Colhoun, especially after he gained admission to a distinguished four-year college. It happened to be the University of Wisconsin; the counterculture and antiwar movement would take hold of the Madison campus.

At Wisconsin, Jack Colhoun did a full about-face. Later, those who knew him in Sackets would read about the All-American kid who became a draft resister, turned down his ROTC lieutenant's commission, and fled to Canada, where he became a leader of the expatriate antiwar movement. In 1971, Colhoun told his own story in *Newsweek* magazine while still living in exile in Toronto.

At first, Colhoun pursued the course expected of him: he signed up for ROTC, even as he listened to campus lecturers who expressed doubts about both the morality and the tactics of the war, and he watched bloody confrontations between police and antiwar demonstrators. Then, in 1967, the Dow Chemical demonstrations took place in Madison. Colhoun learned about the civilian toll of napalm, the flaming chemical jelly produced by Dow for the defense department. He watched as fellow ROTC officers staged a counterdemonstration in which they paraded a sign that said, NAPALM IS GOOD FOR VC ACNE.

Colhoun spent his senior year hoping for a disqualification from his commission and casting about for alternatives, such as cutting his finger off, getting himself arrested on a morals charge, or committing himself to a mental institution. That spring, Nixon ordered the invasion of Cambodia, and the campuses went crazy. While other guys from Sackets reported for duty, Colhoun made a decision: he would report to Canada. He joined one of an estimated 50,000 to 70,000 draft resisters who crossed the border, and he wouldn't come home again until 1977, spending the next seven years as an activist, eventually campaigning for amnesty. "It was a middle-class birthright to explore the many options for avoiding the draft," Colhoun would later tell the *New York Times*.

The guys of Sackets Harbor had lingering complexities of feeling about Colhoun. Jack Knowlton would remain good friends with him and never question his decision. Others, like Jean and J.P., felt that to go to Canada was a profound evasion. J.P. hadn't wanted to go to Vietnam, either. But he didn't know how anyone could live with the shame of desertion. Yet J.P. had sympathy for those who had gone to Canada, too; for what they had done to themselves and their lives. In the end, J.P. was all in favor of amnesty.

If some people were confused by that, well, so be it. It had been a confusing time. If guys like J.P. and Eric and Jean didn't want to go to war, they saw no contradiction in having served. They were unthinkingly proud to continue the tradition of the men in their family who had fought.

What the knowledge class couldn't understand was that most guys went over there and worked as hard as they could and endured huge risks because *that's what you were supposed to do.*

But for once, the guys of Sackets Harbor wanted to do something they weren't supposed to.

On Memorial Day in 1995, after the annual parade made its way down Main Street and ended at the harbor, the male residents of Hounsfield Street emerged from their houses and strolled toward J.P. Constance's beflagged front porch.

Harold Cring walked up the street, deeply confused. He had intended to tell the guys he wasn't interested in buying a horse. So why was he going to this meeting—and why, of all things, had he folded a check into his pocket just before he left the house?

Jean came out of his front door and watched Harold walking up the street, hands in his pockets and staring down at the ground. Next, Mark Phillips ambled up beside them.

"Harold, what are you doing here?" Mark asked. "The other day, you said 'No way.'"

Harold shrugged. He had no answer. Together, they walked up

to J.P.'s porch and took chairs. The others had already arrived. The group consisted of Mark, Peter, Harold, Jean, and J.P., all of them nursing hangovers. There was one no-show: somehow, Larry Reinhardt hadn't gotten the message about the meeting.

Jack, meanwhile, had already loaded up their car and headed back to Saratoga with Dorothy. As they drove away, Jack said, "You're not going to believe it, but I think these guys really want to do this. They're going to think about it, and they'll give me a call."

J.P. passed around beverages. Each week, this same consortium of old school buddies gathered on the porch to drink, talk, and argue, but there was a tension at this meeting that was out of the ordinary. When everyone was settled into their chairs with their drinks, they looked at J.P. expectantly.

"Okay," J.P. said. "Who's in?"

J.P. went over the facts once again, what it would cost, and what they could lose. Jack maintained that they needed at least thirty thousand dollars; most businesses failed because they were under-capitalized, and Jack wanted to make sure that didn't happen in this instance. They would seek to buy a horse for twenty thousand dollars, and keep the extra ten thousand dollars to pay expenses. That meant at least six people would have to buy in to make it affordable. So the question was: who was willing to write a check for five thousand dollars?

Harold shook his head. "I could put that money in a tin can and bury it in the backyard, and it would be smarter," he said.

Harold hadn't made a foolish decision since he decided to be a lifeguard in high school. That had lasted just one summer. Ever since then, he'd been a model of conscientiousness, responsibility, and metronome-like consistency, and now he owned a construction firm that employed half the people in Sackets Harbor. But there was something suppressed in Harold's careful demeanor, too. For years he'd had a quiet yearning, never indulged, to own a Harley-Davidson.

Harold had grown up on a farm just outside of town, and the farm helped to feed all the Cring kids. They had chickens, and fresh vegetables from the garden, and every once in a while a pig to slaughter. His mother baked once a week, covering the whole counter: bread, doughnuts, cookies, everything for the kids' breakfast and for their sandwiches.

When Harold got out of high school and joined the Army Reserve in 1968, he decided he didn't want to be a carpenter. He told his father, Kenneth, that he was tired of swinging that hammer and wanted a break, so he was getting a job as a lifeguard at the lake. Harold quit—and Kenneth quit speaking to him. Harold spent the summer at the beach, but when he didn't get hired as a lifeguard because he was a lousy swimmer, he had to go groveling to his father and ask for a job. Kenneth rehired him—but he still wouldn't speak to him. For weeks, they drove back and forth to work every day in silence.

There was no nepotism with Kenneth. In lean times, Harold always got laid off first. It was Kenneth's way of impressing on his son how lucky he was to have a good, paying job.

Harold learned his lesson, and he would never shirk again. For the first ten years of his marriage to Stephanie, Harold never called in sick, not one day. He was laid off twice, but he was never sick. He took exactly one long weekend off, so he could drive Stephanie to Niagara Falls. That was it.

By 1985, Harold and Stephanie had three kids, Richard aged seven, Cheryl five, and Joseph three. But then all of Kenneth's lessons about the value of a steady job hit home when the company

Harold worked for went bust. Harold was overseeing a project in Coral Springs, Florida, and had just moved his family down when it happened.

Harold had no paycheck, nothing to fall back on. Stephanie and the children went back to Sackets and moved in with her mother. Harold frantically looked for work and made a promise to God: if he found a new full-time job, he would be in church every Sunday.

Five weeks later, Harold landed a job with a Watertown construction company. He flew back North and went right to work, and that Sunday, he took his family to church. The new company built large commercial structures, mostly stores or industrial buildings, and Harold's job was to oversee the construction of a prison. The company was eligible for a bonus from New York State if the job was finished early, and Harold got it done. Next, he helped build the local Wal-Mart and an addition to the junior college. Harold got a percentage of the bonuses, and suddenly, the Cring family was financially secure for the first time.

Harold put the money in the bank, but he and Stephanie felt obliged to do something more with it: to give something back. Stephanie suggested adoption; they wanted a larger family and now that they had means, why not open the circle of their home? Harold and Stephanie spent long evenings discussing whether they could love an adopted child as well as their natural children, and the answer was yes. They adopted two small girls in Korea, sisters aged five and four, whom they named Kimberly and Elizabeth. Over the next ten years, the Crings adopted three more children: Gregory, from Guatemala, and Andre and Dioney from Colombia.

By Memorial Day of 1995, the Crings were trying to figure out how to put them all through college. One daughter was already in junior college, another was about to graduate from high school, and their eldest son, Richard, was getting married and going into the Air Force. So when Harold came home from the Memorial Day picnic and said he was thinking about buying into a racehorse, Stephanie was not enthusiastic.

But Stephanie didn't have the heart to tell Harold no, either. There was only one thing to which she had ever said "Absolutely not," and that was the Harley. Stephanie was seven years younger than Harold, an energetic woman with warm auburn hair who had met her husband while walking down Main Street one day, and even after several years of marriage amid the bedlam of eight children, she exuded the faint sense of still having a crush on her husband. She also had an acute awareness of how dedicated he was; he had gone to work every day for twenty years without a single self-indulgence. So if he wanted to spend some of his hard-earned money, she was inclined to let him.

Harold tried to explain why owning a racehorse appealed to him: it was something completely different, a departure from the sameness of his life. You couldn't find anybody else within a fifty-mile radius of Sackets who would consider doing something so crazy. "I know it's a lot of money, but it really sounds like something that could be fun or interesting," he said.

Just before Harold left the house for J.P.'s porch, Stephanie said, "Okay. I really don't think you should do it, but if you want to, go ahead." With his wife's approval, Harold tore a check out of his checkbook.

J.P.'s wife, Karen, was concerned about the idea of owning a horse, not because they couldn't spare five thousand dollars; they could probably afford it. It was the ongoing cost that worried her. "I worry about how much a horse *eats*," she said.

But Karen also believed that J.P. had spent years doing things for everybody but himself. J.P.'s plea to Karen about the stable was very straightforward. "Can you think of any reason we *shouldn't* do it?" The truth was, Karen couldn't.

After J.P. had gotten out of the Marine Corps, he had come home to a new baby, and he'd gone right to work. J.P. was home all of two days when he started selling glasses and hearing aids as a temporary employee at a shop in Watertown. He also went back to school part-time, helped by the GI Bill, and took a second job pumping gas from three o'clock to midnight.

Eventually, the optical shop hired J.P. full-time. His starting salary was $10,000, and on the night he got the job he met his father for dinner, eager to tell him what he would be earning. But before J.P. could make his announcement, Forrest said to him, "I hit a milestone. I got a raise, and I now make ten thousand dollars a year." J.P. just stared at his father, and couldn't bear to tell him it was his starting salary.

One by one, the other Sackets boys had come back home from college or the military and gone to work. The village they returned to was a place of unmowed lawns in front of abandoned buildings. Feral cats prowled, and pigeons fluttered in the eaves of roofless structures and crumbling façades scrawled with graffiti. The only people who seemed to want to come there anymore were bikers, passing through.

But even at its worst, the village had a naturally beautiful setting: the silver-blue disc of Lake Ontario, shimmering at the foot of the town. "If only we could do something about Main Street," people would say.

A generation of Sackets residents did something about it. As they settled into their adult lives, it became clear that the only way Sackets was going to become a decent place to live again was if the people who lived there made it so with their own hands. They couldn't afford to live anywhere else, so they had to improve what they had.

Jean joined the Village Board of Trustees, and then ran for mayor and won, and during his tenure he secured a series of grants from the state for improvements, which were then carried on by J.P. in turn. The people of Sackets upgraded zoning laws, brought water and sewage lines to the village, and put in new streetlamps. Soon Sackets had good pipes, new parking lots, and a row of beautiful wrought-iron lampposts that led down to the harbor.

Civic-minded residents rebuilt the village throughout the '70s, '80s, and '90s. It seemed like everybody who lived there served in some capacity. Pete Phillips was president of the Board of Education for twenty years, and a member of the Village Board of Trustees, as was Jean. Mark Phillips was on the Zoning Board of Appeals, and he coached and umpired local youth baseball teams. Harold was chairman of the Planning Board and a trustee on the parish finance committee at St. Andrews Church. Larry Reinhardt was a volunteer fireman and coached Little League, and his brother, Lee, was a fire chief.

They went to Saturday-morning meetings at the school, because Pete needed to raise money for the band. They raised a volunteer crew to build a shingled concert gazebo, a romantic structure straight out of Rodgers and Hammerstein. They worked after work and on Saturdays and Sundays to get it built. Jean Derouin's brother laid the paving stones in front of the gazebo. The stones were purchased with money donated by American Legion Post 1757.

The improvements continued into the 1990s. The school was

renovated and additions were built. Bed-and-breakfasts started to appear on Main Street in old Victorians. Small shops opened. People began to move to Sackets, and the new residents caught the improvement craze. Gradually, Sackets went from being one of the poorest villages in Jefferson County to having the highest income per capita. Pretty soon they were adding anywhere from one million to $2.5 million a year to the tax rolls. People kept coming, buying lots, building, and opening businesses. Bookshops, bakeries, breweries. A developer came in and turned some of the old abandoned stone Madison Barracks residence halls into apartments.

Eventually, Sackets became a charming resort village with restored old Federal homes and gingerbread Victorians. There was hardly anything left to fix. The lots near Madison Barracks were selling for $85,000 each, and people were building $400,000 homes on them. A couple bought the old stone mill and restored it into a gorgeous lakeside residence with a walled garden. The gazebo was booked through the summer of 2004 for weddings.

While his old high school friends served their community in Sackets, Jackson Knowlton served the public in Albany. He spent fifteen years as a bipartisan adviser and a dogged problem-solver in state politics, a guy who would work late into the night at the capitol. He worked for Republicans in the Senate, and for a Democratic governor as a Medicaid administrator, until he had a row of certificates on his wall that attested to his skill. But after a while, the psychic rewards began to wear off. Jack wasn't one of those who needed to be near the center of power, he just liked to get things done. The most he'd ever made in government was maybe fifty thousand dollars. He woke up one morning tired of tackling huge problems for small rewards, and decided to strike out for the private sector.

After watching Jack labor all those years at a desk, Dorothy Knowlton, like Stephanie Cring and Karen Constance, figured he had earned the right to throw a little money away. There had been times when she had misgivings about Jack's horseplaying, especially early when they were both working full-time and had small children. Dorothy delivered babies at a local hospital, and she took just six weeks off after the birth of each of her own kids, and every check went into the bank so they could buy their first house for $33,000 in 1973. She'd passed up a million manicures trying to save money, so when Jack gambled too much, she resented it. "Enough is enough," she'd say. "How could you risk three hundred dollars at the track?"

But as their income grew, Dorothy reconciled herself to the fact that the horses were Jack's chief pleasure, apart from his family. She decided she'd better love them, too, because they weren't going away. She learned to read the programs and follow the charts. If Jack wanted to own a thoroughbred, Dorothy wasn't going to stand in his way; he worked hard and he didn't buy boats.

Most of the wives felt much the same; if they had their reservations, they also believed their husbands were entitled to a little abandon. The men weren't gamblers by nature, and they didn't fritter money away. They were hamburger and sausage people, to whom gambling was an occasional raffle ticket, or betting pool, or a visit to Atlantic City to pull some quarter-slots levers.

Pete Phillips had the full backing of his wife, Bonnie, who tended to be as ebullient and ever youthful as her husband. At heart, she was still one of those high-spirited Cring kids who liked to run around the block after curfew. Bonnie and Pete had just finished raising five boys, separated in age by just eight years, and had put them all through college. It was time to do something for themselves.

As Mark Phillips sat on J.P.'s porch, he fought a sense of guilt. Mark had chosen not to tell his wife, Gwen, about the meeting. His excuse for not talking to her was that she would have said "No way," and he was right about that part of it. They were in the midst of putting three daughters through college at four-year institutions, on teachers' salaries. Mark taught math at a high school in a nearby town, while Gwen presided over the third grade at the local Sackets grade school, and the kids' tuitions were running them $2,500 to $3,000 each semester out of their pockets. Mark simply hadn't been brought up to accept bank loans; he couldn't shake the memory of his father, George, rejecting unemployment and selling shoes door-to-door.

Under the circumstances, they could ill afford to lose five thousand dollars on a whim. But Mark was tired of being so habitually careful, and he didn't intend to sit out an adventure. He had always handled the bills and Gwen never questioned him, so he knew she'd never know the money was gone. That morning, he stuck a check in his wallet and told Gwen he was going for a walk over to J.P.'s, failing to mention that he hoped to come home the proud owner of a rather large animal.

This was the backdrop of circumstances against which the guys of Sackets Harbor weighed whether to spend five thousand dollars of their life savings on something as foolish as a thoroughbred horse. J.P. led the argument in favor: this would be just another extension of their friendship, he argued; another way to do something together, much like their barbecues. What better reason for a road trip than to see their own horse run at Saratoga or Belmont?

"If we break even, and have a lot of fun, what's the harm?" he said.

"Well, I still don't know," Harold said.

Now J.P. lost his patience, and leaned forward in his chair.

"Harold J. Cring, you better think about this," J.P. said. "When they write your obituary, why wouldn't you want them to say, amongst all the other good things, that you dabbled in thoroughbred horse racing, and actually won a race or two?"

Harold thought for a moment. Suddenly, J.P. had summarized exactly why, against all of his better judgment, he had brought that check.

"You know what?" Harold said.

"What?"

"That's the most sensible thing anybody's said since I've been here. It might be the smartest thing you ever said."

Harold pulled the check out of his pocket, and clicked his pen. He wrote a check for five thousand dollars. Harold Cring, of all people, was first in.

As soon as Harold took the dive, everyone else did, too. Each man wrote a check and turned it over to J.P. Now they looked at one another, unsure of what to do next. How did you start a stable?

They called Jack and told him the news: they were all in. "Oh-kay," Jack said, "let's get started." There was a lot to do: they would have to register their stable with the Jockey Club. They would have to select a trainer for their stable. And then, of course, they had to find a horse to put *in* the stable. Jack had already come up with a suggestion for what to name the stable: Sackatoga, the perfect description of the ownership, a combination of Sackets Harbor and Saratoga.

Over the several days, the residents of Hounsfield Street delighted in sitting on J.P.'s porch and refining the details of their Sackatoga venture. J.P. and Karen came up with the colors for the jockey silks: the school colors of Sackets High, a deep maroon and gray, in a checkered pattern. It was an easy choice, since J.P. was the president of the Sackets Harbor Alumni Association and Karen was on the board.

Jack, delighted, registered the colors with the Jockey Club. Next, he called a young trainer he knew from the Saratoga backstretch, Tim Kelly. Jack explained that he and his friends wanted Tim to help them establish a thoroughbred stable.

"Timmy, I've gotten together some money with these guys, and we want to buy a horse. Can you find us a horse?"

Jack explained what they were looking for. They wanted a reasonably priced New York–bred that they could watch run at Saratoga. And they wanted a decent chance not to go bust.

"We've only got thirty thousand dollars," Jack said, "and maybe you could not spend all of that."

Back in Sackets, word got around town that Jack Knowlton had convinced the guys to buy a racehorse. The teasing started immediately. Eric Constance said, "Oh my God, Jack finally talked you into it." Most of their neighbors greeted the news with bemusement, or jokes.

"Why don't you name the horse Alpo?" Eric said.

But when Larry Reinhardt heard, he was sorry to be left out. "If you ever need another partner, I want in," he said.

Jean sent off his monthly finances to his accountant, including the canceled $5,000 check. The accountant called him up the very next day, concerned. "Uh, Jean," he said, "does Jeannie know about this?" Jean just laughed and assured him she did.

But there was one spouse who still didn't know what was going on. After a few days, Mark realized he would have to tell Gwen; there was no way he could keep the secret when everyone on the street knew about it but his own wife. "We're in on the stable," he said. As Gwen leveled him with a look, and the tears welled up, Mark knew that his life was going to be hell. It wasn't just the money—although that didn't make her happy—it was that he'd treated her as if she didn't count. She'd been left out, and everyone on Hounsfield Street knew it.

For the next few days, whenever someone wanted to talk about the Sackatoga Stable, they knew better than to do it if Gwen was within earshot. When Mark tried to invite her to the business meetings, she refused. "Don't ask me," she'd say, sarcastically. "What do I have to do with it?"

Then one day, Jack called J.P. with momentous news: Tim Kelly had found them a horse. He was an unraced three-year-old, a bay gelding with decent bloodlines, available for $22,000. Jack had bought him.

They owned a horse. They didn't know their way around a racetrack, and they didn't even know what the bell meant. They just thought it was a clanging sound. But they owned a thoroughbred horse. He was a cheap one, and there was nothing wonderfully distinctive about him, but he was theirs. They named him Sackets Six, after one another.

PART II

Yearling

4.

Pinhookers and
Handicappers

See, here's the deal: The horse doesn't know what it costs. He doesn't know. Owners put the price on horses, okay?

—NICK ZITO, trainer

While Jack and his partners were learning about thoroughbred racehorses, Funny Cide was learning how to *be* a thoroughbred racehorse. Tony Everard's sixty-five-acre farm, the New Episode Training Center in Ocala, was a sort of school. The colt arrived at the farm never having been so much as shod before, but now he would learn everything from how to wear a saddle to how to burst from a starting gate. He would learn how to act like a racehorse, and look the part, too.

As with any formative experience, there was a certain amount of adolescent trauma involved in a young horse's training, and the trauma was exacerbated by the fact that what he was being trained to do was unnatural. It wasn't natural for a colt to have nails hammered into his feet, or to have a metal bit placed in his mouth, or to be galloped in a single direction around an oval of dirt, when what he really wanted to do was zigzag crazily across an open field. The kind of handling he received in the next few months would determine whether the animal became a sound, cooperative racehorse, or a sore, twitchy miscreant.

The probabilities were against Funny Cide making it to the track: two-thirds of his generation would not race as two-year-olds, for reasons that were as various as they were many. Some went lame, or simply decided they didn't want to run. Their ranks dwindled due to bruises, cracks, strains, breathing problems, stomach ulcers, laminitis, pneumonia, or even West Nile. But pure stupidity and bad handling on the part of humans would get a lot of them.

At New Episode, the humans tried to avoid stupidity. Tony and his wife and fellow trainer, Liz Zemp, were touchy about their young horses, literally handsy with them. The term "breaking" horses was a misnomer. Modern horse-training methods had nothing in common with the bronco-busting portrayed in old Westerns. Like any sensible trainers, Tony and Liz didn't manhandle or hurry the yearlings into anything. "You hit them with the stick, it gets in their heads and stays there," Tony instructed his riders. The thing about horses was, they could easily decide they didn't like the game, and quit. There was a saying, "Never spur a free horse." Tony once caught a rider hitting a young horse, whipping him with a stick and calling him a "son of a bitch." He fired the guy on the spot. If you put an impatient rider on them and whacked them with a stick, they resented it, and they stopped. Just like teenagers. Hit a young horse, and you had a problem horse.

Tony was a sixty-six-year-old Irishman with a thick welt of graying brown hair that ran sideways over his head, and a young face inside his middle-aged one. On any given day, you could find him wearing slacks, black mud-splashed boots, and a short-sleeved Hawaiian shirt, surveying the yearlings as they ambled in the pastures. "Harmony" was what he strived for on the farm, he said in his pleasant brogue, and harmony was what he usually achieved.

Funny Cide arrived at New Episode on a sweltering day in August of 2001. The colt stepped from a van and was led to his new home, a stall in a long, white-painted shed row with neatly painted black posts and a tin roof. Horses poked their heads out of adjoining stalls, swinging their noses back and forth, interested. The barn was populated with other animals, too: cats, ducks, and a goat named Cissy picked through the stalls. The colts and fillies didn't like being in their stalls alone, so the critters were put there by Tony and Liz to keep them company. Goats were especially suited for a horse barn, because they tended to stand in one place and didn't get underfoot, and they ate what the horses ate.

In the stall, the colt had his temperature and his health records checked, and a foreman made notes of identifying marks on an index card. Each new horse had a card, noting cowlicks, or stars, so that if it lost its halter, they would know which one it was from among the 120 or so horses they kept on the premises.

Tony surveyed his acquisition: he was a chestnut with hardly any white on him, and he had a good frame, though a little narrow and immature. If he muscled out, he'd be a good-looking horse. If he didn't, well, that was the risk a pinhooker took.

Tony had been pinhooking for more than thirty years, but it didn't matter if it was a thousand years, he still saw things in young horses that he'd never seen before. Pinhooking was one of the more unpredictable livings a person could choose in the horse business.

A pinhooker hoped to spot young horses and improve them in the same way a real-estate speculator looked for a house with good value, renovated it, and turned it over for twice what he paid for it. The problem was, horses were more changeable, malleable. Houses stood still.

Success depended on his eye and his abilities as a trainer. Tony had an eye. But if you asked him to explain exactly what he looked for in a horse, he couldn't really say. He looked for an impression. A good horse had a certain air about it; there was just something that was striking, in its movement, and its eyes.

Tony liked a big girth, and bright eyes, and bone structure. He was relatively underwhelmed by pedigree; a horse could have a frame without pedigree, but he couldn't have all pedigree and no frame. The best pedigree in the world didn't matter if a horse had light, fine bones, because as soon as you breezed him hard, he'd break. A horse needed structure that would hold up under the pressure of 1,100 galloping pounds.

Tony looked for good moves. A horse that could run had an easy action, as if it were on roller skates, its feet seeming barely to come off the ground. But then again, Tony had seen some ugly horses that could really move. The odd stranger still turned up.

Ultimately, Tony didn't have the whole answer. If he knew for sure which of the creatures were going to be runners, he'd be a millionaire many times over. It was a great game when he was right, and an awful one when he was wrong.

Most of the horses Tony bought were in the $10,000-to-$30,000 range, and he bought five or six annually. But pinhooking had a huge downside. It was risky. All a horse had to do was snap his leg out in the field some morning, playing around with the other horses, or get kicked in the wrong place, or step in a gopher hole, and Tony would never see his money again. Horses didn't get worker's comp, and Tony didn't get unemployment.

Sometimes the horses just weren't good enough. If an animal wasn't a runner, Tony refused to sell it; he would ruin his reputation if he did. When you sold a horse that couldn't run, it upset people, and they didn't want to do business with you anymore, whereas if you sold a good horse, you had a client for life. So when a horse couldn't run, Tony practically had to give it away.

He couldn't afford to make too many mistakes. Tony and Liz were two more members of the middle-class of horse racing, a class that was constantly vulnerable financially. New Episode had 120 stalls, and more than 200 horses a year passed through their hands, and their payroll was $30,000 a week. They had two secretaries, a night watchman, and ten exercise riders, along with twenty more grooms and hotwalkers. Tony and Liz paid themselves a salary of $700 a week each, and the farm did well, enough so that they could stand a bad year. But they weren't the kind of farm that could afford two or three bad years in a row. Only the wealthy, or the large commercial operations, could do that.

In order to make ends meet, Tony and Liz also broke horses. An owner or trainer sent a tousled, awkward yearling to Tony and Liz, and a few months later, for a fee of fifty dollars a day, they gave you back a broken and trained two-year-old that was ready to race. It only had to be led to the track and loaded into the gate. The fees from schooling horses helped pay the bills. They were good at it, and it provided a financial security that pinhooking couldn't.

Tony and Liz's methods weren't fancy. They treated horses like horses. After a day in his stall, the new yearling was put in a pen

with two or three other new arrivals, to get acquainted. The yearling hashed it out with his new friends, wrestled and kicked, and
pawed. Once the horses had gotten to know one another and cooled
down, they were moved to a large, far pasture, where another fifty
or so yearlings had been turned out.

For the next few weeks, the yearling would have no responsibility other than to play and to become accustomed to his new surroundings. He found himself in a grassy, open space circled by
oaks and filled with flocks of white egrets. Thick clusters of oaks
drooped with dark glossy leaves, and gray moss chandeliered almost to the grass.

Sometimes, Tony would traipse out into the pasture and wander
through the yearlings, trying to figure which of them would be the
real runners. He pushed through the crowd of velvety bodies and
honeyed eyes, and the horses would nudge him back and smell
him. Soon, a dozen of them at a time would crowd around, nosing
at him, sniffing at his pockets or his shoes. Some of them just stood
quietly behind him and breathed gently in his hair, inhaling and
exhaling, and nuzzling his neck.

It didn't matter what had been paid for them; they were all in
the same field together, $20,000 horses with $100,000 horses,
Florida-breds, California-breds, Kentucky-breds, and New York–
breds, all mixed up. After a few days in the pasture, with their fancy
leather harnesses removed, one looked as scroungy as the next.

In the pasture, the horses were antic. They would brake and
dodge, stomp and cut. Some of them went completely wild, flying
around like jet planes, making a shimmering, dusty circle of
reddish-brown-black color. They pushed and shoved, rolled on
their backs, and squealed, and chased one another.

They were curious creatures, inquisitive. They wanted to investigate everything—although they weren't as bad as the incorrigible goats. The vet didn't park his truck too close to the barn, because between the goats and the horses, they would pull out everything from the back of the truck and try to eat it.

Their heads swung toward any noise or visitor. If a paper bag drifted into the pasture, they'd look at it for a moment, and the next thing you knew, they were jumping up and down on it, a dozen thoroughbred colts pawing it with their hooves.

After a few days, the yearling's coat was more rusty than shiny, with dull patches like a car with the paint rubbed off. He was bleached from lounging in the sun, and matted from rolling in scratchy dry grass. His mane was sparse and tangled, and in places it stood up and went awry. He was crusty and mussed up, and that's how Tony and Liz wanted him to be, for the time being.

Spending a few weeks in the pasture made a horse easier to handle once training started. A colt that had stampeded around a field with the other horses wasn't as easily frightened. Some trainers raised young thoroughbreds like hothouse plants; million-dollar, blue-blood progeny were too valuable to put in a pasture to fight, and potentially to run through a fence and hurt themselves. But a horse that had been isolated, Tony believed, tended to be highly strung and harder to manage, whereas horses that had roughhoused in the pastures tended to be leaner, and better-spirited, and more socialized. Occasionally, one of Tony's clients wanted their horses kept separately, and he obliged and put those in separate pens, but he didn't like doing it. It was Tony's experience that a horse that had been sequestered was intimidated when you put it around other horses and tried to teach it to run.

Tony's experience was long: he had been working horses since he was eight years old, in Ratoath, Ireland, near Dublin. It seemed like every village in Ireland had a track, and all the villagers were involved with horses in some way. His father was a meat-cutter who also owned horses—and who'd had an unfortunate and incurable passion for gambling. When Tony was eleven, his father lost everything gambling. It was a horrible shame for the family, but they got over it, and Tony liked to say, "I was glad he went broke because it changed my life." Otherwise, he'd probably be a meat-cutter like his dad in the old country, selling steak and eating too much. Instead he went to work at the track as an exercise rider and by the age of sixteen was a steeplechase jockey. "And ended up in a life that I'd live over again," he said.

He came to the U.S. from Ireland in 1958 with his older brother, Joe, with the intention of finding work as butchers in New York and saving their money to buy a horse farm. Joe walked the sidewalks for six months before he finally found a job with a grocer on Long Island. Tony found work with the horses, galloping them, training them, and assisting on a brood farm in Rhode Island. In three years, they saved twenty thousand.

Tony found his way to Ocala in 1960, and he discovered a horseman's paradise with land for cheap. An acre went for three hundred dollars, and some of it you couldn't give away—the soil was too sandy, and what was that good for? Horses, that's what. Soon, others were figuring that out, too. Ocala was quickly becoming a prime locale for horse breeders: the weather meant that horses could be turned out all year; they didn't have to be pent up in barns, and that helped them to develop better. The grass was full of limestone, and the ground was perpetually damp and warm, and it never got icy and hard. Eventually, eight hundred thoroughbred farms would grow up in the area, employing 29,000 farmhands, grooms, riders, and hotwalkers. Among the superstar horses that were bred in Florida were a trio of Kentucky Derby winners: Silver Charm, Real Quiet, and Monarchos.

Tony worked for a while as a trainer at the Florida tracks, but the life was too nomadic, particularly after he married and had a son, Brian. Instead he took a job as racing director of George Steinbrenner's Ocala horse farm, Kinsman Farm, so he could settle his family in one place. Eventually, he saved enough to buy his own property, but when Steinbrenner found out, he fired him. Tony had just brought a string of horses back to Kinsman Farm after winning a couple of races when he got a call from Steinbrenner, who wanted to see him. *I think I'm fired,* he thought.

"You bought a farm?" Steinbrenner said.

"Yeah. I bought a farm."

"Why didn't you tell me?"

"It's none of your business. That's my personal business."

"Well, you can't have a farm and work for me."

"Okay. Then I don't work for you."

Steinbrenner indeed fired him, but the two remained amicable. Tony moved down the road to his own place, which he had bought for one thousand dollars an acre, with barns already on it, and named it Another Episode, in honor of a new beginning. For the next twenty-five years, he and his wife and son built the farm, and his career as a pinhooker thrived.

In 1997, he bought a second farm, and he named this one New Episode, once again to signify a change in his life: his second marriage, to Elizabeth. She was a fellow trainer he had known and worked with for years. She had grown up in Camden, South Carolina—a historically horse-crazed town—the daughter of a Navy doctor and a housewife. She started showing horses as a girl, along with her younger sister Shannon, and one morning her mother took them to the racetrack to see the thoroughbreds gallop. "I want to do that," Liz said. She got a job galloping them in the mornings, and from then on it was all she wanted to do. She was an alternate on the 1968 Olympic equestrian team, and then she drifted into training at Finger Lakes racetrack in western New York, where she was known as a handler who could do wonders with horses with bad legs. When one of Tony's New York horses wasn't good enough, if it couldn't run at Belmont or Aqueduct, he would send it on to Liz at Finger Lakes. "Race 'em, sell 'em, but don't send 'em home," he'd tell her.

He had been separated for almost ten years when they began dating. It was hard to find someone who understood the life of a horse trainer, who didn't expect to be taken nightclubbing until midnight. But Liz was like Tony; when he wanted to talk to her at Finger Lakes, he called her at five in the morning and knew she would already be at the barn.

They wed in 1997, and he began all over again with New Episode. Liz didn't like being apart from the horses any more than Tony did. Even when they went on vacation, they missed the horses. They took a week off at Christmas, and in the summertime they went to Del Mar to spend a couple of weeks at the beach, but they were always anxious to get back to the barn. "It's a disease," Tony liked to say.

Tony and Liz rose at four A.M. and were at the barn an hour before dawn. By five A.M. there was a line of cars parked in the grass—vans, pickups, and battered old sedans that had carried the grooms and exercise riders to work. They went about their tasks in dim yellow light, carrying saddles from the tack rooms, bandaging the legs of the horses, and leading them to the track or the pens for their morning lessons.

New Episode had an excellent track for galloping, with a twelve-inch base of packed red clay and half a foot of loam. A computerized watering system kept it the right consistency. (Nothing was more dangerous to a horse than false ground; even a soft spot, when a horse was changing his leads, could blow a tendon, and heavy sand or deep mud could pull the muscles.) Tony had put in lampposts to light the track in the dark, and he'd bought his own starting gate for about forty thousand dollars. It was the perfect setup to simulate race conditions.

Horses galloped in circles through the dark mist, their riders casting repeating shadows under the lampposts, like a ghostly carousel. At the rail, Tony could hear the horses before he could see them, their hard breathing and tromping as they breezed.

Funny Cide's first real training began quietly one morning in the predawn in his stall. Exercise rider Emanuel "Manny" Gonzales slid the door back and stepped inside, carrying a bridle with no ring, and what looked like an oversized tea towel with a cloth strap dangling from it. He laid the piece of cloth over the colt's back, then drew a strap underneath his belly and cinched it.

This was a surcingle, a preliminary to a saddle, and it would get the colt used to having something around his girth. Manny stayed in the stall for a few minutes, playing with him. He pushed Funny gently by his head, leaning on him. This was the first step toward teaching the horse to turn on command.

The horse wasn't having it. Not any of it. Manny pushed, and Funny refused. He jerked his head away and stared at the rider implacably. Manny tried again. The horse was unmoving. "He didn't want to do anything," Manny would remember later. "He wanted to be the boss all the time."

They did this sort of thing for a week. Eventually, the horse deigned to turn circles in his stall, first one way, and then the other. Next, Manny got a saddle on him and a bit in his mouth. Manny clucked and murmured to the horse, and pushed him, and patted him, until he taught him to circle and then to change direction.

Other than a need to be in charge, the horse was easy and smart. He learned everything the first time he was taught: he accepted the saddle and the bit, and each day he grew more accustomed to the tack; to feeling the leather and the metal. He treated it as if it were his own. He chewed on his shank like a snack.

At some point, the colt also acquired his name. Tony's sister-in-law, Ellen, gave it to him. Funny Cide: to her, it was an obvious derivation of his parents' names, Distorted Humor and Belle's Good Cide, and it seemed to connote a kind of dark irreverence, a twisted sense of humor.

Funny's training continued at a leisurely, almost playful pace. Manny put a foot in the stirrup and pulled himself up and lay across the saddle, gradually getting the colt accustomed to his weight. Within another week, Manny or Liz's sister, Shannon, could get on his back and turn him in his stall. Next, the horse learned to carry a rider around the shed row, walking slowly in circles, accompanied by a pony.

If the horse got a little spooky, or bucked, they backed off. They were working with a mind not yet two years old, and there was only so much the colt could absorb in a day. But once the horse was over his spookiness, and could negotiate the shed row, he went on to the corral. Here, he joined three or four other horses and learned how to do figure eights and change leads. Just as importantly, the colt also learned how to stand still and relax in the company of other horses and riders, and not be afraid.

They could tell he was a good horse early on because he handled everything calmly. At times, Shannon and Manny had the sense that they were dealing with an older, more mature horse as he moved around the small circular pen. When he got lazy, Shannon instructed him, just like a schoolteacher. "Pick your feet up and pay attention, feet up, up, up. Quit messing around." When he found his rhythm, his rider rewarded him with praise. "That's it. *Now* we're training a racehorse."

After three weeks, the colt was ready for the racetrack. At first he went slowly, just jogging—if he was rushed, a horse might dump his rider and go through the fence. But Funny was confident and aggressive, his action smooth, and soon they could work him for a quarter mile. They watched Funny's eating habits, to be sure he was relaxed and happy in his training—if they were pushing the colt too hard, he might back off of his feed—but this colt always wanted to do more.

In the meantime, Funny had begun to look like a thoroughbred, as well as behave like one. His stall was in a barn overseen personally by Liz, and Liz had her own methods. She was a superb horsewoman, with hands that knew how to manage a horse firmly without fighting, and she knew how to bring out the handsomeness in a horse, too. Funny Cide was lathered with luxurious suds, rubbed with large soft wads of sponge, and put on a program of vitamins and conditioners that made his coat shine. Liz and Tony laughingly called them beauty products, but the truth was, horses had to look the part when it was time to go to the sales. "No one buys an ugly horse," Tony liked to say.

After ten weeks, Tony decided it was time to address the problem of the colt's un-descended testicle. He consulted with his vet,

Phil Hammock, a bright young doctor from Cornell by way of Dubai, where he had spent a couple of years as the personal surgeon for the thoroughbreds of Sheik Maktoum.

Hammock and Everard reached the same conclusion: the horse should be gelded. There were three reasons to geld a horse: first, to repair a testicle problem; second, to retard the hormonal development of a horse who is becoming too strong in his chest and shoulders and therefore puts too much weight on his front legs; and third, to correct obstreperous, untrainable behavior. In Funny Cide's case, it was strictly a medical decision.

An un-descended testicle didn't overtly lame a stallion, but it could certainly hold one back. When he reached full stride, or went into a turn, it would pull and hurt, and the horse might think, *Well, I'm not going to be in a hurry changing my leads, because I don't want to feel the pain again.* The pain was enough to convince a horse to slow down—he wouldn't try for you.

If they'd had any inkling that the horse was a potential contender in the Triple Crown races, they wouldn't have touched him. A stallion that won any of the three races was worth millions in stud fees. In 2000, Fusiachi Pegasus would sell for $60 million after winning just one leg of the Triple Crown, and he would earn $125,000 per stud session with upward of one hundred mares a year.

But there was nothing in this horse's breeding or appearance to suggest he'd ever be a valuable stallion. He might, however, be a nice stakes horse if he was gelded. Geldings made fine, and sometimes even great, racehorses, and they could run for years: Kelso had been a five-time Horse of the Year who won thirty-nine races in sixty-three starts and earned nearly two million dollars in purses between 1959 and 1966. John Henry won thirty-nine victories in eighty-three starts from 1977 to 1984, for $6.6 million, including the Santa Anita Handicap at the age of nine. Forego won thirty-four races in fifty-seven starts from 1973 to 1978, for $1.9 million.

So they gelded him. On the night of October 26, 2001, Funny was vanned a few miles up the road to the Ferguson and Associates Equine Clinic, where Hammock practiced. Hammock anesthetized the horse and, when he was unconscious, had him moved to an operating table via a hoist-like machine. The procedure took all of twenty minutes, and then the horse was put into a padded stall, the equine version of a recovery room.

Within an hour, the horse struggled back to his feet, officially a gelding.

Sackets Six broke his leg.

The horse ran just four races before he injured himself. The partners all came down to Saratoga to see their horse run, and when he finished third, ridden by Pat Day, it was as thrilling as Jack had promised. Next, they tried him on the turf, and he shot ahead of the field by ten lengths, running like hell. The Sackets crew went crazy, though Jack knew better and said, "He's going to die like a dog." Which he did, finishing far behind, out of the money.

But then he injured himself. Fortunately, it was a clean fracture, reparable by surgery. He underwent a procedure to place screws in his leg, and they spent a year paying the vet bills. Tim Kelly patiently worked the horse back to health, but it was just the beginning of his physical problems. He came back and won a race—only to fracture a different leg. Tim nursed him back to health once more, this time without surgery being performed.

It was worth it. Sackets Six won two more races for them, and he finished second on four other occasions. To walk in the Saratoga paddock with their horse made them feel like millionaires, and so did the clubhouse seats. None of them had ever had good seats at Saratoga before—they were used to sitting on folding chairs in the picnic area. Usually, Jack and Jean would rise at six A.M. and go to the track to grab possession of three or four picnic tables and set up their camp for the day with coolers full of beer and sandwiches. Now, as owners, they had parking stickers and clubhouse passes, and they could watch from the covered green box seats in the clubhouse when their horse ran.

But it soon became clear that Sackets Six was in over his head physically, and racing would only injure him further. They decided to sell him, though they were reluctant to do it. The horse had been just good enough to tantalize them, to keep them interested, and he had rewarded them as much as he cost them. In three years, he'd won three times, earned $110,000—enough to pay most of his own bills. If the horse had buried them financially, they'd never have stayed with it. It would have been the end of their short careers as owners.

Also, the horse gave them a sense of adventure they wouldn't have had otherwise. They took field trips together. They'd drive down to New York to watch their horse run at Belmont or Aqueduct, and eat dinner together on Saturday night, and maybe go to a New York Giants game on Sunday. It was a way to do things as a group, to keep the bow tied, at a time when they were all getting older and might have drifted.

In Sackets Harbor, they took turns hosting Friday-night parties to discuss stable business. The Crings or Constances or Phillipses would put out smoked salmon, cheese and crackers, beer and wine, and everyone knew to bring their checkbooks. Somebody would say, "Okay, J.P., how much this time?"

"Another three hundred fifty dollars apiece."

But the success of Sackets Six notwithstanding, it was also apparent to them that the Sackatoga stable wouldn't be in the thoroughbred business for long without some help financially. There was no way they could continue to write checks for a new horse, veterinary care, and feed bills. They decided to bring in more partners, and Jack set about finding them.

From then on, the makeup of Sackatoga changed regularly. While the core group would remain basically the same, others came and went. Friends and business acquaintances would buy in for a share or a piece of a share, and then get out again when the vet bills became too expensive for them, or if they suffered a business reversal. Mark and Gwen Phillips, for instance, didn't participate in every horse, simply because they didn't have the money or were reluctant to buy in too deep. "Show me a paycheck," Gwen said. "When are you going to get a paycheck?" Every now and then a small check came, but most of the money went back into the stable.

Jean Derouin got out. The Derouins wanted to help one of their sons financially, and they couldn't do it on Jean's income as a manufacturer's rep, while also buying racehorses, without straining their finances. He and his wife, Jeannie, talked about it. "No more horses," she said. Jean told the partners he just couldn't take the chance.

One afternoon, Larry Reinhardt's phone rang, and it was J.P. "Hey, you have a chance to get in," he said. There was a horse named Phone Solicitor, and they were offering Larry a 4 percent share, since Jean didn't want in. "Okay, I'm in," Larry said.

The wives referred to themselves as The Underground. They would find out what one or the other of the husbands had said, and they'd piece together what was going on. It was the only way they could learn anything. When Jean Derouin got out of the group, they talked about whether it was wiser to stay in, or to tell their husbands they'd had enough. But the rest of them decided to hang in there—so far, the guys weren't betting the grocery money.

Jack was the managing partner: he kept the books, paid all the bills, handled the headaches, discussed strategy with trainer Tim Kelly, raised money from other investors, and kept everyone informed. He did it for free, and the truth was, if he could've afforded to quit the health-care business and just own horses, he would have. He had one quirk: he did his bookkeeping in longhand, and he sent the partners statements written out in black ink on legal stationery. Dorothy tried to set up a computer program for him, but he preferred the old-fashioned way.

When Jack looked for other partners, he didn't have to look far—he found them in his friends and acquaintances at the Carousel Bar in the Saratoga clubhouse: Gus Williams, a retired house builder in his seventies; Dave Mahan, a caterer who was in his early fifties; and Lew Titterton, the president of a health-care company, in his mid-fifties. They were like-minded people, guys who worked hard for their money but who liked a sporting wager.

Gus Williams had been a fixture at the Carousel forever. He was the garrulous guy who always had a story and a joke, which he told with a *ba-da-bing* delivery. Each racing season, Gus attended the Travers Stakes, the highlight of the meet, in a shimmering getup of canary-yellow slacks and a black-and-yellow checked blazer. Gus loved to do three things: drink beer, bet horses, and hang out with his buddies at the bar or the VFW. It became Jack's habit to take a bar stool next to Gus, who regaled him with stories of hard luck and big bets.

Gus reminded Jack of his own father, who had spent so much time at the VFW in Watertown. Gus, he learned, was a self-made man, an Italian immigrant's kid and a World War II vet who had served from 1943 to 1945 in the Army Air Corps. He still wouldn't buy a Japanese-made car. "They tried to kill me once," he said. When he came home, it was to a job in construction. Eventually, Gus made good money in the house-building business, and he built a small home for himself and his wife, Annie, in Saratoga, just a couple of blocks from the backstretch. He had owned some horses back in the 1960s, but now he was strictly a bettor, and a partier. Every Sunday morning, Gus would host a party for his backstretch friends at his house, because no place served alcohol before noon. He would get a couple of kegs of beer, and Bloody Mary mix, and then invite his pals to come eat and drink before the track opened for business. You'd find all kinds of people in Gus's house: handicappers, jockeys, trainers, owners, hotwalkers, and grooms. Everybody in Saratoga knew Gus. There were the people who wanted to know him, and the people who didn't want to know him. Jack became a regular.

When Jack founded Sackatoga with his partners after the 1995 Memorial Day picnic, he had invited Gus in on the deal. But Gus's wife, Annie, didn't want him to. "He ain't buying no horse," she said. Three years later, when Sackatoga Stable needed some outside financing, she relented. "Want to get back in the game?" Jack asked. This time, Gus was in.

Lew Titterton was a self-made businessman whom Jack had

known for twenty years in the health-care business. Like many of the Sackatoga partners, he was a child of the Vietnam era; he'd served as a full lieutenant on a 1,200-ton spy ship that monitored Russian missile shots, and he cruised out of Pearl Harbor to Vietnam. When he'd left the Navy, he founded a high-tech company that built computer systems for the health industry, which was how he'd met Jack. Lew eventually sold his company, and he and his wife Pat were looking for something to have fun with when Jack proposed that he come in on Sackatoga.

Lew didn't necessarily love the horses, and he wasn't a big bettor. He had briefly bought into a harness horse with Jack named The Red Ghost, who tried to drown himself while doing hydro-training in a pool, and that cured Lew from owning for a while. Lew was more involved with the rich Saratoga cultural world than with the track, but he enjoyed the clubhouse milieu and the privilege that came with owning, so when Jack invited him in, he said yes.

Lew also loved Gus's Sunday-morning gatherings. For one thing, you could pick up a good tip. Lew had a rule: he never bet more than two thousand dollars in the six-week racing season at Saratoga. But one year, after he lost a grand in the first week, he was looking for a way to get even. Lew went to Gus's weekly party and began chatting with an assistant to the renowned trainer Sonny Hine, who would make Skip Away into the Horse of the Year in 1998. The assistant trainer was already smashed and feeling talkative. "Bet on my horse in the first race," he announced to anyone who would listen. Lew opened the *Daily Racing Form*, and saw that the horse had run twelve times and never won.

"Why should I bet on your horse?" Lew asked.

"Because of the jockey," the trainer said. Sonny Hine was unhappy with the jockey. He felt the rider had cost them a couple of victories with poor rides. "Sonny told him if he doesn't win the race, he's fired and will never ride for him again. And he'll make sure he never rides for anyone else, either."

That afternoon, Lew took one thousand dollars to a betting window on the backstretch and put it on the jockey. When the horse came down the track, he was fourteen lengths in the lead and the rider was practicing standing on the horse's head, beating him to death. Lew won a lot of money, and he thought to himself, *This isn't bad.* He could learn a lot at Gus's parties.

Jack wanted to buy a higher quality of horse for Sackatoga, so together, Jack, Lew, Gus, and some of the Sackatoga partners purchased a $50,000 dark bay colt they named Carrtoga. But Carrtoga was a most unsuccessful horse. He ran only five times before he got hurt. In his first race, a $100,000 New York Stallion Series stakes race, he came in dead last. He raced four more times for them, never winning anything, before he developed a tendon problem. In the end, they gave him away; he was unsellable as a racehorse, though he later became a good show horse. It was an expensive lesson.

The stable acquired two more horses with promising names: Harbor's End and Phone Solicitor. But neither of them duplicated the early success of Sackets Six, and the costs were mounting while the purses were few and far between. By the spring of '99, the owners all felt that they were spending too much money. They weren't buying or racing very good horses, and they weren't having much fun, either.

Tim Kelly had been with them for the four years, through four horses. He was a good, patient trainer who had learned the business from his father, T. J. Kelly, a Hall of Famer who had trained horses for fifty years. But now there were two options: they could sell out, or try a new trainer.

They decided to look for a new trainer who might help them upgrade their quality of horses. Jack and Gus went to Tim's barn at Belmont and apologetically told him the bad news. "Tim, things just aren't working out and we feel we need to make a change and we hope you understand," Jack said. Tim said he did, though he was disappointed to lose the horses. They remained friends, and Tim later went to work for the New York Racing Association.

Jack and Gus consulted with knowledgeable backstretch people, and they came up with the names of three trainers who might be available. Jack then put out the calls. The first guy he talked to said he was too busy; he couldn't take care of his current clients, much less add another. The second trainer called Jack back, and requested that he fax over information on the two horses, which Jack did. Jack never heard from him again.

The third trainer was Barclay Tagg. Jack had noticed Barclay long before he met him, because he'd won a third of the races he entered at Saratoga, an excellent percentage, when he shipped turf horses up from Maryland. Jack bet a Barclay Tagg horse every time he saw one in the program. Barclay would ship his unsung horses in, and they'd jump up and pay fifteen or twenty-five dollars. His reputation was that of a hardworking trainer who'd had plenty of success despite the fact that he never had big-name horses.

Jack called up Barclay at his barn office and said, "I've got a couple of horses, and I'm looking for a new trainer."

Barclay was polite but noncommittal. "Well, tell me about your horses."

Jack briefly described them: Phone Solicitor had some decent breeding, but Harbor's End was by a mediocre New York sire, and they'd paid more money for him than they should have.

Barclay had two empty stalls at Belmont. The New York Racing Association awarded stalls to trainers based on a variety of factors, including their track records and their level of cooperativeness when an extra horse was needed to fill a race. Barclay figured he could use the day rate on two more horses, and maybe they would win and make some money, though he doubted it from the sound of them.

"Well, I've got two stalls open," he said. "I could take them. You want to come down and make the transfer?"

They turned Harbor's End and Phone Solicitor over to Barclay, and they began to hunt for yet another horse. But a new horse meant they needed more capital, and now Jack recruited another Carousel habitué, Dave Mahan, a tall, sleek fellow with brushed-back blond hair and an easy laugh. Mahan was another self-made businessman, a caterer from Connecticut who rewarded himself for his hard work each year with a trip to Saratoga. He rented a small house and spent the summer handicapping and betting the races, and he usually won enough to pay for his vacation.

Initially, Dave had stayed on the far side of the bar from Jack and Gus. He thought the old guy had a pretty loud mouth, so he would go to the opposite end of the establishment and try to ignore the shouted jokes and high-pitched laughter coming from Gus's circle. But eventually the commotion was too much to resist, so Dave sidled down the bar and joined in. He gained a creeping affection for Gus, and they discovered they had a lot in common: they were both hardworking guys who couldn't say no to the horses, even when they broke your heart or emptied your wallet.

Dave had started going to fairgrounds races in Great Barrington, Massachusetts, when he was thirteen years old. His father was a welder and steamfitter, and his mother was a secretary who could make a beef roast last for a week. Dave had discovered Saratoga when he was an undergrad at Thomas College in Maine and he'd found himself spending more and more of each season there. He'd always wanted to be a horse owner, and he'd tell his pals, "I'm going to buy a horse someday."

"Yeah, who's got that kind of money?" they said.

He sold drilling equipment all over the world, traveling to more than fifty countries in Europe, Asia, India, South Africa, and Indonesia, and probably spent a third of his life in hotels. But in 1982, the bottom fell out of the drilling business, and the bottom fell out of Dave's personal life, too. He lost his job, and his marriage fell apart. He moved back home to Watertown, Connecticut, to look for work, but he had trouble finding any in the midst of the recession. One day his father called and mentioned that there was a local catering business for sale. "Dad, what do I know about catering?" he asked.

"Well, you always liked to cook."

"Yeah, for eight people."

The next day, Dave went over to the Crystal Room to check out the property, and by the end of the day he had bought it. He rebuilt his business life, catering weddings, anniversaries, and birthdays. He saved his money, and did so well that now he had earned enough to buy into thoroughbreds.

Like all naïve newcomers, he got cheated. He bought his first horse, a weanling filly, with a couple of friends in 1991 and became deeply attached to her. But a crooked trainer ruined her feet, and then tried to sell the horse out from under him.

Dave wouldn't be defrauded again. He named his stable Kurant, after a brand of vodka, learned as he went, and eventually acquired a respectable string of horses. He experimented with breeding, purchasing a broodmare named Cherylina, who was in foal to a prominent stallion, Devil His Due. She gave him three great foals, and she was pregnant with another one when, in 1999, he decided to expand his catering business. He had an opportunity to buy a twenty-acre estate in Wolcott, Connecticut, with a 30,000-square-foot facility, but it meant he would have to sell all his toys to pay for it, including his 1963 Corvette split-window coupe, a treasure.

While he didn't think of horses as toys, they sure weren't business, either. At a Kentucky sale for horses of all ages, he put his pregnant mare and a sweet filly on the market. He put a shank on the filly and led her himself to the sales pavilion, tears coursing down his face. There were all kinds of tough buyers and sellers in the pavilion, and here came a grown man leading a little filly like a boy at the 4-H Club who didn't want to sell his pet. It broke his heart.

He continued to go to Saratoga every summer, though strictly as a handicapper, and allowed himself to wager no more than four hundred dollars a day. To bet well took a lot of work, in Dave's opinion. He gathered all the data and analyzed it, talked to people on the backstretch and appraised the track conditions, and then he had to bet in the right *way,* choose the exacta or a trifecta, to minimize his risk. A lot of people were good handicappers but bad bettors. Dave was proud to say that he had lost on only one race meet in a decade.

He remarried, and hardly a day went by that Dave didn't congratulate himself on his good fortune in meeting his wife, Nadine, a lissome blonde who bred and showed purebred dogs. There were lots of wives who might view the track as a threat, or something irresponsible and reckless to do with one's money. There weren't lots of wives who would allow their husbands to go to Saratoga for six weeks every summer. But Nadine was easy about it, and even actively enjoyed it. She never once asked, "How much money are you spending?" or "How did you do at the track today?" and nor had she ever said, "You know, you're having way too much fun without me."

With his business and personal life in good shape, Dave felt the old impulse to buy a horse again. Betting seemed like a comparatively empty gesture without an ownership stake. At every opportunity at the Carousel, he said to Jack and Gus, "If you guys ever need another partner . . ." Jack finally asked Dave to buy into Sackatoga on a horse named Blow the Blues. They were at a joint called the Pour House near Belmont Park when Dave wrote his first check.

With Barclay and Robin Smullen as their trainers, the stable immediately enjoyed success. Phone Solicitor had won just one race and wasn't running well when she came to Barclay's barn. He decided to try one of his standard methods for getting a horse to run. He would put her on the turf. Barclay was a big believer in grass, because it was what horses were *supposed* to run on; it was in their nature to sink their hooves into a soft bed of chlorophyll-rich grass.

He'd had the horse about a week when he entered her in a turf race at Belmont Park.

She went off at about 114–1. Gus went to watch the simulcast at Saratoga raceway and studied the odds. He bet four hundred dollars on her, some of it in exotic bets (exactas or trifectas), and the rest to win, place, and show. A friend of his said, "Why did you bet four hundred dollars, at those odds, on that horse?"

"Because I have a hard head," Gus said.

Phone Solicitor finished second. She paid seventy dollars for second, and thirty-six dollars for third. Imagine if she had won. As it was, he collected ten thousand dollars. He was a jaunty, smiling winner.

"Well, if she'da won, what would I have done with all the money? They wouldn't have had enough money to pay me," he said.

If you asked Gus why he loved the track, he said, "Money. Get the money."

But that was the height of their success with Phone Solicitor. In the fall, after the Saratoga season had ended, Barclay leveled with them. "You know, these two horses you've got are not very good. I can do my best for them, but you're just not going to get what you want to get out of them." Barclay suggested they sell out and start new.

"Look, I know what you guys want," he said. "You want to have some fun."

Barclay began looking for horses that would suit his Sackatoga owners. When Harbor's End went lame, they sent the animal to a farm in Virginia to recuperate, and found him a new home through Rerun, an organization that places retired racehorses. Phone Solicitor was sold to a woman in Charlestown, West Virginia, an acquaintance of Robin's who entered her in cheaper races and then bred her.

In October of 2000, Barclay called Jack with something that interested him. "I think I've found a horse you could have some fun with," he said.

The horse was a filly named Bail Money, and another of Barclay's owners was willing to sell her. The owner was a Virginian who wasn't interested in shipping to Florida for the winter, but Barclay was convinced the horse would do well there. She was just sitting in the barn in New York. "You don't need a forty-thousand-dollar horse, and these guys want to have some action over the winter," Barclay said. "How about letting them buy her?"

It was a done deal. Sackatoga bought Bail Money, and Barclay and Robin took the horse to Florida. As soon as they got there, Barclay put Bail Money in an $80,000 claiming race, and she finished second. From then on, she would finish in the money in exactly half the races Barclay entered her in.

In the meantime, Barclay also introduced the Sackatogans to a new partner. Eric Dattner, Barclay said, "wants to play the game." Barclay knew him; he was a mild-mannered, unintrusive, but knowledgeable horseman, and he was dependable.

Dattner, sixty-seven, was a retired mechanical engineer who lived just a few minutes from Belmont and stopped by there on an almost daily basis to watch the horses train. Over the years, he had shared ownership of some horses in Barclay's care, and he liked to hang around the barn. He would bring coffee and doughnuts to the hot-walkers, and he'd observe as the horses were exercised and groomed.

Eric had first gotten involved with horses in 1971, when he saw an ad in the *New York Times* business-opportunity section offering a partnership in horse racing. Eric bought a 50 percent interest in a three-horse stable for $7,500. Which was more than what the horses were worth, but he didn't know that. He learned the hard way, the way all lessons in the horse business are learned.

One of the horses won in his second start, but after that, everything went downhill. It turned out that Eric's partner wasn't paying the bills, so their trainer moved out of town with the horses, overnight, without telling him. Eric went down to Belmont one morning and the stalls were empty.

Eric traced the horses to a small track in Narragansett, where he managed to reclaim one of them, a benighted creature named Rub Out. Eric ran him a couple of times in $1,500 claimers, which was as low as it could get, and he finished second once and third

once, but the horse wasn't well. Eric sent him off to a farm in Box-
ford, Massachusetts, to recuperate, where he was lost in a barn fire.

After that, Eric signed up for an adult-education course on
horses that was being offered at a high school in Deer Park, Long
Island, and he began to study the game seriously. In addition to
classes, he would work around the barns, learning the breeding
business from the ground up. But really, there was no sure or easy
way to avoid misadventures. Mares failed to get in foal, or foals
were born with maladies. He and some partners bred to a horse
named Arts and Letters, a Belmont Stakes champion, for a $10,000
stud fee. The foal was born live—but with a rare intestinal defor-
mity, and he was operated on twice and lived for only about six
weeks before they had to put him down.

By 2000, Eric was at loose ends, without an ownership stake in
any horse, but despite his mishaps, he missed it. He missed having a rooting interest at his home track. He asked Barclay to keep
an eye out for him, should he come across a syndicate looking for
an additional partner.

Barclay thought about Sackatoga and how the ownership
changed on almost every horse. He called Jack and explained that
he had a potential partner for them, if they wanted one. "I don't like
to do this, and I don't normally do it," he said. "But I know you
guys, and I know Eric, and I think it would be a good fit." It was.
Eric bought into Sackatoga on a $39,000 bay filly named, promis-
ingly enough, Diamond Flight, at a sale in Timonium, Maryland.
Despite the cost of the filly, Eric told the group he was prepared to
buy into another horse, if they found a good one.

In that summer of 2001, Barclay took Jack, Eric, and Dave to
the Fasig Tipton sale in Saratoga. It was the same sale in which
Funny Cide was offered by the McMahons and WinStar. All of

them looked right past the awkward colt, wearing hip number 22, while Barclay noticed nothing except the suspect-looking feet. Instead, Barclay steered them to a filly wearing hip number 26. They bought her, for eighteen thousand dollars. They named her Wed in Dixie, and Barclay decided to ship her to Tony Everard's farm. Ironically, she would be in the same horse van as Funny Cide.

By now, Sackatoga Stable had consisted of eight horses and numerous different owners, and for every victory at the track, it seemed as though there had been an offsetting problem. Diamond Flight, one of their most expensive horses to date, contracted a fever disease in a barn in Delaware, and it cost ten thousand dollars in vet bills to treat her. Robin had to race up the turnpike to meet the vet to get the medication that saved her life. The owners weren't in the kind of financial stratosphere that permitted them to continue to buy horses without some return.

But they had Bail Money. In 2001, Bail Money started in nine races and finished in the money in five of them, earning $64,460, including one victory. In 2002, she gave them another first-place finish, and $44,070 more in earnings. She was the pride of the partnership, beloved by the owners, because every time she entered a race, she gave them a shot and always brought in a purse. At least they had her.

After four months at New Episode, Funny Cide was ready to breeze on the track. Usually, Tony and Liz had to teach a horse to go faster, but Funny Cide just decided to go. He galloped through the dark and the mist turned faint yellow by the dim lamps, and that's when he started to show himself.

Afterward, Manny told everyone, "Oh, that's a nice horse." You could feel it, Manny said. He flowed. He was like a high-performance engine, so fast and aggressive it was hard to hold him. At three-eighths of a mile, he had demonstrated real honest-to-goodness speed.

Still, you didn't know about a horse until he took the starting gate. It was time to teach the unraced two-year-old how to respond to the slamming open of those doors and the bell, to race on command. A lot of good horses, as Tony put it, "lost their brain" when they came to the gate.

It was still dark one morning when Funny Cide was taken to the practice gate for the first time. The gate was a spring contraption that weighed ten tons, an enlarged precision instrument of ball bearings and magnets and coils, and it was Tony's pride and joy. At first, they didn't put the colt in the gate; they just let him smell the big piece of steel. Tony banged the steel doors together to try to get him accustomed to the noise. They held the horse by a shank until he got used to the sounds, until it was "kind of like music to him," as Tony said, in his typically lyrical way.

After two days, they could bang the doors and the horse didn't shake or try to pull away. They loaded him. Funny walked right into the gate and stood there confidently, as if he would wait there all day if they wanted him to.

Tony's assistants closed the gates behind him; there was a creak and a clang, and he was in. Tony reached over and locked the doors. For a long minute, Funny stood in the gate, in the dark, the only illumination a yellow leaky light. This horse was still steady, Tony noticed.

Then the mechanism swung into action: the doors shot open,

and Tony yelled "Hyaaaaahh!" The horse broke from the gate and galloped into the darkness. Tony stared after him as he tore down the track.

The horse ran freely, on a path straight as an arrow. He didn't look around or veer sideways; he just went. His coat was shining, and his legs were bandaged in clean white linen, and he looked like a million-dollar horse.

It was obvious that the horse knew what he was doing: the object of the game was to come out of that gate and run. To Funny Cide, dirt was for running. "He just got the idea that the track was for going fast," Liz marveled.

Early the next morning, Tony picked up the phone and dialed Barclay's number. When Tony wanted to talk to Barclay, he called him at a quarter to five, because he knew that Barclay and Robin, like Tony and Liz themselves, would already be at the barn. Over the years, the two couples had become good friends as well as business associates.

"When are you coming down here?" Tony asked. "We got a horse."

Barclay trusted Tony's judgment. He often bought horses from Tony for his owners, and he placed his yearlings with Tony and Liz for training, too. He and Robin made it a point to stop through New Episode each winter on their annual migration from Belmont to Florida for the winter racing. They would wander through the pastures and look at the yearlings, or watch horses gallop, and then stay for dinner and visit with Tony and Liz.

Barclay believed Tony had a superb eye for medium-priced horses. If you were looking to keep the price down but the quality high, New Episode was a good place to find a horse. You wouldn't find Citation at Tony's place—but when you bought an animal from him, it came at a good price and was almost always sound.

Barclay liked to tell his owners, "The best place to buy a good horse is anywhere it shows up."

At the Kentucky sales, buyers often have only five to fifteen minutes to inspect each of the up to four thousand horses in the sale. But the truth was, nobody who bought a young horse had any idea if it could really run, even at the lowest end of the game. Trainers had broken a lot of wealthy people by pretending an expensive young horse was a sure thing. Wealthy owners who bought the finest two-year-olds every year were going to win some big races eventually, but they lost a lot, too.

For instance, some of them matured the wrong way. Young horses changed all the time. They developed splints, from galloping. A horse looked great in November, but when you went back in March, he'd turned into a rat. They got sore or sick—if a young horse got pneumonia, its lungs were never the same. There were other unseen things that could happen to them, too. When the weather changed, they could get pharyngitis, a sore throat, and that affected their breathing and could paralyze their palates. They got ulcers in the eye, from something as simple as banging the hay net and poking themselves. A small clot developed, and soon an ulcer could turn the entire eye gray, and you had to treat the animal six times a day and keep it inside until it healed.

Barclay preferred to study young horses, if he could, and at Tony's place he had that leisure. He could see a horse two or three times over a period of months and watch how it developed.

In late 2001, Barclay and Robin came to New Episode for their regular visit on their drive from New York. That afternoon, they walked out into the pasture among the babies; often that was when they first noticed something in a horse. The horses brushed up against them, and they patted them or stroked their faces.

Barclay paused and looked at a skinny red horse, not the most magnificent animal he'd ever seen, but with brightness in his eyes, and upright ears, and something thick and sturdy in his legs, and a nice long step.

"Who's that?" Barclay asked Tony.

Tony told him it was a colt from the McMahons, out of Distorted Humor. Barclay remembered the horse, but he didn't remember him being this nice to look at. The foot problem had disappeared, and he had good shoulders.

Barclay rejoined Robin and said, "Did you see the Distorted Humor horse?"

"I didn't notice him," Robin said.

"Well, look at him, because he's a pretty nice horse," Barclay said.

Robin saw a handsome but slender animal with a nice walk. He was the sort of horse they liked to look at, form-wise. There was no such thing as a perfect horse; there were only preferences. Some people liked a horse with huge hips and hind end and a big gasket, a large form, but that wasn't Barclay and Robin's style. They liked a narrower and more athletic horse. Like this one. He had all of the dimensions in balance, and a six-inch overstep (the term that described how a horse put its hind foot where its front foot had been), and a ballet-like, toe-heel walk.

No horse had all the parts—but this one came close. They asked the price on him, and Tony quoted $40,000. Barclay just nodded, and filed it away in the back of his mind. The Sackatoga group was always interested in New York–breds, but at the moment they had all the horses they could afford.

Three months later, Robin and Barclay swung back by Tony's place. They rose early in the morning and went to the barn to watch the horses work. They stood by the rail, and every couple of minutes the soft rhythmic thud of hooves in the soil announced another colt or filly approaching.

Liz galloped the chestnut colt toward them, and Barclay and Robin watched his action carefully. His coat shimmered; he had blossomed into an eye-catcher. His gallop was so smooth and easy that it seemed one rolling motion instead of four separate legs. They glanced at each other.

"This is a *really* nice horse," Barclay said.

Tony could tell from the look on Barclay's face that he liked the horse. As Liz slowed the horse and moved him off the track, once again they noticed his walk. He had a better walk than just about any horse Robin had seen, an elegant, measured stride.

Again, Barclay asked Tony, "How much?"

"Fifty thousand," Tony said.

The price had gone up—but it was still a good price. Tony knew what he had; the horse's workouts kept getting better and better, and all signs were that the horse was maturing in the right direction.

Barclay and Robin still weren't in position to make an offer, but they left the farm that day convinced that the horse would be a good buy for Sackatoga. Barclay called Jack Knowlton. "I've seen an awfully talented New York–bred at Tony Everard's," he said.

Jack was intrigued, but he said, "Well, we don't really have the money." Even if they could get it together, it would take some time, Jack said. But he promised he would take it up with his partners.

All Barclay and Robin could do was wait and see. As interested as the trainers were in the gelding, they knew better than to let a good-looking two-year-old break their hearts. Anybody could come along and buy him, any minute. Tony wasn't going to say, "I'll save him for you until you make up your mind." A lot of good horsemen looked for an animal at Tony's, and they came from everywhere. They had eyes, too.

But for the moment, there were no takers. A bloodstock agent offered the colt to several of his owners, but none of them was interested. "I would rather have a mule than a New York–bred gelding," one owner declared. Another seemed vaguely interested, but wouldn't go above forty thousand dollars. "We don't want to spend that much money," the trainer told Tony.

"Well, you know, I'd like to sell him to you cheap, but I have to make money on the good ones," Tony replied.

The horse remained at New Episode, and a month later, Barclay came back for yet another look. For the third time in four months, he stood by the rail and admired the horse. But he was just standing and looking, and not able to pay, while the horse got better and better. Each time Barclay saw him, he found more that he liked. The ugly little foal with the bad feet now had a great shoulder, nice hips, and excellent bones. He was a very well-put-together horse.

The price had gone up to $75,000.

"Every time you look at him, he gets more expensive," Tony said.

Barclay wasn't offended. Tony had taken all the risk on the horse for eight months; he'd broken him, and trained him, and fed him, and doctored him. Anything could happen to a horse in the paddock—he could snap his leg in an instant. The longer he stayed on Tony's farm, and the faster his workouts became, the more he would cost. Barclay was realistic: his money truck hadn't shown up. In April, Tony would offer the horse at a spring sale, and he'd probably get what he asked.

But then one of those chance coincidences occurred, one of those "ifs" that, much later, would cause everyone to ponder the difference between chance and providence. Some of the owners would ascribe what happened next to fate, and others to sheer blind luck—although at the time, it looked like *bad* luck, not good.

In March of 2000, Barclay and Robin entered Sackatoga's favorite horse, Bail Money, in a $62,500 claiming race on the turf at Gulfstream Park. In a claiming race, horses are entered at a specific price, and can be "claimed," meaning bought, at that price, by any other owner or trainer racing in the meet. The idea is to make sure all the horses entered in a race are of similar value, so that owners of quality horses aren't tempted to beat up on bum competition just for the purses.

Bail Money was claimed. In the space of a single afternoon, she was no longer Sackatoga's horse. She now belonged to someone else. The owners were crestfallen; the windfall of cash was small solace for losing their favorite and most successful horse, a creature that had given them so many thrilling afternoons at the track, and the irreplaceable feeling of being winners. She'd never finished worse than fifth, and in her last three starts for them at Gulfstream she had finished first, second, and third, raking in the purse money. She would never run as well again as she did for Barclay and Sackatoga, either. After changing hands, she'd be winless in nine starts.

But where the owners saw a loss, Barclay saw an opportunity.

He picked up the phone and called Jack. What the Sackatoga owners ought to do, he told Jack, was buy a new horse immediately with the cash from the claiming race. And the horse he had in mind was the gelding at Tony's farm. The horse just got better and better, and they were lucky no one had bought him yet, he said. If they didn't get him now, Barclay warned, he would go in the April sales and, probably, for a much higher price. In Barclay's estimation, the horse could be worth double what Tony was asking.

"We've looked at this horse all winter," Barclay said. "He's a New York–bred, a strong-looking horse, just the type we like, and his price keeps going up. I think he's worth it. I know what your limits are and you might not want to go any higher, but you ought to grab this horse while you can."

Jack discussed it with his partners: How did they feel about owning a gelding? They decided that it didn't matter to them; they wanted a racehorse, not a stallion. "As far as I'm concerned, it just means fewer memories," Dave joked.

Jack called Barclay back. "Okay, let's go get that horse," he said. "If you like him so much, then go buy him."

Jack called the partners, and they agreed on how to distribute the percentages: Jack, Dave, and Gus each bought a full share for fifteen thousand dollars. Eric Dattner and Lew Titterton each bought in for a half share. The Sackets crew would split another full share, giving them 4 percent each of the new horse.

Tony congratulated himself on the sale; it was about as good as a pinhooker could do. He'd bought the horse for $22,000 and sold him for $75,000. Still, he and Liz didn't watch the horse load into the van for shipping without a pang. Often, a horse that left New Episode won its first race, and when it did, Tony and Liz felt they could take a little of the credit. After all, the horse had learned to trot, canter, gallop, and breeze, to change leads and burst from a gate, at their farm.

When you taught them from babies, you got attached, and you stayed attached. Tony knew when his protégés were running years after they'd left the farm. The walls of Tony's office were lined with wood-framed pictures of beautiful horses in full racing stride, crossing the wire. Tony helped develop Timely Writer, the 1982 Florida Derby and Flamingo Stakes winner. The 1985 Kentucky Derby runner-up, Tejano Run, was an alum of his, too.

But Tony's favorite alumnus was a New York racing legend named Fourstardave, who'd passed through his hands as a yearling in 1986. Fourstardave became such a stalwart champion that he won a race at Saratoga racecourse for eight consecutive years, and every winter, the horse would come back to Tony's farm in Ocala for his rest. As soon as the horse stepped from the trailer to the turf, he would drop down and roll, like he was kissing the ground. When Fourstardave finally died in 1999, Tony mourned him like he was a person.

Tony watched Funny Cide load into the van for the trip to Belmont Park that spring, certain that he would hear about the horse in the winner's circle, perhaps even that summer. Maybe the colt would be another Fourstardave. He figured when Fourstardave died, maybe God gave him Funny Cide.

Funny Cide arrived at Belmont and took his stall in Barclay Tagg's barn. Barclay loved the look of his new acquisition: the first time Funny Cide breezed at Saratoga, he galloped past everything on the track. Robin was in Delaware looking after another string of horses, but she could hear the enthusiasm in his voice over the phone. "He does everything so easy," Barclay said. But he also reported that the horse was difficult to control, and he was tired of watching ninety-pound exercise riders saw at the horse's mouth. He told Robin to come home; he needed her to handle this horse, and didn't want anyone exercising him but Robin. Barclay felt about Robin the way Tony did about Liz: she was a superb horsewoman who knew how to handle a horse without fighting.

Barclay's fear came true one morning: Funny Cide broke loose from his handlers and took off. To Funny Cide, the track was for running, and when his hooves hit the dirt, he tore around the track. By the time they got to him, he'd "bucked" his shins. Bucked shins occurred when the stress of running caused a soft section of a horse's shins to pull away from the bone and become inflamed.

Barclay called Tony. "The horse ran off with his rider," Barclay said.

"Oh, yeah," Tony said, lilting easily. "He ran off with everybody at the farm, too."

"Now you tell us that?" Barclay said.

"Oh, yeah," Tony lilted. "No one can hold him."

Barclay started laughing. All Tony had ever said about Funny Cide until that moment was "Oh, he's a *fine* horse."

Barclay had to tell the owners the horse wouldn't be ready to run that summer; there was nothing to do for bucked shins except repair the injury and let the horse rest until it had fully, properly healed. Otherwise, Funny Cide was liable to be just another statistic, one of the 21,725 thoroughbreds that would not make starts as two-year-olds.

One morning, some of the gelding's new owners came to the barn at Saratoga to see their new acquisition. They were disappointed; they wouldn't get to see the horse run at Saratoga that summer, and they'd have to wait until racing returned to Belmont in September. Still, they were curious about the expensive new creature that had so impressed Barclay and Robin.

Barclay didn't mind having these owners around the barn so much. They were green, and they had a way of getting underfoot sometimes when they wanted to feed peppermints to the horses. But they were good-natured workingmen who were easy to deal with, and they had senses of humor.

Dave Mahan decided he didn't like the horse's name. He wanted to rename him Fully Loaded. But Gus said, "Let him alone. He knows his name already. You want to give him a name that he don't know? You're crazy. He won't be able to talk to you."

"All right, all right," Dave said, laughing.

Lew Titterton gazed around the shed row. His eye stopped on a gleaming, coppery horse that was tied to a post.

"Is that Funny Cide?" Lew asked.

"That's my pony, Lew," Barclay said, rolling his eyes.

"Oh, boy," Lew said.

5.

The Trainer

There are a lot of trainers out there that have had a lot of horses capable of being Funny Cides come through their barns, but they didn't handle them correctly. What makes Barclay good is that he identified the horse, and had the talent to train him for the classic distances. We've had a bunch of horses, all of us, that started up the road, but they never quite made it. They got on the wrong elevator. They never got to the penthouse.

—JOHN WARD, trainer of 2000
Kentucky Derby winner, Monarchos

It was a hard thing for Barclay Tagg to admit that luck played a part in life, because once he admitted to that, he also had to admit to the accompanying possibility that success was randomly distributed. Luck rendered hard work irrelevant. Luck meant you could hit a jackpot or win a gumball, but it also meant you could fall down a manhole or get killed by lightning. It meant that rich people weren't necessarily virtuous, and that beautiful people could be inwardly corrupt. It meant that you didn't necessarily get what you merited, while other people got more than they deserved.

The people who won in horse racing weren't always inherently good-natured, Barclay had learned. In fact, he had met some real rotten bastards. Just because someone liked the game didn't necessarily mean he liked animals. Some people just liked the mathematics of betting, and they didn't care whether they were betting on kangaroos or cars. Horses were just the medium. Some trainers were excellent at what they did and won thousands of races, and yet they gave horses deplorable care. The animals got a bed of straw to sleep on, and three meals a day, but the trainers didn't know one horse from another. They had no more feeling for them than someone in a slaughterhouse. The horses were just meat.

Barclay had a feeling for horses. But it hadn't made him rich, had it?

He had chosen a profession in which luck figured heavily, in which hard work was seldom equitably rewarded, and in which he could expect to lose about 80 percent of the races he entered. He worked all day, every day, and he did everything right, and things still went wrong. Funny Cide was a perfect example: Barclay had found a gem of a horse, but when Funny Cide arrived at Belmont that spring, the horse seemed to be moving stiffly. On closer examination, it turned out he had sore suspensories in his legs. So Funny Cide spent his first month in Barclay's barn standing in tubs of ice every morning. Then, just when the horse was feeling good again, he ran off and bucked his shins. "Jesus Christ, why can't something go right?" Barclay muttered.

That July, while Barclay and Robin ran their horses in Saratoga during the six-week racing season, the gelding continued to stand idle, recuperating in his stall or in a pen. "Do you know how discouraging it is when the best horse you got in your stable can't get on the track?" Barclay said to his Sackatoga owners.

The horse's best friends were a couple of cats who prowled the barn—Freckles and Tuna. Sometimes Barclay or Robin would peer inside the stall and see the horse and the cats sleeping together, nose to nose. When they brought Funny Cide out into the yard, he would try to follow the cats around. He had a lovely temperament; nothing seemed to bother him—commotion, traffic, or the activity of a racing barn.

By now Funny Cide was nearly full-grown, and he stood 16 hands, 2 inches, only a moderate-sized horse. He was narrow for a thoroughbred, slim from his shoulders to his flanks. Even his handsome copper-brown head seemed narrow, which according to conventional wisdom was not a sign of intelligence. But he *was* smart. His owners gave him peppermints, and he learned to expect the crinkle of the cellophane. As soon as he heard a wrapper, he shot his head out of the stall expectantly.

Steadily, over several weeks, Barclay and Robin worked Funny Cide back into racing shape. Then, one Monday morning in August, Barclay decided it was time to breeze the horse. Breezing was the fastest, most intense form of workout, and the horse's performance would tell them whether he was ready to race.

Barclay wanted a light rider to keep the weight off Funny Cide's back because of his lingering shin and ligament problems. He looked around for a jockey to work the horse. Barclay's first thought was to call Edgar Prado; he believed in starting with the best, and Prado was one of the best. But Prado's agent said he was unavailable.

Barclay cast around for another rider, but it wasn't easy to find one. The following morning would be a Tuesday, and the track was dark, and a lot of jockeys didn't want to work on their day off. Just then, Barclay noticed Mike "The Cop" Sellito strolling near the barn.

"Hey, Mike, I need someone to work a horse tomorrow," Barclay said.

Mike the Cop knew all about Funny Cide, and he'd been waiting for the opportunity to put his jockey, Jose Santos, aboard the horse. It was his job as Santos's agent to find good mounts, and the way to do that was to mingle with people at the track and collect gossip and word of mouth on which horses could run. Mike the Cop had been sitting in the track kitchen at five o'clock that morning talking to a girl he knew, when she started telling him about the two-year-old New York–bred that Tony Everard had sent to Barclay Tagg. The word on the horse was that he was fast. "The horse pretty much beat up on everything it worked against at the farm," she said. After the conversation, Mike the Cop had made it a point to wander by the Tagg barn and hang around.

Mike the Cop instantly told Barclay that Santos was available and would be there the following morning. "What time do you want him?" he asked. Barclay said that eight-thirty A.M. would be fine.

Mike took out his cell phone and called Santos and told him that he had a mount. "Tomorrow morning you got to go work a horse for Barclay Tagg," he said. But there was a pause on the other end of the line. Santos balked.

"Do I have to work for that grouchy son of a bitch?" Santos asked.

Some people thought Barclay would have preferred that horses run by themselves, without jockeys on their backs, and they were partly right. It wasn't that Barclay disliked jockeys; he just thought they got a lot of money and credit for doing comparatively little. A well-trained and rested thoroughbred only ran every four to six weeks, and a trainer worked day and night to get the animal fit and ready. If a jockey messed up a two-minute ride, he went on to the next mount, and might ride as many as sixty horses a week. Meanwhile, Barclay had to stare at an idle horse and a lost opportunity for a month.

Barclay wasn't shy about confronting a jockey who screwed up. A typical example: once, when one of Barclay's horses got bumped coming out of the gate, the jockey responded by taking the horse to the outside. Barclay watched helpless in the stands as the jockey let the horse gallop wide, uselessly, until the race was over.

"Jesus Christ, why didn't you put him in the race?" Barclay asked afterward.

"I didn't want him running up on somebody's heels."

"Well, that's what you're getting paid big money for."

"I'm not going to get killed."

"Well, nobody is asking you to get killed. Put the horse into the race. That's your job. That's what you get paid for."

Santos was one of those jockeys Barclay had growled at in the past for not running a good race, and he wasn't sure he wanted to feel that ire again. But Santos wasn't exactly in the position to say no. He was riding all kinds of lousy mounts to rebuild his career, picking up long shots and exercising horses at five A.M. Most of them were nothing special, average horses, but some of them were really bad acts. One in particular tried to dump him whenever they got in the starting gate. As soon as the horse was led near the big metal frame, he would start freaking out. It took ten minutes to load him. Then, once Santos got the animal in the gate, it tried to roll over on him.

Mike the Cop explained that the word on the new Tagg horse was too good to turn the job down. Given the choice between a good horse and a gruff trainer, Santos chose the horse, although not without misgivings.

"Oh, man," Santos told Mike the Cop. "That guy don't like me."

"Listen," Mike said. "Just go work the horse. Be there at eight-thirty."

The next morning, Santos showed up at the barn, and Barclay gave him terse instructions. "I don't want you to go too fast," he said. "Just a nice half-mile in forty-nine is fine."

"Okay," Santos said, and guided the horse to the track.

They walked the horse around the oval. Barclay sat erect and stock-still on his chestnut horse and watched from beneath the brim of his slouch hat as they went into a gallop.

Immediately, Santos felt the pull in his arms. Beneath him, the action of the horse was awesome, a rolling, effortless sensation. He sat easily on Funny Cide's back while the horse ate up the ground in front of him; the other horses exercising on the track ahead seemed to labor, compared to Funny Cide.

After the half-mile mark, Santos slowed the mount. He settled into a canter, and then a trot, and then a walk, cooling down. He turned the gelding around and walked in reverse around the turn and rejoined Barclay, who still sat motionless astride his pony.

"What were you doing out there?" Barclay snapped.

"What do you mean, what was I doing? You said you wanted an easy workout."

"Yeah, but you went forty-six and four."

Santos gaped at him. He had covered the half-mile in 46.4 seconds? That seemed impossible.

"I didn't go that fast."

"Yeah, you did. You went that fast."

In that moment, Santos knew the horse was better than anything he'd been on in a long time. Santos had a good interior clock, and he was sure the horse had run the half-mile in forty-nine. The horse had covered the ground so effortlessly, with that long stride, that he'd fooled Santos by almost two and a half seconds. Any unraced two-year-old that could cover a half mile in forty-six and change and make it seem slow was something special.

"He saw the horse in front of him, and he just took off," Santos explained to Barclay. "But I know him now. It won't happen again."

Santos walked the horse back to the barn for his bath and grooming. A number of the owners were standing around, including Dave Mahan and Jack Knowlton, who had come out to see their new acquisition in his first serious workout. They wanted to know what Santos thought. Santos decided to be conservative. "It's a nice horse," he said. Once the word on the horse spread, other jockeys would try to wrest him away, and Santos intended to keep this one secret, for himself.

Santos chatted with the owners for a few minutes, and then he and Mike the Cop walked away. "How'd the horse go?" Mike asked.

The jockey put a finger to his lips. "Shhhhhhhh," he said.

"That good?"

"Listen. Whatever you do, don't lose this horse. Keep me on this horse."

For the next several days, Funny Cide just jogged. But when Barclay wanted a jockey to breeze the horse again, Santos got the call. Once again he showed up at the barn early in the morning and received his instructions. Barclay said, "I want you to go forty-nine. I don't want you going forty-six, I want you going forty-nine."

This time, Santos worked the horse a half-mile in fifty seconds. Barclay, sitting on his pony by the outer rail, watched the horse glide around the track. The horse moved more sedately, maybe too sedately. Barclay, ever on the lookout for a setback, wondered, *What's wrong?*

When Santos returned to the side of the track, Barclay was waiting.

"Last time you went forty-six, and this time you went fifty," Barclay said. "Is he all right?"

He was fine, maybe even better than fine. Once again, the horse had covered the ground so easily that Santos had the sense he had barely exerted himself. "He was just cantering," Santos said.

The horse was ready to race, Santos told Barclay. What's more, Santos had an odd sensation of familiarity with the animal. Years earlier, he had ridden Funny Cide's sire, Distorted Humor, to his first victory. "I broke his father's maiden, and he's just like his father," Santos told Barclay. "I know this horse. He's going to win first time out."

Barclay didn't comment; he just turned his pony around and returned to the barn. But it confirmed what he had been thinking about the horse.

In an unguarded moment, Barclay told Lew Titterton, "The horse is a freak."

"What's wrong with him?" Lew said.

Barclay laughed and explained that "freak," in horse terms, was not an insult but a compliment. It meant that the horse was out of the blue. He was an unforeseen and inexplicable freak of nature. "It means he's fast," Barclay said. "The horse is very fast."

Normally, Barclay didn't believe in raising expectations when it came to horses. The majority of them didn't pan out, and if you made the mistake of getting too excited about one, you just looked silly. But there was no mistaking that this gelding had talent, a lot of it, and he was finally healthy, too. It was time to debut him.

Barclay and Robin surveyed the race schedule and made their plans. By then Saratoga was drawing to a close, and there was nothing in which to enter an unraced two-year-old. Instead, they chose something small at Belmont, a maiden special weight for New York–breds in the first week of September. Barclay informed the owners that if they came to New York, they would finally get to see their prodigy run.

On September 8, 2002, Jack and Dorothy Knowlton made the trip to New York to see Funny Cide's debut, and they were joined by Dave Mahan and Eric and Jean Dattner. On the morning of the race, the owners visited the Tagg barn. Dave asked Robin what she thought.

"I'd be devastated if this horse doesn't win right out of the box," she said.

While Barclay and Robin prepared the horse, the owners went to the clubhouse to find their seats. The horses began to load into the gate. Funny Cide had drawn the twelfth post position out of twelve. That was both good and bad: he would be a long way out from the rail, but there was less trouble running on the outside, too. Shortly before the last horse was loaded, Robin and Barclay took their seats with the owners.

The bell went off. Funny Cide came out of the gate awkwardly, and he bumped another horse. He swung back to the outside, and almost immediately fell five lengths behind.

But as he came around the turn, he began to pass horses one after another. From a distance, the other horses looked as if their feet were planted in the dirt, compared to the gelding. Funny Cide reached the stretch well in the lead—and the lead kept lengthening. The owners stared at him through binoculars as he drew away, by five lengths, six, then seven.

"Holy smoke," Dave said.

At the eighth pole, the horse was already ten lengths in front, and now he pulled away by nearly fifteen. At that moment, Barclay leaned over and spoke to Robin quietly.

"Look at him," Barclay said. "He looks like Secretariat."

"What?" Robin said.

She stared at Barclay, dumbfounded. The statement was utterly out of character for him. Normally he kept his feelings tamped down. He of all people knew better than to expect too much: you were just sure you had a runner, and then it turned out not to be. One minute you had a great prospect, and the next minute the horse was injured, or coughing, or fretting with ulcers. Nevertheless, Barclay had said it, and said it with something like hope in his voice.

On September 8, 2002, Funny Cide, with Jose Santos aboard, won his debut at Belmont by fourteen and three-quarters lengths.

Barclay Tagg had seen a lot of horses, good and bad. He had been on a mount of one kind of another since the age of eleven, when he learned and took to heart the famous saying: "There's something about the outside of a horse that's good for the inside of a man."

He was born in Lancaster, Pennsylvania, on December 30, 1937, into a middle-class suburban home, and he had no reason ever to set foot in a stirrup, yet the horses captivated him in pictures, in books, and in his imagination long before he actually saw one in person. While the other kids read Buck Rogers comic books, Barclay read Westerns given to him to by his father, who was one of two partners in a local manufacturing plant that made heavy-duty mufflers. His father was the man in the gray flannel suit, who went to the same job every day and came home every night and had the same cocktail. To Barclay, he seemed bored to death, and boredom was a state his son was intent on avoiding.

Barclay was an eleven-year-old kid riding his bike in the Pennsylvania countryside one afternoon when he pulled over to the side of the road to stare at a real cowboy, or anyway, what passed for a cowboy in Abington, Pennsylvania, outside of Philadelphia. The man was in his fifties and wore elegant riding boots and breeches, and he was standing by a stone barn, and next to the barn was a riding ring, and wandering in a paddock were some horses.

Barclay got off his bike, introduced himself, and pointed to the horses and said, "Can I learn to ride?"

The old man said, "Sure."

The lessons cost him three dollars and fifteen cents each. The old man didn't like to teach riding in the middle of the ring, standing there tapping his boot with a whip. Instead, he put the boy on a horse and got on one himself, and they went for a two-hour trail ride. Barclay spent his life savings, nine dollars and forty-five cents, learning to ride, and when his money ran out after three lessons, he figured he was done. "Thank you very much," he said. But the old man said, "You come back anyway, and I'll put you to work. Go in that barn and start cleaning out that stall, and you can earn the money for lessons." Barclay showed up the next day and mucked out the stalls, and from then on, for the next five years, he spent every afternoon at the barn, caring for the horses and riding them, and eventually he began giving lessons to other kids.

Gradually he learned the old man's story. Lincoln Sharpless was from a Main Line Philadelphia family, and he'd gone out west when he was young to become a rancher. He returned east to recuperate from health problems, but he missed the horses, so he rented this vast horse farm, with several barns and wooded trails. He cleared the trails with a Jeep, and converted a hay barn to an indoor ring so he could exercise the horses in bad weather.

Sharpless was a well-bred gentleman who was also a stern and thorough horseman from whom Barclay got his first lesson in the harsher realities of a farm. One afternoon, Barclay stood by and watched Sharpless kill a sick horse. The animal was down in its stall, fatally ill with an infection. Sharpless couldn't shoot it in the barn because the gunshot would scare the other horses, so he picked up a sledgehammer and did what he had to do.

Barclay was animal-sensitive, so much so that he once slept on the porch with the family beagle when it got sick, and to him the horse world seemed one of semi-constant tragedies. Some of them were inevitable and some of them were ugly and unnecessary, and Barclay would never become quite inured to either. On one occasion, a trainer who rented a barn from Sharpless hired a couple of meat-packers to get rid of his thoroughbreds. Two men arrived in a truck, and they took mare after mare after mare out back and shot each one behind the ear, fifteen horses dead in one afternoon. It was the sort of memory that stayed in Barclay's head more than fifty years later.

But a prettier memory stayed in his head, too. One autumn when he was thirteen, his family traveled to Saratoga Springs to visit relatives. Barclay went out for a walk after supper and saw lights in the distance, which he followed until he came to what looked like a fairground, with tents and a grandstand. Barclay climbed up the grandstand and peered at a dazzling sight: throngs of people milling around in tuxedos and evening gowns, as thoroughbred yearlings were paraded at auction. Everything shone under the lights, the jewels and the coats of the thoroughbreds, and he thought it was heaven. He hung on the back of the grandstand until almost midnight, watching the horse sale.

The next morning he rose at dawn, climbed out of bed, and went back out to the Saratoga Race Course, to discover that the tents were empty and everyone had gone. But he heard music playing, and buckets rattling, and horses neighing. He followed the noises. He began to see horses go by, walking to the training track for their morning workouts. The horses issued exhalations that sounded like huge sighs, and their warm breath streamed into the cool autumn air in plumes. Barclay didn't know where he was, but he knew he was in the right place.

Back home in Abington, Barclay found a job with another riding stable, where he began to gallop thoroughbreds, and he discovered how different they were, in both their sheer speed and their exceptional beauty. They just felt different. Quicker, in everything they did. They *moved*.

Some kids had their own horses, well trained, and well bred, but Barclay earned his way as a stall-mucker, and won ribbons on borrowed horses, traveling to horse shows where he met his first wealthy people and got his first taste of luxury. He would go away to a competition and stay overnight, and the next morning, he'd be served toast that had real butter on it instead of margarine.

He went to Penn State and majored in animal husbandry in the veterinary program, and he ran track for two years. Then he met a girl named Judy who loved horses the way he did, but she lived in Louisville, so he followed her there. He left school and took a job working construction. Day after day, he lugged cement blocks, but he was too skinny to stick to that work for long.

He returned to Penn State and finished his degree in 1961, got married to Judy, and had two baby daughters. Next he found a job managing a vast farm in the wealthy hunt-club enclave of Unionville, Pennsylvania, caring for barns full of hundreds of animals—thoroughbreds, show horses, and polo ponies, as well as cattle and sheep.

Barclay was plunged into the local hunt-club society. At the Rolling Rock Hunt Club, there were timber races, pheasant-shooting, golf, and every other kind of old-fashioned sport, on 100,000 acres perfectly manicured for country living. Eventually he got tired of managing all those animals and wanted to compete, so he became an amateur steeplechaser at the club, which had a dormitory on the top floor with fifty-four brass beds, next to mahogany nightstands with brass lamps on them. Each nightstand had a private telephone, with which to call up and order Bloody Marys.

Barclay loved the open acreage, and the baying hounds, and the ratcheting up of excitement, and the negotiating of terrain at high speed. He also dabbled in show horses, but that cured him of anything involving judging: the fat girl bounced up and down on the horse and got the ribbon. Racing was simple; if you crossed the line first, you won. He began riding timber races professionally, building a respectable record for prominent trainers Jonathan Sheppard and Burly Cocks. Despite its outward elegance, it was a physically brutal sport. The first few bad spills he took, he'd lie there for a minute and then get up and stagger around and tell himself he wasn't hurt. Even when the ambulance came and took him to the hospital, he'd insist he was fine. But the concussions and fractures mounted, and by 1971, he was full of steel pins, and his body wasn't the only thing breaking up; so was his marriage. He'd busted himself up enough; it was time to try something new.

Barclay decided to become a thoroughbred trainer. He had no horses, no contacts, and no backing, but he applied for a license just the same. He looked around for a horse to train, and realized he wasn't going get anywhere in Unionville, Pennsylvania, in the wintertime. Instead, he decided to go to Maryland. A local stable owner loaned him a mare and said, "Why don't you see if you can win a race with her?"

Barclay borrowed a van, loaded the mare, and drove her down to Maryland, and he wandered around the tracks until he found a stall. He'd gallop horses as an exercise rider in the morning and then work his own horse. He earned $125 a week, plus feed for the mare. He finally ran the mare at the end of December, and she finished second and first in two starts, and got claimed.

Next, a local Pennsylvania doctor named Jay Platt gave him a five-year-old has-been horse with badly crippled legs. Platt was a green owner who'd been cheated by shysters, so when Barclay charged him a fair fee to nurse the horse until he was healthy, and then won a race, the doctor was overjoyed. He gave Barclay $400 in cash, in addition to his 10 percent cut of the winnings—and Barclay and his children never had to pay for another doctor's appointment, either.

By 1973, Barclay had three bad horses, two of them crippled, and no prospects. He was doing everything himself, from bandaging the horses' legs, to picking out their feet, to galloping them and washing them and walking them. He courted abject poverty, and he was so hungry that on one occasion he went into a restaurant with no money and hoped a bread roll would fall on the floor.

In need of a job, he called Frank Whiteley, Jr., a demanding Hall of Fame trainer, and asked for work. Whiteley knew Barclay vaguely because they had once been stabled near each other in Delaware.

"Do you need an assistant?" Barclay asked.

"Yeah, I could use one," Whiteley said.

"Can you tell me how much you can pay me?' Because I've got a wife and kids to feed."

"That's not my damn fault."

"Okay."

"I'll give you a hundred and seventy-five a week."

"Frank, my child support's a hundred a week. By the time the government takes my taxes out, I'll have a hundred and thirty dollars left, and I have to send a hundred to my wife."

"That's not my damn fault either."

"Okay."

Barclay joined Whiteley in Camden, South Carolina. The bills never stopped coming, and he was flat broke, but under Whiteley he learned the basics of how to train a top thoroughbred. That year a preternaturally fast two-year-old filly came to Whiteley's barn: her name was Ruffian. Barclay took his turn galloping her, and he'd never felt anything like that underneath him. He galloped her all winter, and then watched from the barn, thrilled, as she became the greatest filly to race that spring. It was his first contact with a truly great horse.

Barclay learned minimalism from observing Whiteley. If he couldn't get a horse to look good, and its coat remained dull no matter what he was feeding it or how many vitamins he gave it, that meant the horse was overtraining. If he backed down in the training and let it graze, the horse would come around. Everybody wanted to run to the vet for medicines and vitamins, but Whiteley didn't believe in artificial health, and in fact believed it could weaken a horse's already nearly nonexistent immune system.

Whiteley didn't do anything special, he just had good horses and took good care of them. He made the feed himself every day, and he grazed them every afternoon, and he didn't care what they grazed on, whether tree bark or roses or grass or soil, because he figured it was something they needed.

Barclay also learned that even a top trainer suffered the vagaries of the business. Whiteley went through months when he was down to ten or eleven horses and had to fire most of the help. But then the new yearlings would come into the barn in November, and by May, Whiteley would be winning all the big races in New York. If a horse couldn't run, he sent it home. He didn't fool around and try to run an untalented horse for $50,000, and he straight-talked the owners.

"This one isn't going to make it. You don't have much here, Mrs. Bancroft."

"But what's wrong with him, Frank?"

"He can't run!"

After a year, Barclay left Whiteley and struck out on his own again, racing horses on the mid-Atlantic circuit. Later, he'd wonder if he'd gone about things all wrong; perhaps his career would have been easier if he'd stayed with Whiteley for a few years. Most trainers were crusty old guys who didn't want a young trainer to come along and do better than they did. Barclay was alone, with no help or advice. Instead, he ground out small victories with low-quality horses for people who couldn't really afford it. He fought for barn space at Pimlico.

He had to beg for a few stalls from the track manager, and when he got them it was with the understanding that he could be bumped by the Anheuser-Busch Clydesdales. One afternoon, the Clydesdales showed up. Barclay and his horses were sent over to Timonium, a five-eighths-of-a-mile ring in the suburbs.

The closest Barclay got to a Triple Crown race was when he'd watch the Preakness from the roof of a barn on the backstretch at

Pimlico. The barn roof had a perfect view of the five-eighths pole, and it was from there that he saw Secretariat streak to victory.

He'd build up a string of horses, and then they'd just evaporate. He'd be doing okay with a dozen or so horses in his barn, and the next thing he knew, he'd have nothing again. Once, he was spending Thanksgiving with his older brother Scott, a retired businessman and now an antiques dealer in Pennsylvania, when the phone rang. It was an owner announcing he was taking back his five horses and giving them to another trainer. Barclay had only six horses in his barn; there went 90 percent of his income.

He was down to just one horse, a turf-runner. He vanned the horse from Maryland to Penn National through the snow, wondering if the van was going to make it through the bad weather. He made it to the barn, and sat there under a blanket, bitterly cold and worried sick that they'd take the race off the grass, because of the weather.

Things got even tougher when his two teenaged daughters, Taryn, sixteen, and Tiffany, thirteen, came to live with him. He and the girls rented a small tenant house in Maryland, and he continued to keep his modest string of horses at Pimlico. He would train all day, and then come home and check on the kids before running horses at night, driving them in a little truck and trailer to Penn National.

He was lucky; his ex-wife, Judy, had run her own farm, and his daughters cared for horses as much as he did, and they were no strangers to work. They did well in school and stayed out of trouble. He had just one scare, when Tiffany ran off. He came home one night from the track, and there was dinner, but no kid. She'd set the table and fixed supper for the both of them, including dessert, but she was gone. She and a friend who had a car had impulsively decided to drive to California.

Barclay was frantic. He hunted for her for six days, in every bar and hangout in the state of Maryland, and he hired a detective who proved useless. Barclay would drive twenty-five miles to a bar and tear the place apart, choking people and trying to get answers. He half-expected to find her lying in the gutter somewhere, or her body in the woods. Finally, he tracked her to Silver City, New Mexico, where she was in the hands of juvenile authorities. He flew out there and picked her up, but first he had to ask a judge to return her to his custody. The judge said, "Now, is there any more crap? Because I want to go fishing." Barclay collected his daughter, and together they flew home.

"Didn't you think I was going to worry about you and wonder where you were?" he asked.

"Yeah, I knew you'd be upset," she answered. She wasn't angry at him or unhappy, she explained; she knew he had to work all the time with the horses. She just wanted to see California. She certainly wouldn't have made Barclay dinner and dessert and set a table for two if she was planning on breaking his heart. She was just being a kid. "Do me a favor, don't ever put family in the hands of the government again," he said. "Just don't do that, because it makes me helpless."

Barclay marched on, running his modest string of horses in New York, Maryland, and Florida. He didn't play golf, and he didn't bowl; all he did was work and raise his daughters. He won the odd stakes race, and put up with the caprices of the game, and carved out a decent living. In 1982, his horses won a total of ten races for $68,239 in purses, and he was putting Taryn and Tiffany through college. He'd leave Maryland at ten o'clock at night and arrive in Saratoga at six A.M. "Gallop 'em, wash 'em off, and ice 'em till the afternoon." Those were his methods.

He might have done better had he been able to put owners ahead of the horses, but he couldn't make himself do it. The phone would ring, and he'd hear an owner's voice on the other line telling him how to run a horse, and he couldn't tolerate it. "I'm the kind of guy that when somebody tells me what to do, I instantly don't want to do it," he once said of himself. "It's not a good trait to have."

But then came Bonner Young, a different kind of owner. A Virginian with a voice soft as a fern, she brought him a creature named Highland Springs, and together they won four stakes races and $403,579. In the 1989 Breeders' Cup Mile, Highland Springs was in front down the stretch. For a moment, it looked like the horse was going to win, and Barclay could taste the $1 million that would come with the victory. But jockey Kent Desormeaux dropped his stick at the sixteenth pole, and the horse finished seventh, though beaten by just two and quarter lengths. *Bad luck.*

Barclay continued to try to beat the odds, even though horses got hurt, or inexplicably quit running. Instead, he did more with less. In some years, his win rate was above 30 percent, and that was saying something. In 1991, he won the Grade 1 Gamely Handicap at Hollywood Park with Miss Josh, and in 1994 he won the Man o' War Stakes at Belmont with Royal Mountain Inn, both of them on the turf. The most money his stable ever made was in 1999, when it brought in $1.9 million, though most of that went back to the owners.

After more than thirty years, Barclay was still working fourteen hours a day, seven days a week, and charging $75 a day, and that covered only the basic cost of boarding and feeding a horse. Some years, Barclay barely broke even. Some years, he ended up behind. Hard work and bad times had taken the buoyancy out of him and made him curt. He sometimes reminded people of Tom Smith, the laconic trainer of the Depression-era hero-horse Seabiscuit.

But by the time Funny Cide arrived in the barn, Barclay was unshakably sure of his methods. He remained a small, hands-on operation, with the help of Robin. Every single morning, Barclay arrived at the barn in the darkness and checked the horses' legs himself in the dim light of the stalls. He ran his hands over them, feeling for stiffness, or heat, in a tendon. Robin liked to say that Barclay knew a horse was sore before the horse knew it.

Barclay insisted that things be done his way, in everything, and the routine in his barn was so regimented and detailed that it was almost petty. But this fell under the category of preventive care, because Barclay by now had too much experience with the small things that could go wrong. Nothing was trivial in caring for a thoroughbred; if one item was out of place and a horse stepped on it, whether a piece of straw or a thumbtack, it was a potentially major problem. Unlucky? Spectacular Bid lost the Triple Crown when he stepped on a safety pin in his own stall and injured his foot the day before the Belmont.

The feet of a thoroughbred were a world of potential bad luck in and of themselves. Barclay stood them in hot water with Epsom salts every day. He painted their feet with turpentine, or he put magnetic boots on them, or he supplemented their feed with something called Shoers' Friend, all to strengthen their hooves and improve their circulation.

There was another reason to be particular, too: Barclay had to watch every penny. He couldn't afford to waste anything, and he didn't. When the grooms washed the horses, Barclay set the soap-pump dispenser on exactly two pumps. A roll of bandages cost $2.50 from the equine supplier across the street from Belmont, but Robin scoured the catalogs until she found a supplier that sold it for $1.29.

Barclay hated to waste even a nail. When it was time to move the horses to Florida for the winter, Barclay insisted that every movable nail be taken with them, down to the screw eyes in the wall from which the water bucket hung. "Don't forget anything," he insisted. After the crew was done, Barclay would walk along the stalls, checking to see if they'd left behind a single shank or tie chain. Once, he found fifteen screw eyes that the staff had forgotten to remove.

"What did I tell you?" he demanded. "Where's the couple of bucks you owe me?"

The grooms stared back at him. "Hey," he said. "These things cost thirty cents each."

The luxuries went to the horses. Funny Cide had a shiny brass nameplate on his halter, with gleaming buckles and chains. He was primped and combed until his coat was dappled, and he got treatments once a week from a chiropractor, the closest thing a horse had to a masseur. Each day, Barclay practically spoon-fed him. The horses ate at four-thirty every afternoon, and that meant four-thirty P.M. on the dot, he told the staff, "not four-twenty-five or four-thirty-five." The trainer prepared the meals himself, measuring the ingredients precisely: oats, sweet feed, salt, molasses, corn oil, linseed oil. He poured hot water in it to soften the oats, and topped it with bran.

The richness and immaculateness of Funny Cide's stall in Barn 6 at Belmont Park was in perfect contrast to the small, dilapidated barn office where Barclay and Robin spent much of their time. It was a freestanding cinder-block room, from which they conducted the more mundane business of training a string of thoroughbreds: they called owners, conferred with vets, ordered supplies, collected weather reports, decided on race schedules, hired exercise riders, contacted jockey agents, handled the payroll, and balanced the books—if they could be balanced.

The only light came from a couple of small windows with bars on them, and a fluorescent overhead bar that served as a flytrap. For comfort, they had thrown down a couple of braided rag rugs on the cracked old linoleum floor, which was peeling and revealed the concrete foundation. The room was furnished with what seemed to be castoffs from an old schoolroom. Barclay worked at a battered old metal schoolteacher's desk next to the front door, from which he could keep an eye on the grooms as they bathed the horses in a small gravel area, while Robin worked at an old tin table shoved against a wall. Hanging above their desks were clipboards holding race charts, shoeing charts, and medical charts. Scattered on their desks were bottles of medicines, and under the desks were sets of muddy riding boots, spurs attached. Hanging on a series of nails in the wall were flak jackets, rain slickers, goggles, and jockey silks.

The items strewn about on the shelves and the floor bespoke their nomadic, hardscrabble, painstaking, hand-and-foot-calloused lives: kits full of horse brushes, bags of peppermints, a stack of buckets, pairs of binoculars, bandannas, chaps, and leather gloves.

There was just one decoration in the room to which some attention had been given: crowding each of the four walls were dozens of framed photographs of gleaming horses in mid-stride, crossing the wire.

As Barclay sat in his barn office and prepared Funny Cide for his second race, he believed, with uncharacteristic optimism, that this horse could be the best of the winners on his wall. This was the one that could make it all worth it. He had trained thirty-eight stakes winners and numerous other lesser-rans, and each had a

The "Sackets Harbor Six" in high school. From top left: Jack Knowlton, Mark Phillips, Peter Phillips, Harold Cring, Larry Reinhardt, and Jon Constance. *(Author family photos)*

September 1995: Sackatoga Stable's first horse, named—appropriately—
Sackets Six. Here with *(right to left)* Pete, Harold, Jack, and Jon.
(Courtesy Sackatoga Stable)

The first win for Sackatoga Stable: Sackets Six at Belmont Park, September 22,
1996, Eddie Maple up. *(Bob Coglianese Photos Inc.)*

Anne and Joe McMahon (here with their horse Regal Classic), owners of McMahon of Saratoga Thoroughbreds, where Funny Cide was born. *(AP/Wide World Photo)*

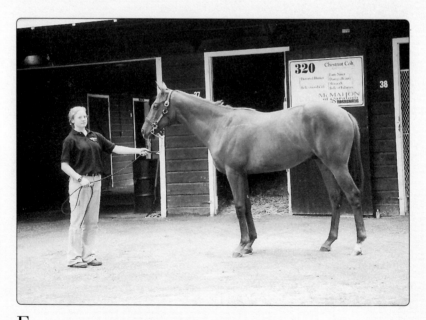

Funny Cide at the Saratoga Preferred Yearling Sale in August 2001, where he sold for $22,000. *(Anne McMahon, courtesy Sackatoga Stable)*

Funny Cide's initial race—and first victory—Belmont Park, September 8, 2002, by nearly fifteen lengths, with Santos riding. *(Bob Coglianese Photos Inc.)*

Funny Cide's first stakes win came only three weeks later. Collecting the trophy, Jack is second from left, Gus Williams is in back of Jose Santos and his two youngest daughters, then come Dave Mahan and Eric Dattner. Jose's oldest daughter, Nadia, is on the far right, next to Barclay Tagg, who'd become our trainer in 1999. *(Bob Coglianese Photos Inc.)*

The famous yellow school bus at the Kentucky Derby, 2003. Look at the other buses! *(Nadine Mahan, courtesy Sackatoga Stable)*

Dave Mahan giving Funny Cide candy and his instructions for the Derby. *(Skip Dickstein)*

Funny Cide passes Peace Rules at the Derby. *(Dave Harmon)*

Funny Cide takes charge. *(Skip Dickstein)*

And *down* the stretch they come!
(Skip Dickstein)

Jose celebrates.
(Skip Dickstein)

Sackatogans cheer. *(AP/Wide World Photo)*

The blanket of roses. *(Skip Dickstein)*

Jack hugs Jose.
(Skip Dickstein)

Jose Junior celebrates on the
shoulders of Mike McMahon.
(Skip Dickstein)

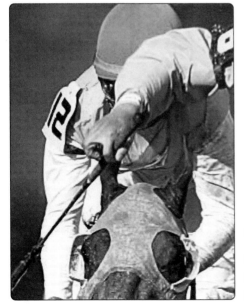

The famous photo that caused the
investigation—until it became clear
the only thing Jose was carrying was
his whip. *(James Squire/Getty Images)*

Funny Cide feeling frisky
two days after the Derby.
(AP/Wide World Photo)

The Preakness. Funny Cide makes his move. *(Dave Harmon)*

Funny Cide leaves them all behind . . . *(Skip Dickstein)*

. . . and wins by 9¾ lengths, the second-largest margin in Preakness history.

(Skip Dickstein)

A happy Jose Santos trots back. *(Dave Harmon)*

Barclay Tagg leads the procession to the winner's circle. *(Dave Harmon)*

Dave and Gus kiss the trophy. *(Skip Dickstein)*

Painting the Sackatoga colors on the weather vane.
(Skip Dickstein)

Robin Smullen
and Barclay Tagg.
(Skip Dickstein)

Sackatoga makes the TV rounds the day before the Belmont Stakes. Left to right: Jon Constance, Harold Cring, Larry Reinhardt, Mark Phillips, Pete Phillips, Dave Mahan, and Eric Dattner.
(Courtesy Sackatoga Stable)

Belmont Stakes day. Funny Cide fans of all ages.
(AP/Wide World Photos)

Sackets Harbor cheers on Funny Cide. Most of West Main Street was closed off, with large-screen televisions set up. *(AP/Wide World Photo)*

But it was not to be. The Funny Cide Team applauds the winner, knowing there'll be other days, other races . . . *(AP/Wide World Photo)*

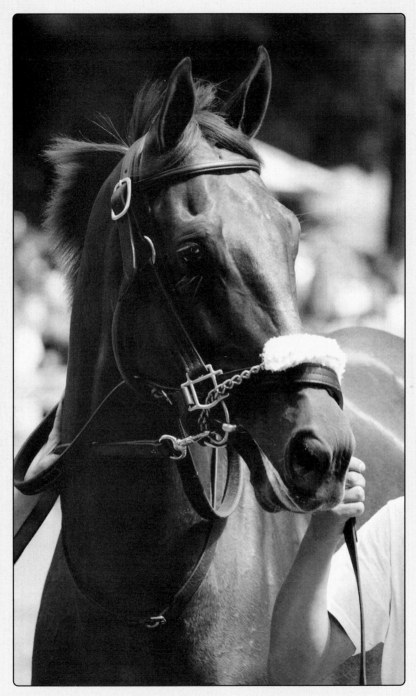

. . . for "The People's Horse." *(Dave Harmon)*

place of equal importance to him. It was hard to rank one victory over another—and it was hard to rank one form of heartbreak above another, too. If there was no deeper joy than Highland Springs, there was no deeper heartbreak than to have a nice horse like Roo Art taken away from him, simply because he'd tried to do the right thing by the animal.

Once, at a low point, Barclay called his brother Scott and ran through his litany of misfortunes and hard luck, the lame horses, the traitorous owners, the cost of it all.

"Why do you do it?" Scott asked.

The question forced Barclay to articulate an answer. Barclay could be extremely eloquent when he chose to be, and anyone who considered him devoid of sentiment hadn't seen him stroke the face of a thoroughbred. He loved his work, even when it made him miserable, precisely because of the constant intrusion of the unexpected. Barclay had given luck an entry to his existence, called it down on his own head, by getting into the horse business in the first place. He could have been the man in the gray flannel suit, like his father, bored to death, but this was what he had chosen, and while he reserved the right to complain, he wouldn't trade lives.

"I ran a horse last Saturday afternoon that cost ten thousand dollars," Barclay told Scott. "I was running him in a five-hundred-thousand-dollar race, and he went off at three-to-five, to win. You know what that does to you?"

"Yeah," Scott said, "and I haven't had a feeling like that since I can remember."

Would Barclay trade his life for a more average one? No. At the racetrack, there was more of everything. More money, more failure, more tragedy, more exhilaration. If his life was tougher in some ways, it was also more concentrated. Win or lose, how many people had an opportunity to do something as fabulous as race for half a million dollars?

So Barclay continued to rise each morning at four-thirty and personally check the feet and tendons of every horse, no matter what their value, because in the end he was a sufferer of the sad but persistent belief that rewards should be the reflection of thoroughness and decency, and almost no amount of evidence to the contrary had shaken his nagging faith in the idea that the big horse *could* happen to him.

When Barclay looked at Funny Cide, he didn't see a picture-perfect portrait of the greatest racehorse in history. He wasn't a product of Kentucky's Finest Mare by Kentucky's Finest Sire, from Kentucky's Finest Farm. But after all these years, there was one thing Barclay knew about good luck: when it finally came along, you had to recognize it.

It was plain that Funny Cide was a talented horse. The only question was, just how talented? Barclay would learn the answer when the horse ran his second race. The Bertram Bongard was a $75,000 stakes race of seven furlongs at Belmont Park, and it presented a different, tougher challenge for the gelding. The field was full of promising New York–breds, including at least two horses that had already placed in stakes races at Saratoga in open company. Funny Cide would go off as no better than the third favorite, and he'd be running against horses that were already proven.

For the Sackatoga owners, it was a big step up. They had never had a legitimate contender in a stakes race before: this was as close to the top of the game as any of them had come. Jack came down from Saratoga again, as did Gus; Dave and Nadine came in from Connecticut, and Eric and Jean Dattner from Long Island, to enjoy the rare air. They hardly dared to hope that their horse would run in the company of stakes horses the way he had in his first race.

The gates opened. This time, Funny Cide broke cleanly. He soon moved to the front—and stayed there. He ran fluidly, hardly using any energy, until they came around the turn, when he flat ran away from the field. Each time a horse moved up and tried to run in tandem with him, Funny Cide just destroyed it. Santos could have pulled until all the teeth in the horse's mouth fell out, and it wouldn't have slowed him.

Funny Cide won by nine lengths. He ran seven furlongs in a minute and twenty-two seconds and broke the stakes record by a second. In the grandstand, Dave turned to Jack, both of them whooping.

"Boy," Dave hollered. "We got something!"

When Santos brought the horse to the winner's circle, Barclay and Robin were waiting, quietly exultant. "This horse has more class than any two-year-old I ever been on," Santos told the trainers.

Jack took the horse by the shank and led him into the circle, beaming. After the trophy ceremony, the owners and trainers went upstairs into the clubhouse to a luxurious private room, where they were served champagne. A television mounted on the wall replayed the race. "This is what you get?" Dave said, looking around, sipping his champagne. "I didn't know any of this happened."

Meanwhile, Santos found Mike the Cop. "This is the one," he said. "This is the one."

Barclay thought so, too. Even he was taken aback by what a dominant race Funny Cide had run. For one thing, the horse earned a shockingly high Beyer speed figure. Beyer Index figures are calculations broadly used for rating the performance of thorough-breds. A Beyer speed figure took into account variables like track conditions as well as fleetness, and it was widely accepted as an accurate indicator of a horse's potential. The highest Beyer figure that a Sackatoga Stable horse had ever had was when Bail Money ran a 91 on the turf, once.

Funny Cide's Beyer figure for the Bertram Bongard was 103.

No two-year-old in the country had run faster.

Funny Cide was more than just a nice horse. He was more than just a nice New York–bred. He was more than just a nice two-year-old. He was a real, live racehorse. He could seriously run. Even Barclay, ever the conservative, couldn't help telling the owners, "We've got something special."

The question now was what to do about it. Originally, Barclay had intended to start Funny Cide for a third time at Belmont against New York–breds, in the $100,000 Sleepy Hollow Stakes at the end of October. But the horse's performance was so stunning that it was sure to earn him an invitation to the Breeders' Cup Juvenile, the $1 million fall extravaganza that featured only the best two-year-olds in the world.

Over the next two or three days, Barclay began to feel pressure to go to the Breeders' Cup. As word spread, other trainers began to approach Barclay with advice: if he entered the Breeders' Cup and won, it was a career-maker.

One morning, a couple of days after Funny Cide won the Bertram Bongard, John Kimmel, a friend and fellow trainer, said, "You know, it's none of my business, but I'm just going to tell you, from my standpoint, you got the best two-year-old in the country. He's probably good enough to go to the Breeders' Cup. And if you were lucky enough to go to the Breeders' Cup and win it, it will change your life as far as a trainer. You'll get the Eclipse Award right off the bat. And you'd have so many horses that you wouldn't know what to do with them."

The Breeders' Cup was the highest-profile event in the country outside of the Triple Crown races. There was no bigger purse or trophy to be had—only the top horses and trainers would be there, competing for the largest purse in the game. A million versus a hundred thousand? It was tempting.

"You got the horse," Kimmel said. "He's sharp right now. Go."

The very same thing had occurred to the Sackatoga owners: Why not think big? Over the next two or three days, Jack called Barclay a half-dozen times, going over the pros and cons of entering the race. Jack, Dave, and Gus pored over the *Daily Racing Form*, and they compared Funny Cide's Beyer figure to those of the other horses that would be entered. The numbers showed that their horse had as good a chance as any.

"We're in this for the racing," Dave said. "He's a gelding, not a stallion, and racing him is the only way to make money with him. So why not? Why shouldn't we go?"

For one very good reason: the Breeders' Cup Juvenile tended to ruin young horses. Barclay knew the history of what happened to two-year-olds in that race, and it was dismal. They almost invariably performed poorly as three-year-olds, and Barclay understood why: they weren't yet mature enough to stand up to the stress of such a high-pressure race. Funny Cide might be almost full-grown, but his bones and cartilage were still tender.

Barclay was convinced, after thinking it over, that the Breeders' Cup Juvenile would be a mistake. Never particularly shy about offering his opinion to owners, he made no exception this time.

"I don't think you should go," Barclay said.

Barclay explained his reasoning. In addition to its lousy history, the distance for this Juvenile would be a strenuous mile and one-eighth. Funny Cide had never raced around two turns before, much less against a field of so many strong horses. That in itself was a compelling argument not to go. Also, he'd never run against open company, and he'd never been shipped anywhere to race.

A young horse could come out of the Juvenile with bucked shins or bad knees, and it could take a year to nurse him back to health, Barclay warned. "If you want to have a nice three-year-old next year, we probably should go with our original plan," he said. "A lot of them never make it back to the track from that race."

There was a fine line in training an equine athlete, Barclay believed, and in some ways it wasn't much different than training a human runner. Barclay employed the same training philosophy he'd learned peaking for his track races at Penn State: short sharp workouts, with lots of rest. But there was one major difference: Funny Cide was being asked to accept a life that was alien to him. It wasn't natural for him to stand in a stall for twenty-three hours a day, and emerge only to gallop on a dirt track to the point of foaming.

Not only could a trainer ruin a horse physically, he could also ruin a horse's will to run, Barclay believed. Too many times, Barclay had seen what happened when a horse rebelled against the racing life. Example: a filly had come to the barn who didn't like the starting gate. She was a beautiful nutcase of a horse, but if you led her near the gate, she'd start backing up. Robin spent weeks working with her, until she finally began to behave, and they decided to run her at Saratoga. She started fine—and was even in second place through two turns. But then a horse drew up next to her, and she just quit. She settled into last place, and stayed there. Afterward, the jockey dismounted and swore the horse wasn't tired, she just didn't like to run. So the owners sent her home. That's what could happen to a horse.

Barclay wanted to put Funny Cide on a conservative path, he explained to Jack. What he had in mind was a schedule of carefully chosen peaks with lots of long recovery time in between. He wanted to run the horse in the Sleepy Hollow, and then ship him down to Florida for the winter, where he could rest and play for a bit before embarking on a campaign of steadily more ambitious events. He wanted to put him on a path that led, potentially, to the biggest races of all.

"Look, I think you could have a classic horse here," Barclay said.

On the other end of the line, Jack listened intently. He knew what that meant: the classics were the Triple Crown races. The Kentucky Derby, the Preakness, and the Belmont Stakes.

Barclay quickly added that he could be wrong about the horse; he'd experienced innumerable disappointments, and he didn't want the owners' expectations to be too high. When you shot for the moon, it was a setup for failure. Funny Cide was a New York gelding whose sire was a sprinter, and the likelihood was that he didn't have the genes. At any point, he might turn out to be not good enough. But Barclay wanted at least to give him a chance to show what he could do.

There were other factors, too, Barclay thought. *Such as whether you had a patient, understanding owner, or a real bastard who was going to fire you and take the horse away for trying to do the right thing.*

So they had a choice, Barclay said. They could take a conservative approach with him. "Or, you could go ahead with the Breeders' Cup horse and maybe ruin him, and never get your classic horse," Barclay said.

After a moment, Jack said, "Okay." The owners would do what Barclay advised. To Jack it was a no-brainer: they would put the long-term welfare of the horse first. Funny Cide would skip the Breeders' Cup and enter the Sleepy Hollow Stakes for New York–breds, as planned. It was a $100,000 race over one mile, and it would be challenging, but not dangerously so. Funny would get experience, without it killing him.

Barclay was relieved. He didn't have three hundred new horses a year, or even thirty. When a good horse came along, you only got a few shots with him. If you wrecked him, it was because you'd been asked to wreck him.

Barclay didn't intend to wreck Funny Cide. It would be too easy to knock the horse out before winter ever started, and blow his whole campaign. In another, larger barn, Barclay knew, Funny would have been pushed—or perhaps even overlooked altogether. There would have been too many other horses to care for, horses that were bigger, and more imposing, and more expensive.

Instead, just maybe the horse had found the right trainer, and the trainer had found the right horse. A thought that prompted Barclay Tagg, stoic and professional pessimist, lifelong victim of tough luck and unhappy accidents, and trainer of hundreds of also-rans, to turn to Robin one morning and utter one of the most outrageously hopeful statements of his life.

"This is going to be our Derby horse," he said.

6.

The Horsewoman

It's not always the horse with the most class that you remember. It's the ones that tried hardest all the time even though they weren't great horses. You know, I recall those horses. They are just as much my favorites as the champs. Good, honest horses.

—ALLEN JERKENS

Derby, hell," Robin said. "This horse can't breathe."

Funny Cide was blowing hard from exertion, and as he did so, a choking, faintly strangled noise came from deep in his throat. Neither Robin's skepticism nor the panting of the horse was something that Barclay, planning for the Kentucky Derby, particularly wanted to hear.

But if Robin said something was wrong with Funny Cide, Barclay had to believe her. When it came to the physical state of the horses in the Tagg barn, nobody knew more than Robin. Barclay fed them, and watched over them, and felt their tendons, but she rode them on a daily basis. Robin knew their best and worst qualities, and she could tell when they were tired, or if they were sore, and precisely where. Barclay liked to say that racehorses weren't like NFL players: they couldn't whine and tell you when something hurt. Somehow, Barclay had to divine what was going on with an animal, and Robin was his way of doing it.

Robin had the memory of a thousand horses in her gloved hands, and she was rarely mistaken about what they were feeling. A lot of riders rode horses without really sensing them—they got distracted with racetrack gossip, or clowned around with their colleagues—but Robin was always intensely attuned to the animal. If Barclay didn't like the way a horse was moving and suspected something was wrong, he'd say, "Can you get on that horse tomorrow? There's something not right about him. I can't really put my finger on it, but there's something just not right."

Robin would mount the horse and jog him, and Barclay would say, "Do you feel anything funny?"

She'd walk the horse back to Barclay and say, "He's a little stiff in his right hind leg." Or, "It's his knees." Or, "He's got hocks." And she was always right. So if Robin said Funny Cide couldn't breathe, then he couldn't breathe.

As Robin cooled Funny Cide down after his workout, she puzzled over the horse's ragged panting. Had she worked him too hard? She didn't think so. They'd covered a half-mile in no faster than forty-nine seconds, and his pace had even dropped off at the eighth pole. Horses could be deceiving: some could go fast and it felt slow; others made slow feel like a hundred miles an hour. But Funny Cide acted like every stride was an effort and he didn't even want a bit in his mouth. His chest heaved, and the noise in his throat sounded moist and heavy. She thought, *Barclay thinks this is going to be his Derby horse?* This horse wasn't up to it, not with this labored breathing.

Robin knew how highly Barclay thought of Funny Cide, and she was loath to disappoint him. But Funny Cide simply didn't have enough wind to be a Derby contender. She wasn't sure what to say as he walked alongside her on his pony. But, like him, she had never been one to mince words.

"If you think this horse is going to go a mile and a quarter, you're crazy," she said.

"What?"

"The horse can't breathe. He'll never go a step over a mile and a sixteenth. If we can get him to go a mile and sixteen, we'll be lucky. No way is he going any farther than that."

Barclay was crushed. He had tried to keep things in perspective after the Bertram Bongard. "We don't really know how good those other horses were," he told himself. "They could have been the worst ones in the world." But Jose Santos continued to insist he'd never ridden a better horse. "I tell you, he's the best two-year-old I ever been on," Santos said. For better or worse, Barclay had allowed himself to think better and better of Funny Cide.

Now Robin had smashed his hopes for Funny Cide in one sentence. Maybe the horse really wasn't bred well enough for the classics. They had been working him harder, trying to prepare him for longer distances, and for his upcoming race in the $100,000 Sleepy Hollow Stakes. Maybe the pressure had revealed a weakness in him. His father was a sprinter, and it stood to reason that the son would have trouble going farther than a mile, too. Maybe the horse wasn't a freak after all.

But Barclay didn't want to believe it. He thought about Funny

Cide's earlier workouts, and how easy they had seemed. The other possibility was that he was sick.

"Why can't he breathe?" Barclay asked her.

"I don't know. I'm just saying he can't."

When they got back to the barn, Barclay decided to ask the vet to take a look at Funny Cide's lungs as he made his rounds. The vet went into Funny Cide's stall and put a scope down the horse's throat. When he drew the scope up, it was covered in a thick mucus. The horse's throat was full of fluid; no wonder he couldn't breathe. "He must have an infection," the vet said.

Barclay didn't know whether to be relieved or alarmed. "Well, what are we supposed to do?" he asked. "Can he run?" That weekend, Funny Cide was supposed to go off in the Sleepy Hollow as the heavy favorite. "I can put him on some antibiotics for three days," the vet said. "And then you'll have to take him off for the race." According to the vet, the horse should be capable of running a mile comfortably, if they could unclog his throat and get his breathing cleared up in time.

By the afternoon of the race, Funny Cide was somewhat improved, but he still wasn't totally well. Under normal circumstances, the trainers would have scratched the horse. But after discussing it with the vet, they decided to let him run. "He's ninety percent," the vet said. For all their conservatism, there were times when they had to push an animal. Perhaps the hardest thing to learn in horse training was that you couldn't stop and nurse or fix every single sore spot or twinge. The next thing you knew, the horse was six years old and you hadn't won a race with him yet.

Also, Funny Cide needed the experience, Barclay decided. All the horse had ever done was run as hard as he could; he hadn't yet learned to pace himself. In horse-racing parlance, he'd never been "rated" behind other horses. If Funny Cide was going to compete in the classics, he'd have to learn to sit behind the early speed, saving his energy for the finish. It was a critical part of the young horse's education.

Barclay's plan was to rate the horse in the Sleepy Hollow and see how he reacted. Where else were they going to teach him, if they didn't teach him in a New York–bred stakes race? "He should be good enough to win, no matter what happens," Barclay told Santos.

But as post time approached, Barclay and Robin had a bout of nerves. It was "Showcase Day" at Belmont, there was a larger crowd than usual to see the race, and the odds on Funny Cide had dropped until he was listed as a 2–5 favorite. Moreover, all ten of his owners were coming to Belmont to watch their prodigy. "You guys really need to see this horse run," Jack had said. They didn't know that the horse wasn't feeling his best, or that Barclay had instructed Santos to hold the horse back.

In fact, Dave Mahan was so certain Funny Cide would win that he went into the clubhouse and found a betting window and began peeling off bills. He placed one thousand dollars to win on his horse.

Also contributing to the trainers' pre-race jitters was the fact that entered in the Sleepy Hollow field was a horse named Spite the Devil, trained by their great friend Allen Jerkens. The iconoclastic Hall of Famer was a large man with a small voice whose nickname around the barn was simply Chief, and a favorite was never safe in a race against him. Jerkens had pulled off more upsets than perhaps any trainer ever, defeating among others Kelso, Forgo, and Secretariat twice, a feat for which he'd won the Eclipse

Award in 1973. Writer William Leggett once wrote of Jerkens, "He could train a pit bull to meow."

All in all, the circumstances made Robin so nervous that she felt sick: everybody was expecting Funny Cide to win by several lengths, and yet, Robin knew their horse couldn't breathe properly. And here was Jerkens lying in wait for them.

In the paddock, Santos couldn't understand why Robin seemed so worried. "What are you so nervous about?" he asked. "I mean, he's going to win."

Robin just said, "Well, good luck."

As Funny Cide came out of the gate, the owners chattered with excitement, speculating about how many lengths their horse would win by. But within moments their chatter died down. Santos pulled the horse in—and got pinned inside, against the rail. Funny Cide fought with the jockey, furious at being held back, as they headed into the turn.

Now Santos wanted to let him go, but he couldn't, without running up the hind end of the horses in front of him.

The owners and trainers began screaming encouragement, Dave Mahan loudest of all, thinking of his thousand dollars. Finally, as the horses came off the turn, a horse on the rail moved over slightly—just enough. Santos gunned Funny Cide into the small hole of daylight, and got him through.

Just then, Spite the Devil moved alongside Funny Cide and passed him.

Funny Cide flipped his ears back and surged forward, digging into the track. Now he passed Spite the Devil. As they approached the wire, it was Funny Cide in the lead. Spite the Devil tried to come back on him, but it was too late.

Funny Cide won by a long neck. When Santos brought the horse to the winner's circle, he just said to Robin, "Now I know why you were so nervous."

Dave Mahan got to lead Funny Cide off the track to the winner's circle. Nadine teased him, "I've never seen a smile on your face that big. Even when you married me, you never smiled like that."

Barclay and Robin believed it was a significant victory for the horse: he had beaten mature competition, and he had done it with heart, and class, when he wasn't feeling well and had every reason to lose. A lot of horses, when they got headed in the stretch and were as tired as he was, might have given up and said, "Okay, I'm done, I want to go back to the barn now for my bath." Instead, Funny Cide had pushed his ears back and driven to the finish line. "Horses with talent and breeding are a dime a dozen," Robin told the owners. "But few of them have the right attitude. Funny Cide has the personality to go with his speed."

They all trooped upstairs to the private room for their champagne again, and Barclay joined them. "Boy, that was close," he said. "I probably should've scratched the horse, because he was a little sick. But I figured even sick, he's still good enough to beat these horses."

"What?" Dave said.

"He's sick," Barclay said.

"Barclay," Dave said. "You might want to tell me if we got a sick horse—because I may not want to go down and bet a thousand dollars of my money."

"He was ninety percent. I thought ninety percent was good enough."

There was one person who was willing to stake everything he had on Funny Cide, even after the horse's ailing performance in the Sleepy Hollow: Jose Santos. The race only persuaded Santos more than ever that the horse was a potential champion. Santos had ridden in the Kentucky Derby five times, but he'd never finished better than fourth. This horse was going to change his fortune in the race, he confided in his wife, Rita. "I've found my Derby horse," he insisted. Rita was the daughter of a jockey, and the sister of a jockey, Herb Castillo, Jr. She knew horses as well as anybody. She looked at her husband skeptically.

"Are you insane?" she said. "A gelding and a New York–bred?"

But Santos continued to tell anyone who would listen about Funny Cide, even after he went to the Breeders' Cup, held at Arlington Park in Chicago. Thanks in part to Sellito, Santos had managed to procure a mount for the four-million-dollar featured race: a 43–1 long shot named Volponi. Jack and Dorothy Knowlton and Dave and Nadine Mahan flew in to see Santos ride, and on a frigid afternoon, he sat astride Volponi and galloped to a stunning upset victory.

That evening, they all went to the victory party. Jack and Dave worked their way across the room and congratulated Santos and his family. "That was a great race," Jack said.

"Well, thank you very much," Jose said. "Your horse Funny Cide is going to be my Derby horse."

Jack just arched an eyebrow.

But Funny Cide wouldn't be anybody's Derby horse if Barclay and Robin couldn't solve his nagging throat ailment. Two weeks after the Sleepy Hollow, Robin was galloping Funny Cide at Belmont when she heard the familiar wet noise in his breathing. They took him back to the barn and scoped him, and the same glue-like substance came from the back of his throat, a string of mucus so thick it looked like caramel.

Barclay had no choice but to call Jack and tell him the horse was sick and would not be running for a while. "The freakin' thing is back again," he said. "It's worse than ever. His lungs are filled up."

To Barclay and Robin's relief, the owners agreed to let the horse have a long rest. One of the advantages of dealing with self-made businessmen was that they had experience in hiring experts and listening to them, and abiding by their knowledge. Barclay made plenty of mistakes—everybody made mistakes in the horse game— but he was the guy who was at the barn at five o'clock in the morning, and at five o'clock at night, and he had a better chance of being right about the horse than someone sitting in an office somewhere else, trying to second-guess him. Sackatoga Stable, he decided, were the best owners he'd ever had.

Funny Cide would not run again for three months. They put the horse on antibiotics, and his breathing would clear up for a few days at a time, and then, just when they grew hopeful, the clogging fluid would return. The vet had no firm diagnosis for the problem, and no medicine seemed to work. It wasn't a serious illness, but it was a frustrating one.

Robin tried to use the time to educate the horse, and to nurse him through other, smaller nagging physical ailments. Funny Cide was so strong and impatient that he ripped his own mouth open on the bit. He had a narrow jaw, and he pulled so hard that he often came back from the track with a bloody mouth, the skin torn at the corners, leaving two lumps of congealed flesh.

Even when they were jogging, Robin could feel him grab at the rings of the bit. As soon as Funny Cide's hooves touched the dirt, he surged forward, and the jolt would run through her hands. It was a vicious cycle: the more his mouth hurt him, the harder he wanted to run, because his horse's instincts said the way to get away from pain was to go faster. He didn't know how to back off. All he knew was to run from pain.

Robin began to experiment with other bits, determined to find one that was comfortable for him. "Are you going to change it fifteen times?" Barclay teased her. Finally, she found one that didn't torture him, and which had a steel bar below his mouth for better control.

With the new bit, Robin worked on patience with the horse, trying to teach him self-control. Some days, she would walk Funny to the track, and then just stand for a few minutes letting him take it in. She wanted him to relax, to smell the air and look around. They might stand there for as long as fifteen minutes.

None of the other exercise riders could control Funny Cide. But Robin knew there was no holding the horse back with strength—he weighed 1,100 pounds, and it wasn't going to happen. Not that Robin was weak. She was a slender but muscled 130 pounds, without an ounce of fat on her.

The issue with Funny Cide wasn't strength but strategy, and Robin handled him strategically. She knew better than to try to physically restrain the horse. Instead, their workouts became a kind of high-speed negotiation. If she pulled him in too hard, he would respond by swerving to the outside. Then, to keep him from running into the fence, she'd let him go forward. They veered around the track, Robin asking the horse to slow down, and the horse insistent on galloping away, until gradually, he learned how to pace himself. Barclay sat on his pony and watched them, admiringly.

"Robin's the only person who can ride that damn horse," he said.

It was no exaggeration to say that Robin was on horseback even in the womb: her mother won a jumping competition when she was pregnant.

Robin was one of four children of hardscrabble horse people, Ann and Kenny Smullen, who raised show horses and foxhunters on their family spread, Laurel Hill Farm in Oxford, Pennsylvania. The Smullen farm was not too far from Unionville, and every once in a while an erect rider in a slouch hat would ride by their property and raise a hand in greeting. Barclay Tagg rented a piece of land that neighbored the Smullens', and he kept some horses. He knew the Smullens to nod to, and sometimes he would wave at the little girl with the braid and her three brothers working in the stables or paddock.

It was also no exaggeration to say that Robin could ride before she could walk. She was competing in horse shows by the age of four, and at eight, she reached the Junior National Finals and placed fifth in the country among eighteen-and-under riders. Showing horses was an entirely different discipline from racing thoroughbreds, an exercise in painstaking form rather than speed: it was about which horse and rider were the best trained, the cleanest jumpers, and the most composed in their movements. But it was also an exercise in costliness. Robin might have reached the top echelon of show horses, the Grand Prix level—she was probably a good enough rider—but lack of money held her back.

On the Smullen farm, there were no extra funds with which to buy higher-quality horses and prettier tack. Instead, Robin purchased her own horses with money she earned for breaking yearlings. One of her first horses was a wizened, malnourished thing that she bought from her father for two hundred dollars. His name was Barnabas. Her father warned her that he was probably no good for show riding. He was a cheap black horse Ken had acquired for use as a pony at the local track, and when Barnabas arrived on the farm, he was so ASPCA-thin and sickly that he probably should have been put down. Robin said, "Dad, you can't take this horse on the track. First of all, he can't hold your weight." Robin made her dad a bargain: he owed her a couple hundred bucks for chores, but she would take Barnabas instead.

Improbably, Robin turned Barnabas into a prizewinning show horse. He had a background as an amateur jumper, and under Robin's care, he became a sleek and shiny champion with an array of ribbons and gold medals. She was devoted to him, and they competed together for the next four years as she went to high school.

In addition to decorating her bedroom with ribbons, Barnabas helped to distract her from the breakup of her parents' marriage. Ken was an alcoholic who would disappear for hours on end, while Ann presided over the farm and raised the children. Ken would say he'd be home at seven, and the family would sit at the dinner table, waiting, and waiting. Finally, he'd stumble home at two A.M., surly from liquor. He'd ask for coffee, and Ann would put it on, and he'd fall asleep. If Ann got upset, he'd say, "Don't let the door hit you on the ass on your way out."

One evening, Ann packed all of his things and sat them on the porch. This time, when Ken came home after midnight, she opened the door for him. "You're late," she said.

"Uh-huh."

"Your bags are packed and you're leaving this farm with what's in them. I'm finished. Don't let the door hit you on the ass on the way out."

They saw him only periodically after that. Robin and her brothers helped her mother run the farm. Robin broke and trained horses, and sometimes she bought new ones with her own money. By the time she was seventeen, she had five stalls of horses in the family barn that she had purchased and trained herself, a business within the business. In addition, she galloped horses at a neighboring farm; she would rise before dawn and exercise horses, and then come home and clean up for school.

But Barnabas remained her first love, and when he died of an aneurysm, she would feel the loss for the rest of her life. She was schooling him for a horse show one morning, when he simply buckled beneath her. She tried to walk away from the struggling horse, but he kept whinnying after her. She turned around and sat down beside him. He put his head in her lap, and she held him like that until he died.

For days, Robin couldn't go near the barn. She was inconsolable—so much so that within a week she had sold every horse she owned; all five of them. She'd never show a horse again. After Barnabas, she gave up the sport altogether. She continued to help train the show horses for her mother, but she refused to show them herself, swearing she wouldn't be hurt a second time.

Instead, Robin turned to racehorses and decided to make them her living. She had always galloped them as an exercise rider, but now she applied for a license as an assistant trainer and made her way to Charles Town, West Virginia, where she spent the next few years running her own horses. At one point, she worked up to a winning rate of 17 percent—but the purses were so small it hardly mattered, and she barely scraped by.

Despite her vow not to become too attached to a horse again, she was devoted even to the cheapest animals in her stalls. Few people outside of the track understood that. Once, she fell into a relationship with a guy who didn't know anything about thoroughbred racing, and they thought they were in love until one day when one of her horses got colic. Robin was late for dinner. She called up and said, "I'm obviously not there, and I'll be there as soon as I can get there, but I have a sick horse." It was after eight-thirty by the time she reached the restaurant, and he was furious.

"I can't just leave a sick horse," she said.

"Well, you're gonna have to make a decision. It's either me or the horses."

"Wrong answer."

"What does that mean?"

"There is no 'It's me or the horses,' " she said, " 'cause all there are, for me, are horses. You don't even enter into it. You either accept me with the horses, or you don't accept me at all. Because the horses are always going to come first. Always."

Adult humans could care for themselves, but horses were reliant, she tried to explain. It didn't matter: they broke up. Men were going to come and go, Robin decided. The horses would always be there.

Then she met and married an ex-jockey named Michael Saunders, whom she'd gotten to know while training horses in West Virginia. He was already an alcoholic and on his way to becoming a drug addict. She knew she was making a mistake even on her wedding day, but she went through with it because she'd said she would. It lasted three years.

Her husband drank steadily, and drugged increasingly, and grew volatile. He never hit her, but he hit other things. Glass. Furniture. He bashed a hole in the drywall. Once, he got angry while they were sitting in their car, and he punched out the front of the windshield, shattering it with his bare hand.

She understood that she was the child of an alcoholic, and she'd read up on the pathology: she wanted to fix everything for everybody. But she was learning from her marriage what the horses had already taught her: there were some things she couldn't fix. Not only couldn't she fix her husband, she couldn't even make him better temporarily. He was in a vortex, and she could stay in there with him or pull herself out. So she got out. Two years after she left him, he was found dead from complications related to his addiction.

She moved into an apartment for $500 a month, and took two jobs, exercising horses in the pre-dawn and selling tack at a local equine supply shop in the afternoons. With her savings, she bought her own house, a small place in Elkton, Maryland, with a mortgage of $700 a month. She worked six days a week, left home in the dark every morning and got home after dark every night, and did her laundry and cut the grass on Sundays. But the house was hers, the first thing she'd ever owned that wasn't a horse.

For the next few years, Robin quit dating almost entirely. At the track, she was known as the pretty but tough girl trainer who wouldn't say yes to an invitation. *You've got to make better choices,* she told herself. So for a while, she made no choices at all, just lived alone and carried her mortgage, and gradually paid down the house in Elkton.

By the winter of 1997, Robin was working as an assistant to a colleage in the training business, Dr. John R. S. Fisher, looking after a string of four horses for him in Florida. She invited a friend down to stay with her and share a small house she had, rent-free. One afternoon she was walking a horse to the track at Gulfstream Park when she passed Barclay Tagg and said hello. She had a nodding acquaintance with Barclay from her years as a trainer in Maryland, and his barn at Gulfstream was next to Fisher's. He nodded back pleasantly and didn't seem to take any special notice of her. But the next day, he stopped her and asked her out to dinner.

"Well, my girlfriend's here," she said, uncertainly. "And she's not leaving till Friday. But I guess I could go to dinner after that."

"Okay," he said.

On Friday, Robin's phone rang.

"Is she gone?" Barclay said, without introduction.

"Yeah, she's gone."

"Well, let's go to the beach."

Robin had never gone to the beach. She worked, that was all she did, and she didn't even own a bathing suit. But she ran out of the house and bought one. She put it on, over her white skin, and slathered herself with sunblock.

Barclay picked her up and they drove to the beach. They didn't say three words to each other as they laid out a couple of towels. Robin picked up a book and began to read. They lay there all afternoon, sunning, reading, and napping, but without speaking.

After a few hours, Barclay said, "Okay, I got to go back to the barn."

"I do, too."

When they got back to the barns, Robin did her chores. She was just sitting down to make out her set list for exercising the horses the following day, when Barclay reappeared in her doorway.

"Want to go out to dinner?" he asked.

"Yeah, okay. I'll go out to dinner."

They went out to dinner, to a place on the beach, and sat together by the shore, again without really talking.

The next morning, Robin did a little asking around. She had known Barclay wasn't married, or she wouldn't have gone out with him, but now she heard from some barn acquaintances that he had been seeing Charlsie Canty, the attractive, articulate announcer who covered horse racing for NBC. Robin didn't date people who were already involved; it was part of her better-choices policy not to start a relationship before another one had ended. Much as she liked Barclay, she thought, *I'm not going there.*

Later that afternoon, when Barclay was done with his training, he came to Robin's tack room. "So what do you want to do today?" he asked.

"You and I got a problem," Robin said.

"What's up?"

"I didn't realize that you were seeing somebody before I agreed to go out to dinner with you."

"Well, I've already talked to her about that," he said. "She and I are very good friends, and we'll remain very good friends."

Robin had intended to tell him thank you for dinner and she didn't want to see him anymore. But now, instead, she said, "Okay." And they went back to the beach.

There were a lot of horsemen, and just plain men, who had the gift of the gab, and Barclay wasn't one of them. He was not much with people, but if you saw past his brusqueness and looked at what he did and how he did it, then he was the guy for you, Robin decided. He had heart, and honesty. It was pretty straightforward, as far as Robin was concerned.

Barclay liked to say, "We went to dinner, and she never left." And it was almost that simple. The partnership worked. It worked at home, and it worked at work. They saw every sunrise together. They went to the barn before the first sliver of light, and by midafternoon they were done with their work, and free to do what they pleased until it was time to come back to the barn before sunset. "Who could want more?" Robin said.

She rode the horses, and he watched her, and it was as if they experienced the same thing. They didn't take vacations, because if they left for even a week, they missed the horses. They needed the action, to work with the animals and ride them and feel them with their hands.

When they needed a break, they went to one of the balmy, sublime, blue-water Florida beaches, and napped. Usually, Robin didn't even go into the water—she was the world's worst swimmer. Sometimes she would wade into the shallows and stand there for a moment to cool off, and then climb back out and fall asleep. Just the sound of the beach was what she preferred.

The horses still came first for Robin, always, but they came first for Barclay, too, and life was a lot easier, Robin realized, when you understood that about your other half. Neither of them had to stop caring for horses to care for their partner. Maybe that was why much of Barclay's surface irritability around the barn receded once Robin came. He didn't worry as much about all the things that went wrong, because so much was right. Track people noticed it, and they liked to tease Robin about the change she'd wrought in him. "He's much nicer since he met you," they said.

A good horse could win a lot of races, even in the wrong hands. A good horse in the right hands could win even more. It mostly depended on the horse.

But a horse in the thirteenth post position couldn't do much at all.

After several weeks of rest in Florida, Funny Cide was well enough to race again, despite the fact that his trachea still periodically clogged up from his mysterious ailment. He was still on antibiotics intermittently, and his breathing was better, and while he wasn't cured, the horse was now ready for his first start as a three-year-old.

Barclay and Robin entered him in the Holy Bull, a Grade III stakes race of a mile and one-sixteenth at Gulfstream Park. Even with his lingering breathing hitch, they were confident he could win—until he drew the thirteenth post.

A horse couldn't get any farther outside than that. It meant that Funny Cide would be strung way out to the right, and he'd have to run farther than any other horse in the field. Moreover, their young horse had a habit of swinging wide to begin with. Also, one slot inside of him would be Allen Jerkens's horse Spite the Devil, ridden by Jerry Bailey, the foremost jockey in the business.

With a post position like that, almost nothing good could happen. Barclay wanted to scratch him, but he couldn't: the horse needed the race, and it was time to test him against open company.

Nothing good did happen. Finny Cide broke horribly after hitting the side of the gate. Then, he was bumped by Bailey on Spite the Devil. After he got untangled, he responded by veering right, practically to the outside fence.

Funny Cide was six horses wide on the first turn. Santos tried to get back in the race around the second turn, but Funny Cide was bumped again, and Santos took him out wide once more. From there, he just galloped down the middle of the track, with open space in front of him.

He still finished fifth, beaten by five lengths.

In a way, it was an accomplishment. Funny Cide had run everywhere but through the parking lot to get to the finish line, but he'd never stopped trying, and he wasn't beaten to the wire by much. If he had started from any place but the thirteenth post position, he might have won.

Around the track, it was hailed as a courageous race: Funny Cide had overcome several spots of trouble and still run credibly. The way Barclay and Robin figured it, with all of his zigzagging, he had run a mile and an eighth while the other horses ran a mile and a sixteenth.

Others thought so, too. A week later, Jerry Bailey's agent, Ron Anderson, called Barclay, wanting to know if his jockey could ride Funny Cide in the Fountain of Youth. Barclay was speechless. Bailey was the top jockey in the game, and he rode only the best mounts available.

"Well, I don't understand," Barclay said. "Why do you want our horse when you've got your pick of everything out there?"

"Barclay, according to my figures, that horse ran an awesome race in the Holy Bull."

Barclay turned him down. Santos would remain his jockey. At the very least, Funny Cide and the jockey had run well enough to take the next step toward the Kentucky Derby, he had to admit.

Barclay didn't want to be accused of having Derby fever; if Funny Cide wasn't up to it, if he was too common, or if he was at heart a sprinter, a miler at best, the horse shouldn't be pushed. Barclay had never been the sort of trainer who wanted to go to the Derby just for the experience. He didn't care to go to Churchill Downs as a spectator, or as a tourist-trainer, to watch his horse run ninth.

If anything, Barclay kept looking for a reason *not* to go to the Derby. If the horse stopped improving, he was out of it, he told the Sackatoga owners. "We're not going to the Derby just to go to the Derby," Barclay insisted. But so far, the horse kept making his own case.

Barclay and Robin carefully considered what to do with him next. The traditional proving ground for the Derby was the prestigious Wood Memorial at Aqueduct in April, and most of the top Derby hopefuls would be entered, including the exquisitely bred super-horse, Empire Maker. Funny Cide should be in the field, too, the Sackatoga owners and trainers agreed. If Funny Cide wasn't worthy of the Derby, they would know it based on his performance in the Wood. They had to be convinced that Funny Cide had a shot to *win* the Derby, not just enter it.

"Then I'll know whether to go on with him, or to end this foolishness," Barclay said.

But before the Wood, the horse needed one more race. Barclay was inclined to run him at home in the Florida Derby, but Jack Knowlton had another suggestion. The day after the Holy Bull, Jack came out to Gulfstream to see Barclay, and offered his idea: some of the Sackatoga owners enjoyed going to New Orleans for the Louisiana Derby every year. Would Barclay consider entering Funny Cide there?

As usual, Barclay's first impulse was to say, "No, let me train the freaking horse, we're going to do it my way." But it was actually a pretty good idea, when Barclay thought about it. The Louisiana Derby was five weeks before the Wood, and it was a Grade II stakes race for $750,000. It upped the ante, gave the horse a slightly more ambitious race to train for before the Wood. If something went wrong, if the horse got sick again or drew a bad post position, they could always scratch and enter the Florida Derby instead, which was scheduled for a week later. Also, the horse would have to learn to ship sometime, if he was going to be a Derby horse. Barclay and Jack agreed; they would enter him in the Louisiana Derby.

Despite Barclay's caution about overreaching with Funny Cide, Jack and his fellow Sackatoga bettors were already thinking ahead about a trip to Churchill Downs. In early December, Jack and Gus went to Las Vegas to gamble. For fun, they decided to see what kind of future odds were being offered on Funny Cide in the Kentucky Derby. The race wasn't until May, and no one had heard of their horse, so he was certain to be the longest of shots.

Jack called J.P. in Sackets Harbor before the Las Vegas trip to see if any of them wanted in on the action. "Listen, Gus and I are going to Vegas. Ask the guys if they want to put some money down on Funny Cide to win the Derby, at long odds."

J.P. hung up and put the question to his partners. The Sackets partners were such novices in the horse and betting businesses that they misunderstood: they thought the bet was whether Funny would get "in" the Derby, not "win" it. The guys enthusiastically chipped in various amounts. When J.P. called Jack back, he had collected several hundred dollars. The other partners and some of Jack and Gus's friends contributed several hundred dollars more

Jack and Gus went to a casino race book and asked for the odds on the Kentucky Derby.

Funny Cide was listed at 150–1.

"How much can we bet?" Gus asked.

The limit was only two hundred dollars, but still, it was a heavy payoff: if their horse came in first, they would win $30,000. Jack and Gus each got down a $200 bet.

The oddsmakers, in order to protect themselves, immediately lowered the odds. Jack and Gus then took $200 each at 75–1. Now the odds fell again.

Jack and Gus visited race books all over the Vegas strip. By the time they were done, they had wagered $2,000 at odds ranging from 150–1 to 40–1.

But back at the barn, Barclay and Robin weren't willing to bet anything on the horse, given the fact that his breathing still wasn't right. It had now been more than three months since he'd first choked up, and they were no closer to finding an answer. Three different vets had examined him and done throat cultures, but they hadn't found a clue as to what was wrong.

They had tried every kind of antibiotic: Batrol, Amacasin, Genecin, penicillin, and Genecin and penicillin together. The horse was on so many different kinds of antibiotics that he became used to them. Robin could swear that when they came into his stall to treat him each day, he practically rolled his eyes, as if to say, "Oh, God, not that again."

They were beginning to wonder if the horse's condition was not only chronic but incurable, when late one afternoon Barclay wandered into the barn office of an old friend, Dr. Stephen Selway, who was regarded as among the very best veterinary surgeons in the business.

"I have this horse," Barclay said, "and he's the best one I have. But I'm having real problems with him." With that, Barclay launched into a description of Funny Cide's breathing, and the various ways they had treated him. Selway had never seen Funny Cide and didn't know anything about him, but as he listened to Barclay describe the symptoms, they sounded too familiar.

"Does he look like he's sick?" Selway asked.

"No," Barclay said. "He's got dapples all over him."

Dapples, along with eating habits, were a reliable indicator of whether a horse was healthy. A thoroughbred in perfect condition had a magnificent sheen; its coat stretched tightly across its muscled body and reflected every light and dark spot, so that it looked literally like dappled light.

"Take that horse off the antibiotics," Selway said immediately. "There's nothing really wrong with him. I know what he's got."

"How do you know?" Barclay asked, dumbfounded.

Selway explained that he'd had another patient-horse with similar symptoms: Funny Cide was lacking cilia, the tiny hairs that brush mucus and food from the throat. He'd probably had pneumonia as a baby, Selway said, and the ailment had burned away some of the cilia and left bald patches. "He was probably sick for a few days," Selway said, and then he had gotten better and no one had thought any more about it. But the bald patches left by the pneumonia made his throat clog easily.

Selway said there was a simple solution: Funny Cide needed an expectorant—cough medicine. He prescribed a daily injection to help thin the blockage in the horse's throat, and he warned them that it could take some time. Then he piled the medicines in a large box and gave it to Barclay. Gratefully, he accepted it.

Over the next few days, their regular vet, Dr. George Burch, treated the horse, and his breathing began to clear—slowly. Now the question was whether they could get him fully healthy in time to earn his way into the Derby. One morning, as they tended him, Robin came up with an idea. They were basically treating Funny Cide for head-cold symptoms—so why not use the same remedy you'd use on a child?

"What would be wrong with a transpirator?" she asked Barclay.

Robin's idea was to give Funny Cide the horse version of a Vicks vaporizer: a transpirator heated up distilled water to 104 degrees and turned it, and any accompanying medicine, into steam. A mask was fitted over the horse's face, and he breathed in the steam and meds.

"It can't hurt," Barclay said, shrugging. "We're running out of things to do."

Robin ordered a transpirator with the help of Jack Knowlton, who did some research to find a distributor on his home computer, but it arrived broken. She reordered it, and the next one didn't work, either, reinforcing Barclay's belief that few things ever went right. Finally, a third transpirator arrived, just three days before the Louisiana Derby. By then, they decided to wait until after the race to try their experiment.

Funny Cide's throat troubles had cost him some training, so Barclay and Robin didn't have extremely high hopes for the Louisiana Derby. Seven trying weeks after the Holy Bull, they arrived in New Orleans.

Funny Cide set the pace early—and then gave it up and seemed beaten when he dropped back to fourth. But then he made a late charge on the rail and somehow finished third. The winner was Peace Rules, the second-best three-year-old colt in Bobby Frankel's barn, behind Empire Maker.

Afterward, Jose Santos told them he hadn't expected such a strong second effort from Funny Cide. Had he known the horse had it in him, they might've won the race. He slid out of the saddle and said, "He surprised me."

Once again, Funny Cide gave Barclay, Robin, and the rest of the Sackatoga Stable reason to believe he could be a Derby horse. Though he hadn't won, he had finished in the money, despite months of ill health. (The payday became bigger when the second-place finisher, Kafwain, was later disqualified and Funny Cide was automatically elevated to second place.). They were still learning just how much horse they had. What might he do if he ever ran a healthy race as a three-year-old?

They would find out, once and for all, at the Wood Memorial, which would be run over a mile and an eighth at Aqueduct on April 13. They shipped Funny Cide back to Florida and began to treat him with the transpirator.

Every day for the next five weeks, Funny Cide calmly accepted the mask as Robin slipped it over his narrow copper face. The horse stood stock-still and breathed in the warm vapor and medicine, his eyes half-closed. It looked as though he was napping.

Finally, a week before the Wood, Barclay and Robin asked a vet to scope the horse one more time. They stood around and bit their fingernails while he was examined. Finally, the doctor removed the scope—and pronounced Funny Cide's throat 95 percent clean. At last, on the eve of the most important race of their careers, the horse's physical problems seemed to be solved.

The Wood was a hugely prestigious and dramatic race in its own right, apart from the fact that it was historically the route that many horses took to the Derby. But this version of it was supposed to offer little in the way of theater, because Empire Maker was such an overwhelming favorite at 1–2 odds. While Funny Cide had run gamely in the Louisiana Derby to finish third, Empire Maker had destroyed his competition in the Florida Derby to win by several lengths. The victory had prompted Empire Maker's jockey, Jerry Bailey, to make a bold statement: Empire Maker was not only the favorite to win the Wood, *and* the Kentucky Derby, but a possibility to win the Triple Crown, too. "He's the kind of horse that, if luck goes your way, you could think about all three of them," Bailey said.

Everything in Empire Maker's demeanor seemed to reaffirm the opinion. He had the obvious breeding; it was in his bones. He was an imposing horse, a dark bay whose coat rippled with muscle and tendon, a barrel-chested creature who seemed to exhale speed like steam.

But over in the Tagg barn, it was the opinion of Funny Cide's trainers that their horse was finally breathing well—and he seemed to be getting stronger and stronger as a result. Each time Robin exercised him, he seemed more powerful. He was a whole different horse from the gagging, snorting creature who had barely won the Sleepy Hollow.

On a raw April afternoon at Aqueduct, where the track was muddy, Barclay and Robin prepared Funny Cide for the running of the Wood, and all of the Sackatoga owners came to see whether their horse would go to the Kentucky Derby. "If he runs a big race, we go," Barclay promised them.

As the field of eight horses burst from the gate, a horse named New York Hero took the early lead from the first post. But most of the eyes in the crowd of 19,392 were on Empire Maker. The favorite broke sharply, and settled into third place, biding his time.

Robin and Barclay watched Funny Cide, and as they did so, they swelled with pride. Their horse was second place, and what's more, he was allowing Santos to rate him. He had learned his lessons.

On the far turn, Funny Cide overtook New York Hero and gained the lead. Empire Maker also made his move, and came to Funny Cide on the outside. Now Santos let Funny Cide run. The horses hurtled past the three-sixteenths pole together.

Funny Cide had the lead momentarily . . . and then Empire Maker surged past him, a length ahead. Santos asked his horse for one more try—and Funny Cide closed on Empire Maker again.

They crossed the line.

The winner was Empire Maker—but by only one-half of a length. The colt bred in central heat and air-conditioning, trained by the famed Bobby Frankel and ridden by the great Jerry Bailey, had won the race, as he was supposed to. But Funny Cide had run stride for stride with him and almost overtaken him at the end.

In the box seats, Robin's eyes welled up, and she began to cry. "It's okay, it's okay," Barclay kept saying. But then he realized she was crying because she was so happy. She was crying, she tried to explain, because the horse was like her child, and he had done everything perfectly, the way he'd been taught, and she was so proud of him. And she was crying because the horse had finally run freely.

Down in the winner's circle, Empire Maker was celebrated as befitted a favorite and a champion. But afterward, Frankel and Bailey seemed somewhat self-conscious because Funny Cide had made the race so close. Frankel pointed out that Bailey had hardly gone to the stick. "He probably would have won easier if Jerry got after him," Frankel told the press.

The remark would be the beginning of a rivalry, and a class war. As far as Barclay Tagg and Robin Smullen were concerned, Empire Maker's victory had by no means been assured.

At any rate, Funny Cide was going to the Kentucky Derby. "He made the decision for us," Barclay said. "We don't have a choice. At a mile and a quarter, he just might beat that other horse."

PART III

A Classic Horse

7.

The Derby

We were lucky nobody else bought him. We were lucky he
stayed sound all winter. We were lucky that he turned out as
good as he did. I mean, we don't know the son of a bitch can
run. We were just standing there watching this little yearling
walking around the pen, you know. But he was the right type.
He was the right type.

—BARCLAY TAGG

To much of the public, most of
the time, horse racing was a smoky vice that took place at beer-
splashed suburban tracks, where men in bad sport coats crouched
over crumpled sheets full of hieroglyphics. But once a year, a race
was run that the general population understood and cared about:
the Kentucky Derby. It was the first race of the Triple Crown, and
the most elegant, held at handsome old Churchill Downs in
Louisville, whose shingle-and-brick clubhouse with indelible twin
spires had given racing an aura of class ever since it was founded

in 1875, chiefly to prevent gentlemen from racing their horses down Market Street and knocking over the citizens.

Throughout the last days of April, the Kentucky Derby contenders arrived at Churchill Downs, and so did the money. Some of it was oil, some of it was tobacco, some of it was Hollywood, and a lot of it was inherited. The Sackatoga owners gawked at the variety and scale of the wealth that went by, and wondered where they fit in. All around them were luminaries of the thoroughbred world. Here came Saudi prince Khalid Abdullah, owner and breeder of Empire Maker. There went Wayne Lukas of the four Derby victories, and owners Bob and Beverly Lewis, who had twice won the Derby. Here came an Oklahoma gas magnate, and there went a Japanese businessman. Had they gotten in too deep? Another Derby entry, Artswhatimtalknbout, had sold for $900,000 as a yearling and was partly owned by director Steven Spielberg.

The other owners were cool and beautifully dressed, and they had a serene sense of belonging. The sheiks jet-streamed in on private planes and did majestic flybys of the twin spires. The Sackatoga crew came in on supersaver fares. "The hicks from the sticks with our jackets from Kmart," J.P. joked.

Their horse was in the Kentucky Derby, but they were still the crew from Sackets Harbor who had pooled their funds for one babysitter, and gone to one another's houses to party because they didn't have enough money to eat out. It was a financial stretch for some of them to be there. The trip cost them two thousand dollars each, conservatively.

But somehow it seemed worth it. Maybe it was the state of the world that made them less cautious with their money. On Hounsfield Street, the horse paraphernalia decorating their front doors was now joined by American flags and signs that said WE SUPPORT OUR TROOPS. Three families on the street had young men in the service.

Harold and Stephanie Cring's eldest son, Richard, was a staff sergeant in the air force who'd been stationed at McGuire Air Force base in New Jersey on September 11, 2001. When President George W. Bush arrived to view the damage at the World Trade Center, Staff Sergeant Cring was in the security detail that helped secure Air Force One at the air base.

J. P. and Karen Constance's son-in-law, Pat Frank, was in Iraq. Pat was a major in the 101st Airborne and had shipped out to the Middle East in March. J.P. told his daughter, Jennifer, "Honey, majors never get hurt, they stay in command areas and direct troops." But Pat had been overseas for only a few weeks when news came that a deranged soldier had thrown a grenade into Pat's tent, which was full of officers from the 101st. Frantic, Jennifer called J.P. and said, "You lied to me." They sat by the TV for hours before the phone rang: Pat was safe, he hadn't been in the tent because he'd been taking a shower. Now, just four weeks later, the Constances tried to pretend they were on a carefree vacation to the Kentucky Derby. But it was difficult.

They distracted themselves by gawking. In a way, gawking was as much a part of Derby tradition as mint juleps or fancy hats. You could always tell the first-time owners at the Derby, because they had a habit of blocking foot traffic and of tilting their heads to look up at the twin spires. Most people just smiled and stepped around them.

The Sackatoga owners toured Churchill Downs, and they stared with fascination at everything from the scratching of rakes in the hay to the hissing hoses as grooms washed down the other horses.

In Bobby Frankel's barn, Empire Maker stared out of his stall, assured and imperious, in a peel-me-another-grape kind of way. He was so perfect he looked varnished. Over at Bob Baffert's barn, everything had a high sheen, from the Cadillacs and Jaguars parked outside the shed row, to Baffert himself, with his shock of white hair and his pressed linen shirt and his polished, whiskey-colored boots.

The Sackatogans did much of their gawking in the lobby of the historical old Galt House Hotel, where they had a large block of rooms. But not all of them could afford the Galt House, with its appalling rate of $1,050 for three nights. Mark and Gwen Phillips found a Holiday Inn instead, and Eric and Jean Dattner commuted from a motel in Lexington. Larry Reinhardt decided not to go to the Derby at all; the horse was a long shot, and he had already taken his vacation for the year, with his wife to Europe. Instead, he stayed in Sackets Harbor and planned to watch the race at the Boathouse Restaurant, where owner Eric Constance was throwing a Derby party.

They looked for ways to save money. Dave Mahan was in charge of finding a bus to take their large entourage to the track, but when he called the hotel bellman, Chico, the rate for Derby day was $3,200. He was aghast—their group could not afford to throw down that kind of money for a three-mile ride. Dave picked up the phone again and called the hotel bellman back.

"Listen, is there anything else we can do? We ain't the Bafferts or Lewises, you know?"

The bellman said, "Let me do some checking."

A while later, he called back.

"How much pride do you have?" Chico asked.

"That depends on the price," Dave said.

Chico said there was a yellow school bus available for $1,100.

"Perfect."

Dave hung up and called Jack, and explained that he had found a bus to take them to track. The only catch was, it was yellow. It was an old-fashioned yellow school bus.

"I got us a big yellow stretch limo," he said.

Jack burst out laughing. "That's great," he said.

Funny Cide slipped into town late, and unnoticed. Other trainers took their horses to Kentucky days in advance to accustom them to the surroundings, but not Barclay Tagg. He believed in shipping a horse as close to race day as was feasible, so as not to disrupt the animal. Horses were creatures of routine, and Barclay believed Funny Cide would train better and be healthier at home than in a strange barn at Churchill Downs. He had moved horses that way for thirty years, and he saw no reason to change.

Also, Barclay and Robin didn't want to take any chances now that their horse was finally healthy. Ten days after the Wood Memorial, they had asked a vet to scope the horse. The doctor stuck the scope down the animal's throat and said, "What am I looking for?"

"I don't know, you tell me," Robin said.

"Well, he's absolutely clean," the vet said. "Whatever I'm looking for is not there."

Funny Cide was working beautifully at Belmont. Four days before the Derby, he ripped off five furlongs in fifty-eight and two-fifths seconds, and it was all they could do to make him stop running. Robin came back glowing. "Barclay, this horse is doing awesome. He's moving better than he's moved in his life."

Someone else thought so, too. One afternoon, Robin was working around the barn, when an assistant trainer to D. Wayne Lukas
stopped in to chat. "My boss thinks you've got a great shot at the
Derby," he said. Lukas had watched the Wood Memorial, and despite the declarations of Bobby Frankel and Jerry Bailey that Empire Maker had won easily, Lukas had come away with a different
impression. "That other horse was worn out," the assistant said.
Lukas thought Empire Maker had tired in the Wood and that Funny
Cide had a chance to steal the Derby from him. It was no mean en-
dorsement.

Finally, three days before the race, it was time to ship Funny
Cide to Kentucky. Barclay chose the hour of two A.M., when it was
cool and there was no traffic, to move him. Later that morning,
Robin and Barclay flew to Louisville and went to straight to
Churchill Downs to see about settling the horse into his temporary
quarters. They had rented stall No. 6 in Barn 48, from an old friend,
Tony Reinstedler.

Also that morning, Jack Knowlton went to the Derby draw. Each
horse was matched with a number, and the number determined in
what order their trainers chose their positions. Funny Cide pulled
the number two, which was great news. It meant they had second
choice. He called Barclay and Robin, and said, "What post position do you want?"

"Four," Barclay said.

"No, six," Robin said. "If someone scratches on the inside of
us, then that puts us too close to the inside."

"All right, six," Barclay said. "Six. We want six."

Robin felt good about the race for reasons both superstitious and
sensible: they had stall No. 6, and post position No. 6, and no less

a trainer than Wayne Lukas thought they had a chance. Meanwhile, Bobby Frankel did something curious: he chose to put Empire Maker in an outside post position. It meant the horse would have less traffic and less dirt in his face, but it also meant he would have to run farther. Obviously, Frankel was supremely confident in Empire Maker.

So were the experts, the bettors, and the press. Empire Maker was supposed to win the Derby, period. Everybody said so, and they said it might well be the first leg of a Triple Crown, too.

There was one small catch: Empire Maker had come out of the Wood Memorial with a bruised foot, so sore that he had been able to walk only for the last two days. But Frankel declared that the horse was sound again and dismissed all doubts.

"Bet against him at your own risk," Frankel said.

Funny Cide was either ignored or given nearly zero chance in the field of seventeen. No gelding had won the Derby in seventy-four years, and no New York–bred had ever won it, period. Only a handful of reporters ventured over to the barn where Funny Cide was housed. The day after he arrived, Robin was putting Funny Cide's saddle away when they showed up and began asking questions, aiming their tape recorders at her face. *Whoa*, she thought, *what's all this?*

"How was he today?"

"He's fine, everything's okay."

"What do you think your chances are?"

"Well, you know, you don't come unless you think you've got a shot."

On the morning before the race, Robin and Barclay took Funny Cide to the track for a two-mile jog. The horse behaved beautifully, though he was slightly anxious, unused to the crowds in the stands and the cameras at the rail. After he finished, Barclay and Robin walked him toward the starting gate, in order to school him.

As they stood there, Empire Maker galloped past. The colt came around the clubhouse turn, and then suddenly bolted to the outside rail, swerving crazily out of his appointed path. His ears were pinned, and he tried to pull up, as if to say, "I don't like what I'm doing, and I don't want to do it." Then he jogged home to his barn, clearly favoring his bruised foot.

It was obvious to Barclay and Robin that Empire Maker was sore and unhappy. Back in the barn area, the press was waiting for Frankel. The trainer continued to insist that there was no problem and that Empire Maker was the horse to beat. "This is getting like a soap opera," Frankel said. "There ain't nothing wrong with that horse."

But Barclay and Robin saw it differently.

"What do you think?" Robin asked Barclay.

"He's pretty lame. I can't believe he's going to run if he's hurting like that."

"Well, I'll tell you what I think," Robin said. "If that's the horse to beat, we have a shot. He'd better not stub a toe—because if he does, we're right there."

Their own horse was working well, resting well, and eating everything that was put in front of him. Later that morning, Jack wandered by to check on things. "How's the horse doing?" Jack asked. For days, he'd been nervous. So many things could keep a horse out of the Derby at the last second—a cough, or a bad foot. Until they loaded the horse into the starting gate, he would worry.

But Barclay turned to Jack and used a word that Jack didn't

think the trainer had in his vocabulary. A word he'd never heard Barclay use before, on any subject.

"Everything is perfect," Barclay said.

On the morning of the Kentucky Derby, Jose Santos dressed himself in a natty dark suit and then checked on the sartorial progress of his two oldest children. His eight-year-old son, Jose Junior, had put on a dark blazer with a pink shirt and was busily combing his hair. Jose pinched the boy and whispered to him. "Hey, do you know what I dreamed last night?" he said. "I dreamed I won the Kentucky Derby." The boy grinned.

Jose rounded up the rest of his family. "Okay, guys," he announced. "Let's go see Dad win the Kentucky Derby." His daughter Nadia wore her prettiest dress, as did her mother, Rita, who also sported a swooping, wide-brimmed hat. As Jose led them to their car in the hotel parking lot, the girls paused to check themselves in the car mirrors one more time.

"That's right," Jose said. "We're going to be taking a picture today."

Jose's faith that he and Funny Cide would win the Kentucky Derby had been unshakable for months, so much so that he had commuted between New York and Florida on a weekly basis just to gallop the horse and stay in touch with him. Ordinarily, Jose didn't get attached to a horse, because it was a treacherous business. Jockeys lost their favorite rides all the time; they were first to be fired when a horse didn't run well. Trainers blamed them for being insubordinate, or owners blamed them for spoiling expensive breeding with bad tactics. If you developed affection for a mount, you were just asking to be dumped, and disappointed. But Jose had an odd, implacable conviction when it came to Funny Cide. He was supposed to ride this horse.

The belief sprang in part from sheer experience. By the age of forty-two, Jose had ridden every kind of horse, good and bad, and he had ridden them while sober and while hungover, too. He was the oldest son of a struggling jockey in Chile, Manuel Santos, who had been hard-pressed to feed seven children. Manuel put Jose on a horse before he could walk, and turned him into a professional jockey by age twelve.

The family lived in brutal poverty, eleven people sharing a two-bedroom house with a dirt-floor kitchen. There were just four beds, so the children slept head to foot, two down and two up. They had only a single change of clothes each. One night a week, they would wash themselves from a bucket, and Jose's mother, Elena, would stay up till two A.M. laundering and mending their dirty clothes.

Jose was a groom by age eight, and he quit school after the sixth grade to go to work at the Hipico racecourse, earning twenty-five dollars a month for riding horses. He weighed all of eighty-five pounds, but he got little protection or comfort from Manuel, who taught with his boot. The first time Jose was thrown from a horse during a race, he lay on the ground, stunned, waiting for the ambulance to come and pick him up. His father, watching from the rail, stalked onto the track and kicked the boy in the butt as he lay in the dirt.

"Get up!" he said.

"I fell."

"If you don't have no broken bones, you get up right away," Manuel said.

From then on, whenever Jose fell from a horse, he got up quickly, whether he had a broken bone or not.

By 1976, Jose was one of the leading jockeys at the club, a prodigy who had already ridden seventeen winners even though he was still just fifteen. He was so sure of his ability that he began to get a little cocky. Once again, he ran into his father's boot. Jose was winning a race by ten lengths one afternoon, when he took a peek back over his shoulder and, pleased to be so far ahead, struck a series of beautiful poses in the saddle on the way to the wire. It was not just showy but dangerous—that was how a rider lost his concentration and, potentially, his balance.

Jose dismounted and went to the scale to weigh in, and when he came back out of the jockey room, his father was waiting for him. Manuel kicked him in the butt and slapped him on the head.

"The wire is in front of you, not in back of you."

Manuel was as strict off the track as he was on it. Jose had a ten P.M. curfew, and he didn't know what a dance club looked like, and every cent he earned went to his family. But by the time Jose was seventeen, he chafed at his father's rules and wanted his independence. One night, he decided to test the curfew: he came home at ten-thirty P.M.

His father was waiting for him. "One," Manuel said, meaningfully, and went to bed without another word.

Jose tested him again the next night; this time he came home at ten-forty. Again, Manuel was waiting for him. "Two," Manuel said.

About a week later, Jose walked in the door at eleven-thirty. He never heard the word "three." All he heard was the sound of his father's hands as they beat him.

In 1977, Jose was offered a guaranteed contract to race thoroughbreds in Colombia for the princely sum of $200 a month, plus whatever he could earn in purse money. He jumped at it. Colombia not only offered a better living, it offered the chance to escape Manuel's discipline, too. Jose sent his first $200 paycheck back to Chile—but it was the last one Manuel and Helena would get from him for five and a half years.

In Colombia, Jose discovered discotheques, and drugs. For the first time in his life, he began clubbing and drinking, and one evening in a nightclub, he was introduced to cocaine. Alone, out from under Manuel's strictures, he confused independence with dissolution. He spent whatever he earned on coke binges.

Eventually, he became so dissolute that it threatened his career. He was riding a good horse that was considered the favorite to win the Caribbean Classic in Puerto Rico in 1984, but because Jose was drunk half the time, the owner lost confidence in him and fired him from the mount before the trip. "I'm putting a more responsible jockey on him," Jose was told. He had already obtained a three-month visa for Puerto Rico, but now it was useless.

Instead, he decided to use the visa to go to Miami and try his hand at American racing. He booked a flight, and spent his last three days and nights in Colombia partying around the clock. He finally got on the plane with one suitcase, $2,000 in cash, "and a lot of hope," as he put it. He also had a brutal hangover. He swore to himself that he wouldn't touch cocaine again once he set foot on American soil. As soon as he put a shoe down in Miami, he would quit doing drugs.

Jose knew nobody in Miami, and that was a good thing, because it meant there was no one to drink with or to supply him with cocaine. He found a room with a fellow immigrant jockey, and went from barn to barn at Hialeah Race Track, hustling work as an exercise rider. He spoke no English, and lived mostly on bread and eggs, saving his cash to buy riding equipment.

It was months before he got hired to actually ride in a race, and then without much success. He had only a couple of unremarkable second- and third-place finishes and was ready to go back to Colombia when he broke through and won a race at Gulfstream, which persuaded him to stay on a little longer. Three weeks later, he won a $20,000 stakes race, and his career was off and running. He went on to tie for leading rider at the Calder summer meet. After that, everyone wanted his services and he was booked solid.

Jose won the jockey titles at both Gulfstream Park and Hialeah in 1985—and he also won a reputation as a rider so determined to win that he was often disqualified for fouling. Sometimes he fouled on two or three horses a day. Nothing held him back. By 1988, he was one of the nation's leading jockeys; along the way he had gotten married, largely to obtain his green card. Next, he migrated to New York, where for four straight years he was the leading money-winner.

But the long winning streak ended with a terrible spill at Belmont in 1992. Jose was lying third in a turf race behind the late Chris Antley, looking for a chance, when it happened. Antley swerved to the outside, and Jose tried to wedge his horse through a narrow opening at the rail. But just then, Antley moved to the inside again and cut him off.

Jose's horse hit the fence, and they flipped. Horse and rider fell heavily, and three other horses and jockeys went down behind them. Jose's horse broke its shoulder and trampled him. Another of the falling horses landed squarely on Jose's right side, 1,100 pounds of thoroughbred crushing him. He broke eleven bones, all on the right of his body, including his arm, shoulder, collarbone, hip, and foot. Even his eye socket.

The accident derailed his career for the next decade. He spent a year recuperating from the worst of the injuries, but it took far longer to recover from the whispers that he'd never be the same rider. He lost all of his mounts. Other jockeys at the top of the game took his horses, riders like Jerry Bailey and Julie Krone. Jose never got the horses back.

It required two pins and fourteen screws just to put his right arm back together, and six months of rehabilitation just to regain partial motion in it. It was nine months before he rode a horse again, and when he returned, he preferred to ride safe and wide. It was said that he had lost his nerve.

The only horses he could get were long shots. Now, instead of riding 2–1 favorites, he was riding 20–1 mounts, and it made a big difference. Jose thought he had a lot of friends in the training business, but they all disappeared. They were friends of convenience, it turned out—a hard lesson that he would remember.

One good thing happened to him that year: he met Rita Castillo, the daughter and sister of prominent Panamanian jockeys. Jose was hanging around Gulfstream one day, still recovering, when he saw a gorgeous woman walk past the jockey room. "Who is that?" he asked. "Oh, that's Herb Castillo's daughter," someone replied. As a teenager, Rita had worked as a model, but now she was a secretary in the racing office. Jose had to meet her. He introduced himself to her and invited her to lunch. They began eating together two or three times a week, and talking on the phone, and Jose was in love.

Jose's first marriage had collapsed years earlier, despite the births of two children, but he had never gotten divorced. Now that he set about straightening his affairs, he discovered he had a lot less money than he'd thought. He was overextended financially, between supporting a family in the States and helping his family in Chile. Also, he had never learned to write properly in English, and thus couldn't properly oversee his business affairs. He suspected that accountants and lawyers cheated him. Rita moved in, and she started helping him piece his life back together. She had been reared in the States from infancy and knew how to read an American legal contract, and a profit-and-loss statement.

Jose continued to struggle through lean years professionally, but he was personally content. He and Rita wed in 1997, and by the spring of 2002 they had four children, and Jose's teenaged daughter and son from his first marriage often visited. Rita oversaw the household in Hollywood, Florida, while Jose rode, and even when he commuted to New York for the Eastern racing season, he never spent more than two weeks away from her. "She's the mommy and daddy at the same time," Jose would say admiringly of his wife.

He still suffered wild career swings. He won the Travers and the Belmont on Lemon Drop Kid in 1999, only to shatter his wrist badly again in 2001 and lose several more months of rides. Rita helped keep him fit by taking him on power walks in Florida, and with Mike the Cop's guidance, he was starting to get good mounts again. By now, Jose was used to making comebacks—and what better way to show he was back on top than by winning the Kentucky Derby?

Years earlier, when Jose and Rita were first together, they'd visited the museum of racing at Churchill Downs. That day, Jose told her, "When I win this, I'm going to give you the roses."

On the afternoon of May 3, 2003, he intended to keep the promise.

The Sackatoga owners stood in the lobby of the Galt House on Derby Day and regarded the yellow school bus parked out front lot. As they did so, the more well-heeled guests of the hotel stepped around them and into limousines or luxury coaches. J.P. stared at their glistening jewelry and fur coats, and then looked back to the school bus. It seemed small and rickety, not to mention vividly yellow.

"A real bus would have cost us a lot more money," Jack explained.

Dorothy said, "Well, what's the difference?"

"Hey, who hasn't ridden a school bus?" Pete Phillips said, and clambered on.

Harold Cring feigned embarrassment. He lurked around, checking both ways. He did a stroll-by, to be sure nobody was watching. As his fellow owners watched him with rising hilarity, Harold circled the bus. Finally, he darted on with a hand covering his face.

Dave had stocked the bus with coolers full of Bloody Marys and beer, and they sipped their drinks as they departed for the three-mile ride to the track. Dave chatted up their driver along the way. "You gotta bet our horse," he said. "C'mon, twenty bucks." They pulled into the Churchill Downs drop-off area, and the driver pulled out twenty dollars and handed it to Dave.

"Here. Put twenty on the horse across the board."

Dave demurred. "No way," he said. "You bet to win, or you don't bet at all. Here's what we're going to do. You give me your twenty, and I'm going to put twenty on top of it, and we're going to bet it to win for you on our horse."

"You think he's got a shot?"

"Not only has he got a shot, I'm going to bring you back a lot of money."

On the side of the bus, their driver had taped a large sign with block letters that said, FUNNY CIDE. As they disembarked into the Churchill Downs parking lot, pedestrians stopped and pointed, giggling. Through the bus windows, the Sackatogans could read the lips of passersby as they said, "Oh my God, look at those people coming to the Derby on a school bus."

A young man named David Travis watched the Sackatoga owners file off of the yellow bus and couldn't help sharing their antic gaiety. Travis was their official Louisville host. Each owner of a Derby horse was assigned a local volunteer to help them find their way around the track and learn race protocol. No one else had particularly wanted to host the upstart strangers from New York, but Dave, among the more junior volunteers, had said, "I'll take them." For three days, Dave had shown them the sights and tutored them in the ways and history of Churchill Downs. Their free-floating high spirits were a lot more fun than hosting some oilman. And maybe it was his imagination, but he had a feeling about them. Or maybe he was just being starry-eyed; at dusk the evening before, Dave had proposed to his girlfriend in the Churchill Downs paddock.

Dave helped his large crew find their seats, which was no easy job. The owners were scattered all over the clubhouse because there were so many in their party. The Crings and the Constances sat together, and just over from them were the Phillips brothers and their wives, and Jean and Jeannie Derouin.

Dave led the Knowltons and the Mahans to their seats, along with Gus Williams. When they arrived at their box, Dave was jolted by an odd feeling when the usher told them, "You know, I've had the winners in this box for five years in a row." Jack said, "Well, let's hope you have them again."

But before they could win anything, they had to get through the rest of the day. The race would not be until late afternoon, and it was only the brunch hour. They decided to kill some time by eating, and trooped off to a buffet for the owners. They marveled at the food—the carved meats and artichoke salad, and shrimp and grits—and idly discussed their chances.

J.P. just hoped they didn't get embarrassed. Karen kept telling J.P. she thought Funny Cide would win. But J.P.'s response each time was firm. "It's impossible," he said.

Next, they spent an hour or two busily collecting as many souvenir mint-julep glasses as possible. They kept ordering the juleps to get the glasses.

After about the third one, J.P. said to a female bartender, "I'd like two mint juleps, hold the julep, and the ice, and the mint."

"You just want the glasses."

"Right."

The more serious bettors among them studied the racing forms and wagered on other races. J.P. kept up a constant teasing as Dave Mahan hunched over a folded handicapping form.

"He's studying how to lose," J.P. kidded.

There were different kinds of bets, J.P. explained to anyone who would listen. You could guess—that was one kind of bet. You could put your money on a lucky number, or a horse's name, or a presentiment. Or you could bet on a system, a handicapping theory, or a formula.

But if you want to make a smart bet, J.P. announced, "You take that money and put it back in your pocket."

Gus Williams decided to make a side wager with a gentleman behind him, with whom he bantered about Gus's canary-yellow-and-black-checkered sport coat. The gentleman was an owner of Offlee Wild, another horse entered in the Derby. He said, "Oh, I like that coat." Gus said, "Yeah? Well, I like your hat." The gentleman was sporting a distinguished brown derby hat. The more Gus looked at that hat, the more he decided he wanted it to go with his outfit.

"Let's make a bet," Gus growled.

"For how much?"

"That hat."

They struck a deal. If Funny Cide beat Offlee Wild, Gus got the hat. If Funny Cide lost—Gus gave up the jacket.

Peter Phillips was thinking about betting, too. He stared at the fifty-to-one-hundred-dollar betting windows. Pete was used to betting for six or eight dollars. What kind of people bet fifties and hundreds on a horse race? he wondered. Certainly not ordinary people.

Pete walked up to one of the fifty-dollar windows. "Could you cash this hundred-dollar bill for me?" he asked.

"Sure," the cashier said, and handed him two fifties.

Pete walked away from the window, without making a bet.

"What did you do that for?" Bonnie asked.

"I had to go there," he said. "Just once, I had to go to a hundred-dollar window."

On the backstrech of Churchill Downs, Barclay and Robin moved around the barn, performing some chores. But after a while, there was nothing left to do. It wasn't like home, where they had twenty horses to take care of. They had one horse, and he stood in his stall, with his front legs in tubs of ice water, keeping his tissues and tendons cool.

They went to the hotel, took their dirty clothes off and showered, dressed for the race, and went back to the barn. It was still only two o'clock. They read the paper, and looked at the horse. They read books, and looked at the horse. They walked in circles—and looked at the horse.

Barclay went for a walk and found a betting window. The latest odds on Funny Cide were 13–1. He opened his wallet and took out two hundred dollars. He hadn't bet two hundred dollars in his whole life, put together. He trained horses, he didn't bet on them. But he placed two hundred dollars on Funny Cide.

Why did he do it? Maybe because the horse was calmer than they were. Funny Cide was so calm, in fact, that when Robin walked down the shed row to check on him again, he was flat-out sound asleep. The horse lay in the straw, his chest gently rising and falling.

Robin called Bonner Young and said, "Bonner, Bonner, you're not gonna believe it. He's sleeping. Funny Cide is sound asleep." When a horse was that relaxed, it was a good sign. It meant he was saving every ounce of energy for the race.

Bonner said, "You're going to win."

"We are. We're going to win."

The horse had yet to show a sign of anxiety. Early Friday morning, they had schooled him in the paddock, circled him around the track to the brick courtyard, and showed him the saddling stall. The horse just chewed at his shank, as usual, and rubbed up against Barclay.

Finally, it was time to rouse the horse and prepare him for the race. Strangely enough, Funny Cide seemed to know what time it was. As soon as Robin and Barclay started up the shed row, he poked his head out of his stall, as if to say, "Here I am, I'm awake now."

The Sackatoga owners arrived at the barn. After hours of waiting and idly sipping juleps, they were finally excited. They were about to enjoy the penultimate experience at the Kentucky Derby: the walk from the backstrech, around the oval track, to the paddock with their horse in front of an immense, cheering crowd. It was a stroll every thoroughbred owner and trainer yearned to take just once. The more experienced horsemen and -women declined to take the walk and stayed in the clubhouse, saving their shoes from the mud. But the Sackatogans couldn't imagine such detachment. They felt as fresh and green as the horses themselves, who now emerged from the barns, clean and bright and unmarked.

The horses pranced on cleanly bandaged legs, looking like schoolgirls in kneesocks. It was a beautiful deep-blue spring afternoon, and the clubhouse and infield made a gorgeous panorama of twin spires, green grass, roses, and a roaring wall of people. The air smelled like a concoction of animal heat, sweet hay, and Early Times. Dave Mahan thought, *This is my happy spot.* The next time he was in a traffic jam, he would come right back here in his mind.

Lew Titterton brought him back to earth. He glanced down and noticed Dave's shoes. They were alligator loafers that must have cost four hundred dollars, and they were sinking into the damp loam. "Dave, what are you going to do with those after this is over? They're going to be ruined."

"I'm not going to throw them out," Dave said. "I'll never throw these out."

Dave regarded his shoes. The mud was now slopping over into his socks. He didn't mind. It was Derby dirt.

The Phillips brothers paused and looked out at 140,000 people. "What in the world did we ever do to deserve this?" Pete asked. But then they, too, looked down. Mark poked his brother. "Don't walk in that crap," he said.

Now the horses were assembled. Funny Cide was sixth in line, the same as his post position. The procession began. Robin led Funny Cide by a shank on one side, and holding him by a shank on his other side was his groom, Zach Quintana. There were people piled two stories high all the way around the track, and as the horses moved through a gap in the fence and onto the track, an immense roar went up.

Spectators leaned over the balustrades, and banged on the metal rails and whooped. Photographers ran up behind Funny Cide and shot off pictures, click, click, click.

Funny Cide walked into the maelstrom of sound and color and action—and he spooked. He went into a crouch, and he started to back up. Robin, holding tight to the shank, thought, *He's panicking.* As if reading her mind, the horse reared up and pawed at the air.

Dave turned to Jack and said, "Oh my God, I think I'm having a heart attack."

The crowd, excited by the wildness of the horse, only screamed louder. The track curved toward the twin spires, and now the horses were separated from the spectators by just a few feet of fencing. It was like running a gauntlet.

Funny Cide started jigging and running sideways.

Jack began to sweat. The horse was wasting so much energy that he wouldn't have enough left to run a mile and a quarter. He thought, *Christ, we get all the way here . . .*

Funny Cide reared once more, and came down. Robin and Zach were tossed around like rag dolls. A pony rider came alongside Robin, and Barclay said, "Do you want the pony boy to take him?"

"I don't know," Robin said, as Funny reared again.

Their horse was falling apart. Robin tightened her grip on the shank and said to Zach, "Hold on to him." Zach shortened his own grip, but this only made Funny Cide fight harder.

"Don't do this to me now," Robin said to the horse. "Come on Funny, not now. You've never done this before. You're losing it. Come on. You're okay. You're all right."

The horse looked back over his shoulder at her, as if he wanted to say, "Are you sure?" Robin continued to murmur to the horse, trying to calm him. But all she could think was, *How are we going to get to the paddock without getting killed or turning him loose?*

Barclay watched their riled horse, and he thought they were through, too. He'd been waiting for something to go wrong, and now it had. The paddock was still a couple of hundred yards away, and the horse was so unmanageable it seemed they might not get him there. *All of a sudden he's acting like a damn cheap horse at Charlestown,* Barclay thought. *Maybe he's just cheap. Maybe he's really just a cheap horse.*

No wonder he was judged such a long shot.

Robin kept looking back at Barclay with an expression that said, "What do I do? What do I do?" The pony boy started to take hold of Funny Cide, but Barclay worried that the horse would rebel even more. "No," he said. "I don't want the pony boy touching him."

Instead, the pony boy just walked alongside Funny Cide. The presence of the pony seemed to calm the gelding somewhat, and Robin and Zach seized the opportunity to ease the horse away from the crowd, toward the inside rail, where it was quieter.

Funny Cide continued to break into an intermittent jig, but at least he wasn't rearing anymore. Finally, they approached the tunnel to the paddock. "You gotta keep moving, you gotta keep moving," Robin hollered to the horsemen ahead of her, but the reply drifted back, "We can't move, there's nowhere to go." There was a logjam in the tunnel. The line of horses stopped. Once more Funny Cide reared—and stayed on his hind legs so long that Robin feared he would flip over backward.

Just then, the line began moving again. Funny Cide came down, and moved forward. He trotted through the tunnel and into the sunlit paddock. Although the paddock was crowded, it lacked the frenetic energy of the track, and Funny Cide seemed to recognize where he was. As quickly as he'd suffered the onset of nerves, now they disappeared. He calmed down.

Robin walked the horse around the paddock a few times, until she was sure he was relaxed. He wasn't sweating, Robin noticed, relieved. Most horses that became agitated would be dripping with sweat, but Funny Cide didn't seem hot, so maybe he still had a race in him. In fact, it was as if he'd never turned a hair. Robin, on the other hand, was exhausted.

Barclay said, "Just bring him in and let him stand in the stall." That was asking for more trouble, because Funny Cide was not the kind of horse that liked to stand. Usually, he started kicking. But this time, when Robin led the horse into his stall, he stood perfectly still. He just observed the activity of horses, trainers, jockeys, and owners, shifting his ears inquisitively.

There was one other figure that stood still in the throng of people: Jose Santos, Jr. The little boy had managed to find a free space in the crowded paddock, and now he stood by himself, with his head down, praying.

Barclay put the saddle on Funny Cide. This piece of routine the horse was familiar with. Calmly, he chewed on his shank. Jose Sr. appeared alongside the horse, and prepared to hoist himself into the saddle. Jose had been in the jockey room and had missed the tumultuous walk; he didn't know they had nearly been forced to scratch him.

"He's been real nervous," Robin said to the jockey. "But just pat him and talk to him, and he'll listen."

Jose nodded, then turned to Barclay for his final race instructions. "Just keep him close to the pace," the trainer said. "It's a long race, and if he's in the middle of the pack, there'll be too much traffic."

Just then, Dave Mahan touched Barclay on the arm. The trainer turned around. Dave said, "I have some instructions, too." Barclay looked at him like he was crazy: this was hardly the time for a meddlesome owner.

Dave reached over and shook Jose's hand.

"Here are my instructions," Dave said. "Run fast and win."

The first notes of "My Old Kentucky Home" rang across the infield. The melody rose into the spring air, and the thousands of spectators began singing in unison.

As Jose walked Funny Cide out to the track for the post parade, the horse began to sweat and jig again. Jose patted him and leaned down and spoke into his ear.

"It's okay," Jose said, cheerfully. "It's a lot of people. You should be nervous."

The song ended, and Jose galloped the horse down the track, to warm him up. The horse moved strongly beneath him. They settled back to a jog, and then a walk. Jose turned him, and they moved toward the gate, waiting their turn to load. When it was time, Funny Cide moved without the slightest protest into his assigned slot. And then he stood there, perfectly calm, waiting for the doors to open.

As Barclay and Robin climbed the stairs to the clubhouse, they could hear the melody of the Kentucky anthem drifting through the covered, arcade-like clubhouse. They dropped into their seats, dazed. The horse had acted up so badly that the trainers hadn't been able to enjoy a moment of the Derby experience so far. They hadn't dared to look around and see the crowd or the twin spires. Now they took in the view.

The anticipatory roar of the crowd was growing deeper and more frantic. Robin raised her binoculars and scanned the horses as they jogged, or cantered, or waited to be loaded into the starting gate. She looked for signs of anxiousness in Funny Cide. But the horse was perfectly composed.

"I can't believe he lost it," Robin said to Barclay.

"I can't believe it, either."

"But he's got it back together," Robin said.

A few boxes away, Jack and Dave took their seats next to their wives. Jack was still sweating with anxiety over the state of their horse due to his antics on the way to the paddock.

But Dave was oddly serene. He said to Nadine, "We're going to win this right now." Nadine glanced at him and said, "What?"

"We're going to win this race, right now. You watch. When he comes down the stretch, they're not going to catch him. He's just too good."

What Dave saw next was a very clear picture, with no sound. He never heard the crowd at all. He was so focused on the horse that he didn't hear anything but the sound of his own voice and his quickened breathing.

"Good luck, guys," Dorothy said. "Here we go."

In J. P. Constance's box, as they waited for the bell to ring and the gates to open, Karen couldn't see, so she slipped off her shoes and hopped up on her folding chair in her stocking feet.

The bell rang and the gates flew open. Karen screamed and jumped and down on the chair. As she landed, she slapped J.P.'s shoulders with her palms, like a jockey whipping a horse.

They came out of the gate like a cavalry charge.

Funny Cide did not break cleanly. He bumped with Offlee Wild out of the gate, and for an instant, Barclay worried that the horde of horses would close in on him. He looked like such a small red horse amid the fifteen others.

But then Funny Cide seemed to dart forward and find an open space. He settled into the third position from the rail, behind a horse named Brancusi, and Peace Rules, with Edgar Prado aboard.

Robin watched the early progress of the race through her binoculars. As they went into the first turn, Prado swung Peace Rules out wide, and forced Funny Cide slightly wide, too. *Come on, Edgar, give us a little bit of a break here*, she thought.

But Jose panned along, nice and easy around the first turn. They kept their positions through the first quarter mile, and then the half. Jose glanced sideways, looking for Empire Maker. He didn't see him.

Jerry Bailey had Empire Maker half a dozen lengths behind, in eighth place, but with a clear path.

At six furlongs, Prado moved Peace Rules to the front. Now Jose moved Funny Cide up, too—and here came the favorite, Empire Maker, charging up from behind. Jose caught sight of Bailey on the big bay colt from the corner of his eye, for the first time.

They hit the quarter pole in 1:35.75 for the mile.

Robin stared through her binoculars. Bailey had already gone to the whip with Empire Maker. Now Prado went to the stick on Peace Rules. She moved her gaze to Funny Cide. He was gliding along, effortlessly. Jose's whip was frozen in his hand.

Robin lowered the binoculars and told herself *We're gonna win the Kentucky Derby*.

Barclay kept his mouth firmly shut. They would see about that. He stared at the track. Jose had Funny Cide in a perfect position coming off the final turn.

Okay, come on, it's time to go, he said to himself.

They thundered into the stretch at Churchill Downs. Three horses challenged one another: Empire Maker, Funny Cide, and Peace Rules on the inside.

Still Barclay didn't utter a word, keeping his jaw tight. So now they would find out. No one had believed the horse could run in this company, save for his trainers and his jockey and his owners. For months, they had stubbornly believed in him, contradicting common wisdom and their own common sense. Now they would know. The horse either had it, or he didn't. There was only one question.

Is he good enough?

Jose asked the horse for everything he had. He switched the stick to the left hand and hit the horse twice.

Funny Cide pulled slightly ahead.

Peace Rules was beat.

To the outside, Bailey hit Empire Maker with his right hand— and got a small response. Bailey whipped Empire Maker again. The horse made no progress. Bailey switched to his left, then back to his right, and still the horse didn't surge. They had flattened out. They weren't gaining any longer.

Funny Cide had a hundred yards to go to the finish line, and there was a clear and growing space between him and Empire Maker. Funny Cide led by a length . . . and then by more than a length.

Barclay finally spoke. "Robin," he said in wonderment. "We're going to win the Kentucky Derby."

Stephanie Cring kept up a babbling narrative of the horse's progress. "He's in third, he's in third, he's in second, he's in first!" Next to her, Harold heard himself begin to scream as the horse pulled slightly ahead. When he saw there was daylight between his horse and the others, he went numb. Everything was foggy. All he could see were the colors of Sackets High leading the charge toward the finish line.

Karen Constance beat on J.P.'s back, pounding with her fists. J.P. tried to wave her off, and then push her off, but she kept beating him.

As Funny Cide hurtled down the stretch, Jack Knowlton began to chant. To Dorothy it sounded like an incantation: "We're going to win the Derby. Oh my God, Dot, we're going to win Kentucky Derby. We're going to win the Kentucky Derby!"

Funny Cide swept past the twin spires.

On May 3, 2003, a narrowly built, New York–bred, longshot gelding, owned by ten inexperienced and uninitiated owners, won the running of the 129th Kentucky Derby, and in the space of 2:01.19, changed everybody's idea of what was possible and what was not.

Atop the horse, Jose Santos burst into tears.

In the box seats, it was bedlam. As Funny Cide crossed the wire, Barclay and Robin clutched at each other and buried their faces in each other's shoulders.

Dave Mahan whooped and lunged at Jack Knowlton, and the two men caught in a massive bear hug. In between them, Dorothy was crushed, nothing visible of her except her little hat, tilted sideways.

Jose Santos, Jr., shouted and thrashed with joy. "Can you believe it, can you believe it?" he screamed. His sister Nadia collapsed for a moment into the arms of her friend Irene Day, the daughter of jockey Pat Day. Rita, weeping, rocked back and forth saying, "Oh my gosh, oh my gosh." Then she gathered the children and they rushed down to the track.

J. P. Constance stood for a moment, dazed, his shoulders aching from Karen's fists. Everything seemed to be airborne and in slow motion. Jean Derouin moved toward him, guttural sounds coming from his mouth, and hoisted him upward. J.P. felt himself lifted off the ground. Somewhere over Karen's shoulder, he could see the Phillips brothers, their heads thrown back, and they too were screaming. Everyone was screaming, at the tops of their voices, from way down deep in their lungs, huge primal noises.

The chairs in the box were flying around like toothpicks.

The NBC cameras were trained on Bobby Frankel, whose horse had been the sure thing. Frankel had watched impassively as Empire Maker faded. The people around him mouthed, puzzled, "Who won?"

In the box of the governor of Kentucky, various dignitaries and racing officials sat in their seats, stunned. One of them was Tim Smith, the commissioner of the National Thoroughbred Racing Association. Smith struggled to hide his disappointment in the outcome of the race.

Smith was a neat, courtly businessman whose job was to promote thoroughbred racing, and he needed a star, a horse that created some buzz. The Triple Crown races were the most visible and popular events by a mile; the public cared less about the other graded stakes races around the country. The sport depended heavily on a popular Derby winner to boost interest and draw bettors to those windows. Smith wanted a horse that the public would *recognize.*

But nobody had ever heard of this horse. When Funny Cide crossed the wire, Smith was baffled. He had no idea who the owners were. He leafed through his program and saw "Jackson Knowlton, Sackatoga Stable."

Smith turned to his seatmate, Steve Sexton, the president of Churchill Downs.

"Who are these guys?" Smith asked.

Sexton said, "I don't have a clue."

Smith watched as the Sackatoga owners made their way to the winner's circle, whooping like a parade out of control. *Great,* he thought, *racing needs a big horse, and instead we get an obscure long shot.*

Still, it wasn't Smith's job to pull for a specific winner in the Kentucky Derby. It was his job to congratulate the winner gracefully. He rose from his seat and made his way to the winner's circle to conduct the post-race ceremonies.

As he arrived at the podium, there was NBC's Bob Costas, marveling over the unlikelihood of the victory. "I think they own three horses," Costas said.

Suddenly, it dawned on Smith.

Funny Cide might be the best thing that had happened to thoroughbred racing in some time.

The tears coursed down Jose's cheeks, and his life rewound in his mind like a movie, the memories unspooling: his father teaching him to ride, the feel of his father's boot on his backside, the clothes freshly washed by his mother, the splintered bones, and the plaster casts.

He slowed Funny Cide to a trot. An outrider came alongside them and steered them from the dirt track to the turf track beyond the inner rail. They began a long and gloriously sedate walk toward the winner's circle. Jose looked around the track and saw that massive wall of people, cheering. And then he saw something else.

A little boy shot across the infield, screaming in exultation. It was Jose Junior. "My daddy won the Derby!" he howled. "My daddy won the Derby!"

In the first minutes after Funny crossed the wire, Barclay and Robin only cared that the horse was all right. They pushed their way down to the track in a tremendous crush, perfect strangers congratulating them and pounding them on the back, and looked around for Funny Cide and Jose, but they couldn't see them in the throng.

The losers drifted past them, mud-splashed and jogging. One by one, the horses were unsaddled and led toward the barns. Still Funny Cide hadn't returned.

Now Barclay began to worry—had the horse hurt himself? He stared down the track and lifted his binoculars to his eyes. "Why hasn't he come back?" he said aloud.

Robin stared around the dirt track and saw no sign of him. "What happened to him, is everything okay?" she asked.

A security guard pointed: Funny Cide hadn't come back because he was walking down the turf course, en route to the winner's circle. He was about to be draped in roses. Robin and Barclay wanted to run to him. "Okay, can I go get him now?" Robin asked the guard. The guard said, "He's coming. Just wait a minute. He'll be here."

Finally, here they came. The trainers reached him and stroked Funny Cide's neck, and ran their hands across him, gratefully. Robin stretched up and gave Jose a hug. "We did it," Jose said. "We did it." Barclay shook his hand wordlessly—but came close to smiling at him.

Together the trainers, horse, and jockey walked into the winner's circle. Robin wanted to take the tack off of Funny Cide, he was so obviously tired, but there were too many things going on, and the crowd of people in the winner's circle was growing larger by the second.

The crowd closed in around the steaming horse. Roses were draped over him, and the photographers began shouting and jostling.

Funny Cide's leg bandages were splashed with mud, and his head was hanging with exhaustion. But as the photographers lined up for the victory photograph, Funny Cide suddenly swung his head toward them and struck a champion's pose.

"Look at that," Jose laughed.

Bob Baffert had been sitting in the box next to Jack Knowlton and Dave Mahan, and he watched, bemused, as the Funny Cide owners bolted out of their seats, screaming, for the winner's circle. Baffert stared after them, and remembered that shocking newness of winning a Derby for the first time. *How many of us, anymore, experienced newness?*

In 1996, Baffert had experienced his first Derby with Cavonnier. When he had walked the horse from the backstretch to the paddock, he had felt like Wyatt Earp going off to the gunfight at the O.K. Corral.

He had been so electrified when his horse Silver Charm crossed the wire as the winner in 1997 that he'd thrown his arms in the air and screamed, and as he stumbled from the box to the winner's circle, he'd forgotten all of his things. He'd left everything behind, the programs, the traditional mint-julep glasses. He'd come back later to collect his souvenirs, and found they were all gone. Spectators had taken them.

Baffert glanced once more at the winner's circle, now filling up with the ebullient Sackatoga owners. He adjusted his shades and started to stroll out of the box. But he stopped and turned back and spoke to an usher.

"Listen," he said. "Get their stuff together. Take care of it, would you? They're going to want it later."

Karen pushed Harold and J.P. out of the box and toward the winner's circle. But the men didn't know how to get there. They hurtled down an aisle to the right, but someone said, "No, go left," so they went left. They saw Mark Phillips run by, and Harold hollered at him, but Pete had been lost in the shuffle. They jogged down stairways, and passed through wrong doors, while tears rolled down their faces at the same time they laughed and whooped, and people reached out to grab them, slap them on the back, and shout congratulations. Finally, they got down to the track area and squeezed their way through the chaos to the trophy presentation.

In the winner's circle, little Jose Junior came up to Jack, with tears still running down his face. "You made my daddy's dream," he said. "You made my daddy's dream."

Jack leaned over to him and said, "No, Funny Cide made his dream."

"No," Jose Jr. said. "You made my daddy's dream."

Two jacketed track officials appeared by Jack's and Barclay's elbows and asked them to move to the paddock area, where the press was waiting to interview them. As they were ushered away, Jack glanced behind him. Some of his Sackatoga partners were now lying down in the infield.

They were making snow angels in the grass.

Barclay made his way to the paddock and into the interview room. As he took a chair, he felt a hand on his shoulder. He turned around. It was Wayne Lukas.

Lukas shook Barclay's hand, and bent over to whisper in his ear, and patted him on the back.

"Good feeling, isn't it?" Lukas asked. "Enjoy it."

In the winner's circle, the crowd had finally begun to dissipate, and Funny Cide was led away to the barn.

But before he went, Jose Santos plucked some of the roses. He carried them to his wife. "I promised you these ten years ago," he said.

Once more, they both began to cry.

The Sackatoga owners hit the post-race party at the Kentucky Derby Museum like a large roiling wave. At first the security guards at the door tried to say, "Who are you? May I see your passes?" But finally they gave up and let the whole noisy crew in. If it was less than dignified, the Sackatogans were too euphoric to care.

One minute the guests were nibbling hors d'oeuvres from small plates and sipping wine, and the next, the jubilant band from Sackatoga had piled through the door with all of their kids and their kids' friends, and were grabbing sandwiches and champagne glasses, and swigging beers and whooping, "Funny Cide!"

Dorothy drank a glass of champagne, and as soon as she drained it, someone handed her another full glass. She drank that, too. After a while, her head hurt. But it wasn't from the champagne— it was because she was unaccustomed to wearing high heels and a hat all day.

J.P. felt as though he had walked into a black-tie affair wearing blue jeans. There were people in that room, he knew, who must have felt they had no right to win the Kentucky Derby. He surveyed the veteran thoroughbred people in their couture and gems, and wondered if, underneath it all, they were aghast at what had happened to their sport.

Just then, Peter Phillips grabbed him, laughing. Peter had been wandering the room, and he'd overheard a well-dressed woman talking to her circle of friends.

"My God," she said. "Some of them are *schoolteachers!*"

Finally, after many beers and glasses of champagne, the Sackatoga Stable owners reconvened at the yellow school bus. As Dave climbed aboard, he clapped hands with the driver—and then handed him his winnings. His $40 bet had paid off more than $500.

"Next time I guess we can afford the better bus," Dave said.

They rode back to the hotel, hanging out of the bus windows and hollering. When they arrived back at the Galt House, they piled into the elevators and rode them to the top of the hotel, where there was a bar. Dave found a manager. "We're going to need food, and we're going to need drinks, and just run the tab," Dave said.

It was nine-thirty at night, and Barclay and Robin were still at the barn. After the post-race ceremonies and interviews, they had returned to the stable to check on Funny Cide. They went straight to his stall. Barclay ran his hands over the horse's legs, checking for heat, nicks, cuts, or bruises, while Robin patted his neck and told him how proud they were.

The horse's legs were perfectly fine. Next, Barclay checked his feet. One shoe had turned a little bit. Barclay called a blacksmith and booked him for the next morning. Robin mixed a large tub of feed for Funny Cide, who tore into it, hungrily.

They left him that way, happily chewing in his stall. They themselves were starved; they hadn't eaten anything since an early lunch. Just then, Barclay's cell phone rang, and it was Jack Knowlton, calling from the Galt House bar. "Please come for a drink," Jack insisted. "Everyone wants to see you."

The trainers headed over to the hotel, but by the time they got there, the food was gone. Instead, they just had some wine, and clinked glasses with the owners and visited for a while. Dorothy sat down by them, and she asked a question. "What makes Funny Cide such a great horse?"

"He's really, really fast," Barclay said, smiling.

When Jack and Dorothy returned to their room at the Galt House, it was almost two A.M. and there was a huge ice bucket on the counter with a bottle of champagne and congratulations from the hotel. They couldn't bear any more champagne, so they just sat there for a few minutes, saying, "Can you believe it?" And then they went to bed.

They were on such a high that they slept only a few hours before they woke again. Dorothy turned over and looked at the clock: it said seven A.M. She looked at Jack.

"What do you think?" she said.

He said, "Want to get the paper?"

"Yeah. Let's go see if it's real."

Giggling, Dorothy retrieved the paper from the mat in front of their door. They spread the paper open and stared at the front-page headline and a glorious color photo of Jose Santos and Funny Cide heading for the wire, with the twin spires in the background.

"Well, I guess it must be true," Jack said. "It's in the paper."

Robin was too excited to sleep well. At four-thirty A.M., she heard the newspaper arrive outside the hotel-room door. She got up.

Barclay rolled over and said, "What are you doing?"

"I gotta go get the paper."

Robin grabbed the paper and tiptoed into the bathroom, leaving Barclay to go back to sleep. She sat in the bathroom for an hour, reading every story and studying all of the pictures. When she finally came out again, Barclay was still dozing. Robin didn't understand it. How could he sleep? She shook him.

"Come on, let's go, we gotta get up," she said.

"It's five-thirty."

"I know."

"We didn't get in till one."

"Yeah, but we have to be at the barn by seven."

"Robin, it takes five minutes to get over there."

"Yeah. But I want to go see him."

Barclay sighed, and heaved himself out of bed. He shaved and cleaned up, muttering that he couldn't believe she would drag him out of bed on the Sunday morning after the Derby. "We've got all day with nothing to do," he said. Barclay wasn't kidding; Funny Cide was supposed to be loaded into a van for the trip home shortly after seven A.M., but after that they wouldn't know what to do with themselves. There were no flights available out of Louisville until Monday, and no horses to take care of.

They drove to the barn, and Zach walked Funny Cide out of his stall. The first thing the horse did was rear straight up in the air with pure happiness. Robin laughed out loud.

Funny Cide took a stroll around the shed row, and had his shoe fixed by the blacksmith. Zach removed his poultices and washed his legs, and put fresh bandages on. By now a crowd of reporters had showed up, and Robin led Funny Cide to the van in front of an audience.

Barclay pulled the driver of the van aside. He tucked one hundred dollars into the driver's hand. "Whatever you do," he said, "don't let this horse get hurt."

Funny Cide was driven away to catch his plane for New York.

Now Robin and Barclay stood around the barn, not sure what to do with themselves. They killed some time chatting with reporters and well-wishers who wandered by.

Among the visitors to the barn was Joe DeFrancis, the head of Pimlico, home of the Preakness Stakes. DeFrancis and some of his traveling party had stopped by to congratulate them and to say he would see them at the Preakness.

"Is there anything I can do to help you?" DeFrancis asked.

Barclay dryly said, "Well, if you had a plane, you could get me home. I got a lot of stuff to do, but I can't get a flight out until to-morrow."

In fact, DeFrancis did have a plane, sort of. He turned to a member of his group, a gentleman who owned a private plane and who was headed back East. He said, "Well, you can fly with us." They would be happy to take Barclay and Robin to New York.

Within an hour, Barclay and Robin were sitting on a Learjet. They still hadn't eaten anything since lunch a day earlier, but now a flight attendant passed out turkey and ham sandwiches. Between that and some chips and pretzels, it was enough to get home on.

Robin and Barclay landed at Islip that evening, and they immediately made their way to Belmont to check on the horse. They arrived at the barn at feeding time. A security guard was posted outside, as befitted the barn of the Kentucky Derby winner. Barclay had called ahead to make sure that the horse would be protected when he arrived home. "Make sure that nobody is standing around when he gets off the van, so he doesn't get scared and hurt himself," Barclay said.

Barclay and Robin walked into the dark barn, turned on the stall light, and patted Funny Cide. He nipped back at them, and then he got down and rolled in the straw. Barclay made his dinner. The horse plunged his face into the feed bucket.

They'd finished up and were headed home to their apartment when Barclay's cell phone rang. It was their friend Allen Jerkens.

"Are you going home?"

"We'll be there any minute."

"Well, come to Stella's."

Stella's was a semi-local joint where a lot of Belmont trainers and horse people liked to hang out. Barclay and Robin looked at each other and shrugged and smiled. They were still starving. They drove straight from the barn to the restaurant.

They walked in the door, and straight into a party. The entire Jerkens family was there, with a pack of other friends from the track, all crowded around the bar. Allen came striding toward them, and the great big man wrapped his arms around Barclay, and he kissed him. Then he put his head against him and started weeping.

"You did it," Allen said. "You did it. You stuck to your convictions and you did it your way, and you did it. It feels like my own horse won."

Barclay was as moved as at any moment since the horse had won. It meant more to him than any roses or trophies.

The next morning, everybody came by the barn. Trainers, friends, exercise riders, people they hadn't seen or heard from in years. Tommy Walsh, a former fellow steeplechase rider of Barclay's who he hadn't heard from in years, had sat on his couch and watched Barclay's horse win the Derby, and shouted at the screen, "He's one of us! He's one of *us!*"

When Barclay finally had a moment to relax, he called his brother Scotty. "I'm sorry I didn't call earlier," he said. "I was on this damn Learjet, having a Bloody Mary." After Scotty had heartily congratulated him, Barclay hung up, and sat back in his chair, and finally took it all in. *Well*, he thought, *it isn't as if I don't deserve it.* He'd been in the trenches for thirty-two years. How did it make him feel? It made a man feel like he'd been doing something right in all that time, that's how. And it made him feel that if he died tomorrow, at least he would be remembered.

Of course, if he'd died in January, it occurred to him, there'd have been a lot less to remember him by.

8.

The Triple Crown

I think what the horse did was give hope to the un-rich.

—JOHN WARD

Some people said winning the Kentucky Derby made a horse seem bigger. Maybe it was true, or maybe it was just perception, but in the days after the race, the grooms and hotwalkers in the barn swore that Funny Cide grew.

Winning the Derby certainly didn't make the Sackatoga Stable owners and trainers any taller, but it did make them stand up straighter. They'd taken a chance and it had paid off, and that gave them a sense of accomplishment. But what really made them swell with pride was that Funny Cide's win was treated as a universal victory for the middle class. "It was like my own horse won" became a common refrain. Everyone seemed to feel as if they, too, owned a piece of the horse.

On a small route in upstate New York, graffiti appeared on the sign that announced, ENTERING HISTORIC SACKETS HARBOR.

Underneath it, someone had hand-lettered, FUNNY CIDE RULES.

Back in Saratoga, Jane McMahon, the middle of the five McMahon children, took out a large white bedsheet and began painting on it with green barn paint. She made huge block letters:

1ST HOME OF FUNNY CIDE
DERBY WINNER

Then she hung it on the barn.

After a day of sightseeing in Louisville, Jack and Dorothy flew home, and they were taken aback when the flight attendants announced that Funny Cide's owners were aboard and the other passengers broke into applause. On landing, they were met by their daughter Wendy, who showed up with a huge balloon hoseshoe, and their friends Stan and Barbara Yake, who had rented a horse costume, and pranced hilariously just outside the security area. They drove home to find their front porch covered in bouquets of roses, bottles of champagne, and newspapers with front-page headlines announcing Funny Cide's victory.

In Chile, at the family home of Jose Santos, the festivities went on around the clock. Jose called home, and his half-brother Hernand answered the phone. It was nine-thirty in the morning in Chile, and Jose could tell that Hernand was drunk.

"Are you partying this early?" Jose asked.

"We're still celebrating," Hernand said.

Then he put Manuel on the phone. Jose's father was in tears. "You got what you wanted your whole life," he said. Those were the only words he could get out.

When the Constances, Phillipses, and Crings returned home to Sackets, the town fire trucks came out to greet them. It took a few days for the shock of the victory and the haze of the homecoming to clear—and when it did, they suddenly remembered the money they had given Jack and Gus to place that futures bet on Funny Cide in Las Vegas.

They checked their tickets and did the math. The two hundred dollars Jack and Gus had each wagered had paid off to the tune of sixty thousand dollars. J.P. had a ticket at 40–1 that was worth four thousand dollars. Even a twenty-dollar bet returned at least eight hundred dollars.

Larry Reinhardt had unthinkingly thrown his ticket into a container on his desk and never given it a second glance, because he'd thought *no way*. But after the horse won, he was scared to death that he wouldn't be able to find it. He rummaged frantically through every drawer in his desk before he remembered where he had put it.

As for Funny Cide himself, he seemed to understand that he had done something significant. In fact, he *was* still growing physically—horses don't reach their full weight and height until they are four. But he also grew in confidence and presence.

A fellow trainer came by the barn and studied the horse, and said, "He's not very big, is he?"

"You wait. He looks bigger with the tack on," Robin said.

A day later, Robin saddled Funny Cide for his exercise. Now the other trainer looked at the horse again. He said, "I see what you mean. He does look bigger."

But Funny Cide also had his skeptics. To some, he was too much of a long shot, too improbable. How could such an unremarkable-seeming horse, with commonplace lineage, come out of virtually nowhere and win the biggest race in America? Among the doubters was a reporter from the *Miami Herald* named Frank Carlson.

Thanks to Carlson and the *Herald*, the euphoria over Funny Cide came to an abrupt halt. Five days after the Derby, Jose Santos was relaxing with his family in his apartment at the Garden City Hotel when his cell phone rang. It was Carlson, calling on behalf of the *Herald*, and he had a question for Jose.

"Congratulations on your Derby win," the reporter said.

"Thanks," Jose said.

"Let me ask you something," Carlson said. "Other than your whip, were you carrying something else in your hand?"

"Nothing," Jose said. "All I had was my Q-ray."

"What's that?" Carlson asked.

A Q-ray bracelet was a silver hoop that supposedly had curative powers for bone pain and arthritis. It had been a recent birthday gift from Rita.

"It's for arthritis," Jose explained.

"No," the reporter said. "I think you were carrying something else. Were you carrying something with your whip?"

"What are you talking about?"

The question didn't make sense. Why would he carry anything but a whip?

It suddenly dawned on Jose that he was being accused of cheating to win the Kentucky Derby.

"Listen to me, my friend," Jose said. "I don't have time for this nonsense."

He hung up and didn't give it a thought. He had more pressing things on his mind. His horse, Volponi, had lost that day, and he wanted to watch the replay.

He had no time for such silliness.

But the next morning, May 10, Floridians woke up and opened their *Miami Herald* and saw a front-page story that accused Jose Santos of cheating, and with it ran a large photo in which Jose indeed seemed to be grasping a suspicious dark object in his hand, and it was clearly not his whip.

The story suggested that the object he appeared to be holding may have been a device, possibly a battery, to shock the horse into running faster. There was nothing to substantiate the charge, simply the fuzzy picture and a quote from a steward at Churchill Downs, Rick Leigh, saying the photo was "very suspicious."

Jose, his son, and Mike the Cop were sitting in the track kitchen early that morning drinking coffee and eating toast when they learned what the *Herald* had published. Jose was wearing a small television microphone on his collar because he was being followed for an MSNBC documentary. Mike's cell phone rang, and Jose heard him say, "What are you talking about?" The next thing he knew, Mike had torn the microphone off his collar. "You better come outside," he said.

"What's going on?" Jose said.

Mike said, "There's a big write-up in the paper in Miami. This guy wrote a front-page story saying you were carrying a machine in your hand. Tell me the truth. Were you carrying something?"

"What are you, fucking kidding me?"

"There's a picture."

"Yeah, well, I want to *see* the picture."

Mike got back on the phone and had a copy of the story faxed to the track. The piece had two major errors, apart from the central falsity of the accusation itself: the writer misquoted Jose as saying that he carried a "cue ring" to call "outriders." Somehow the writer had misunderstood Jose when he said he wore a Q-ray to help his arthritis.

The damaging part, however, was the photograph. It looked damning. There, in the palm of Jose's hand, was a dark splotch. By eight A.M., TV camera crews and print press began to show up, the picture was on the news, and the story was spreading around the entire track. Jose called Rita at home and explained to her what had happened, trying to minimize it. The *Herald* had accused him of something, he said. "But don't worry about it. It's not that big a deal."

But it was a big deal, and it was getting bigger by the second. Jose's cell phone was now ringing like crazy, trainers and fellow jockeys calling him from Florida to tell him what was in the paper. Jose Junior wandered back and forth, playing. His father did his best to pretend nothing was wrong, that everything was normal. He didn't want to worry his son.

But then the stewards called from Churchill Downs. They were conducting an inquiry into the Derby and had scheduled a hearing. Jose would have to fly to Louisville. He would also need a lawyer.

Jack and Dave arrived at the Tagg barn and heard what had happened. They and Barclay and Robin immediately scoffed at the accusation. Robin said, "Well, that's just crazy." For one thing, Jose had changed his stick hand four or five times coming down the stretch. There was no way he could've been carrying anything. As far as they were concerned, it was impossible that he'd had anything in his hand other than the whip.

Nevertheless, every TV station and publication in the country picked up the story. It was a feeding frenzy at Belmont. Jose was surrounded by press. He called Rita back at nine-thirty. "This is getting bad," he said. "You need to come and pick up Jose, and we have to see an attorney."

"How can this be?" Rita asked.

When Rita arrived at the track, Jose Junior was pacing. He ran toward her. Rita thought, *He knows.* He said, "I know what they're saying. They're accusing my dad of cheating, and he's not a cheater."

Meanwhile, Mike the Cop had an idea. He went over to the local police station, where an old friend of his was the head of detectives. Mike handed over the picture from the *Miami Herald* and asked if the police lab could blow it up. The cops obliged: when the photo was magnified four hundred times, they could clearly see that there was nothing unusual in Jose's hand.

Officials from the New York Racing Association at Belmont Park had the same idea. They did their own enhanced examination of the photo, and it proved Jose's innocence. The mysterious "dark object" was actually a piece of the jockey silks of Jerry Bailey, as he crouched on Empire Maker just behind Funny Cide.

Jack and Dave took a copy of the enhancement and started showing it around the track. Jose directed his son's gaze to the picture. "Look," he said. "You have nothing to worry about."

Jose Junior said, "Yeah, Daddy, it's the colors. It's the colors."

At four P.M., Jack and Dave held a press conference on behalf of the Sackatoga Stable to respond to questions from the press. Surrounded by microphones and cameras, they displayed the NYRA photograph that clearly showed there was no "machine" in the jockey's hand.

Still, suspicion hovered over Jose. People continued to ask questions that day. Even Rita said, "Jose, is there anything you need to tell me? You know I love you and I stand behind you one hundred and fifty percent." For the first time, Jose lost his temper, and he flared up at her.

"Are you crazy?" he said. "You think I'm that stupid? When I know that horse has a great chance to win? And anyway, how am I going to carry something when there's a TV camera on every corner and thousands of pictures?"

"Then let's go meet the attorney."

For seventy-two hours, Jose had to put up with the accusations and the spiraling national media story. On Saturday, he tried to go to work as usual at Belmont. Rita and the kids joined him, but as soon as Rita saw the press crush, she called her brother. "Can you do me a favor and come and get the kids out of here?" she asked. "The press is going crazy, chasing Jose all over the paddock."

All afternoon, throughout the day's race schedule, Jose was heckled by spectators. As he rode his first mount onto the track, someone shouted, "You can't win no more because someone took your battery!" When he won a race called the Nassau County Breeders' Cup Stakes, someone shouted, "Sure. You use your machine just for the stakes races!"

But Jose had already persuaded one important constituency of his innocence: his fellow jockeys. That morning, Jose had arrived early at the jockey room at Belmont, carrying a videotape. He'd slid the tape into a VCR and turned it on. A group of riders gathered around and watched a replay of the race. They were convinced that Jose had nothing in his hand. Word of mouth spread among the riders that Santos was clean, and was getting a raw deal from the press.

That evening, Jose's phone rang again: this time it was Ron

Turcotte, who had ridden Secretariat to the Triple Crown. Jose was deeply moved: the two had never met. "Everything is going to be all right," Turcotte told him.

But Jose still had to convince the stewards at Churchill Downs. On Sunday night, a full week after his Derby triumph, he flew back to Louisville. Meanwhile, at home in Albertson, New York, Rita and two of the children spent the night nervously. They sat propped up in the same bed together, watching the television. Rita kept the kids away from the phones and the news reports. But she couldn't shelter them entirely. Her oldest daughter had been questioned by schoolmates, and the younger children had heard the whispers. It was all around them, it seemed.

Eventually, Rita dozed off, with her children still piled up in the big bed. While Rita slept, her daughter Selena stayed awake and watched a news report about Jose and Funny Cide, and they saw footage of their father arriving in Louisville.

At two A.M., Rita woke up to find her seven-year-old daughter, Selena, upset and unable to sleep. Rita asked her what was wrong. "I'm nervous," Selena said. "I didn't realize my daddy was a bad person."

Rita calmed her daughter down, and eventually they fell back to sleep. The next morning, she reported the conversation to Jose. It was perhaps his lowest moment. He hung up and went to the hearing at Churchill Downs in a state of cold, suppressed anger.

Jose and Mike the Cop, accompanied by a sports attorney, met with the track stewards to review the tapes and photos of the race. It took just one hour before Jose emerged, totally exonerated. But by now, exoneration wasn't good enough for Jose. He wanted more than that.

He wanted to win another race. The Preakness.

B arclay believed that all the commotion took a toll on a horse. It wasn't natural for Funny Cide to face mobs of people, to be led in and out of his stall, and to have flashbulbs go off in his face. The uproar after the Derby could hurt the horse's temperament if Barclay didn't guard against it, he believed, to the point that Funny Cide might decide he didn't like crowds anymore. Barclay didn't want to lead the horse to the track on Preakness day and watch him fall apart again from nerves.

There were exactly two weeks between the Kentucky Derby and the Preakness, and the main task of the trainers was to keep their horse fit and calm. Funny Cide had every chance of winning the Preakness, if they could simply maintain his current happy state. The Preakness was a shorter race than the Derby, a mile and three-sixteenths at Pimlico Race Course, and the field would be just ten horses. Absent would be Empire Maker, whose trainer had conceded he needed a rest. Funny Cide's chief challenger would be Bobby Frankel's other horse, Peace Rules.

Barclay kept Funny Cide sequestered at his Belmont barn, particularly in the wake of the Santos controversy. He put up a gate at the front of the barn and posted a sign barring anyone but employees from the premises. NO ENTRY, EMPLOYEES ONLY, MISTER BARCLAY TAGG, the sign said.

Barclay and Robin were the only guardians the horse had, and they intended to protect him. So many times they had second-guessed themselves as trainers: Why didn't their horse run any better? Racing wasn't an exact science, and from an odds standpoint, it was the toughest game played outdoors. But Funny Cide was their long-awaited affirmation that their methods were correct, and now that they had him, they didn't intend to screw him up.

For instance, Barclay insisted he would not ship Funny Cide to Pimlico until early on the morning of the race. Preakness officials entreated him to bring the horse down to Maryland early: they wanted him on the premises to help promote the race. But Barclay said no. He hadn't done it for the Derby, and he wasn't doing it now.

At his home barn in Belmont, Funny Cide could go about his normal routine, and prepare for the Preakness relatively undisturbed, whereas at Pimlico, the press would ask for him to be paraded out of his stall every day. Barclay wasn't going to move Funny Cide until he absolutely had to.

Meanwhile, Barclay and Robin had their own issues with moving. Funny Cide's stress level was at a minimum, but theirs was soaring. They were essentially homeless. They had been living in a basement apartment near Belmont owned by a fellow trainer, Linda Rice, but six days before the Kentucky Derby, Rice had stopped Barclay on his way out the door and said, "Listen, I hate to say this, but you have to move out."

He said, "Okay. When?"

"By Wednesday."

"By Wednesday, next week?"

"No, by this Wednesday."

It was the day they were supposed to fly to the Derby. Rice explained: she had refinanced the house, and in the process, a bank appraiser had told her the apartment was an illegal rental. Rice asked them to move their things into the garage, so the apartment would be empty when the appraiser came back. She hoped it was just temporary. Barclay and Robin packed what they needed for Kentucky and piled the rest of their belongings in the garage.

But when they returned from the Derby, Rice gave them the bad news: they would have to move out permanently. In the two short weeks between the Kentucky Derby and the Preakness, they had to look for a new apartment. They spent the mornings working at the barn, and then they apartment-hunted in the afternoons. Their belongings remained in a heap. Finally, they found a new rental and turned their attention back to preparing the horse.

Early on the morning of May 16, the day before the Preakness, it began to rain. Barclay stared at the deluge through the open door of the barn office, and said to Robin, "I want to ship today."

"Okay," she said, with equanimity. "When?"

"Right now."

"Right now, as in, like . . . ?"

"Right now."

Robin picked up the phone and called the van company and said, "When can you be ready?"

"When do you want to go?" the driver asked.

"Right now."

"Right *now*?"

"Yeah, right now."

Barclay's change of mind wasn't as sudden as it seemed. He had been watching the weather reports, and the forecast was for the weather to worsen through the night and into the next day. He didn't want to risk shipping the horse on race day in a storm. As he looked around at the deserted barn area, he decided that he'd rather beat the heavier weather. The change in plan had another advantage: no one would be expecting them at Pimlico.

Within twenty minutes, the trainers and grooms were packed and ready to load the van. They were just about to walk Funny Cide out—when the press showed up. The crews gathered at the barred barn gate, waiting for their daily interview with Barclay. Robin regarded them and said to Barclay, "This isn't going to work. You can't walk the horse out the front gate, because they're going to see him leave." If the press knew Funny was shipping to Pimlico, there would be a throng of photographers waiting for him to arrive, a flashbulb circus.

Barclay said, "It will work."

He told the van to pull around to the back of the barn, out of sight, and then he strode out to the barn gate and began chatting with reporters. Funny Cide's groom, Zach, casually led Funny Cide out of the shed row. The press took no notice of them; Funny Cide was so nondescript that from a distance he looked like just another brown horse. While the press was preoccupied with Barclay, Zach slipped Funny Cide into the van.

A reporter said, "When are you shipping?"

"Early in the morning," Barclay lied.

As soon as Barclay got rid of the press, he and Robin grabbed their suitcases, hopped into the car, and started driving. Three hours later, they pulled into Pimlico, about fifteen minutes behind their horse. They quietly walked Funny Cide into the private barn of their friend Mary Eppler. They had chosen to stable the horse in Eppler's barn because it was on a more secluded part of the backstretch, while most of the other horses were in residence at the prominent Stakes barns.

They ushered Funny into his stall and began to prepare his dinner. Just then, a track photographer came jogging toward the barn. He'd been tipped off by track security that Funny Cide had arrived.

As the photographer came running down the shed row, Barclay went out to meet him. "Whoa," he said. Barclay threw his arm out, pointing to the door. "Get out of here," he ordered. The photographer slowed to a walk but kept coming. Barclay said icily, "I'm not going to tell you again, I want you out. No pictures."

Incidents like that didn't endear Barclay to the press and public, but he didn't care. He cared about what was best for the horse. He cared that the horse got settled in and ate his dinner. He cared about routine.

In fact, Funny Cide was probably holding up better than Barclay. The next day, when reporters showed up at the Eppler barn, Barclay confessed that he had tricked them, and that he didn't care for the attention or the pressure. Barclay kidded the press, "I'm trying to enjoy myself without having a heart attack." He couldn't help it, he confessed. Cranky was his habitual demeanor. "I got here by working hard all day, every day," he said. "What can I say? It's the way I am."

The important thing was that Funny Cide was relaxed. While Barclay sparred with reporters, the horse happily tore into his feed bucket. "He's biting everyone and having a grand time," Barclay said.

There was one more reason for the trainers to be stressed. On the Wednesday before the race, Jack Knowlton and Dave Mahan had attended the draw for Funny Cide's post position—and this time they weren't lucky. Funny Cide drew the number ten, giving them the last choice. It was the worst possible result. Nobody wanted to run at Pimlico from the far outside. The race was too short, and a horse in post ten could well be doomed. Jack immediately stepped outside and called Barclay to give him the bad news.

"Well, it is what it is," Jack said. "At least we got it right for the big race [the Derby] when we had to have it."

They got one small break at the draw later that afternoon. Bob

Baffert's horse, a lightly raced long shot named Señor Swinger, had drawn number nine. But instead of taking the ninth post position, Baffert stepped to the podium and announced, "Ten." He wanted the far outside for his horse, apparently in order to keep the dirt out of his face and give him as untroubled a race as possible. But Barclay also wondered if Baffert had done it in part as a gesture of sportsmanship toward Funny Cide. The gelding would run from the ninth position. It was better than ten.

F unny Cide and the Sackatoga Stable owners awoke on the morning of the Preakness in unfamiliar roles: now they were the favorites instead of the long shots. The Sackatoga party had grown to 120, enough to fill not one but two yellow school buses. They had no intention of riding anything else to Pimlico. They carried Playmate coolers, and their clothes were festooned with Funny Cide buttons and pins, which had materialized out of nowhere since the Derby. "Funny Cide, get rowdy! Let's crank this party up!" they chanted on the buses, as they passed beers down the aisle.

"Everybody present and accounted for?" Knowlton asked. He counted heads. "Okay. Let's go." The buses pulled out.

Once again, it was a long day before post time. It was chilly and overcast, and they passed the time having lunch in a private tent and getting their picture taken with the singer Lee Greenwood, who was on hand.

But the day was longest for Barclay and Robin, with their lone sleepy horse nodding in his stall at the Eppler barn on the backstretch. Funny stood, as was customary, with his front legs in tubs of ice water, his eyes half-closed. Barclay and Robin killed a couple of hours just sitting in their car and reading the papers. Barclay reminisced about the old days at Pimlico, when he had perched on a rooftop to watch Secretariat run. "Once," he remembered idly, "a car ran into my barn."

Jose Santos passed the time by playing Ping-Pong in the jockey room and trying to ignore the pressure he felt in his throat. He wanted to run a big race. In his mind, neither he nor his horse had gotten proper credit for their Kentucky Derby victory, because of the *Miami Herald* cheating controversy. He wanted a victory that would kill any lingering doubt that they were a deserving pair of winners. He had been confident before, but now he was determined to blow the race and the short field apart.

Finally, it was time to race. Jose marched to the paddock, where Barclay gave him the instructions he wanted to hear. There was no time in the Preakness to fool around; you had to grab a lead after the first half-mile and hold it. "I don't care where you are early, but you'd better be in front by the time you get to the half-mile pole," Barclay said.

"When he's ready to go," Barclay added, "just *go*."

Funny broke from the gate neatly, and Jose immediately took him from the number nine post position to two places off the rail. As they headed into the first turn, he tucked in behind Peace Rules and a horse named Scrimshaw.

Into the clubhouse turn, Edgar Prado urged Peace Rules into the lead alone, dictating the pace.

Barclay and Robin watched their horse lying third. So far, Funny Cide was running easily. Santos kept the horse on a loose rein, and allowed him to cruise up to Peace Rules. Jose sat high in the saddle, barely moving his hands.

After a half-mile in 47.14, Peace Rules and Funny Cide ran head to head. The race was on as they neared the top of the stretch.

Funny Cide was ready to go. But Jose made himself and the horse wait until the last three-eighths of a mile.

Jose made two clucking noises to his mount. Funny Cide's ears pointed forward—and they were gone. In the bat of an eye, the horse opened up two lengths. They gunned down the stretch, opening more distance with every stride in the soft earth.

Two lengths. Three. Peace Rules was a plodding memory. Now Funny Cide led by five lengths . . . and then six, and seven, and eight.

Jack Knowlton's son, Aaron, turned around and began shouting to the massive crowd in the clubhouse seats. "Thanks for coming!" he screamed.

Funny Cide and Jose came to the wire. As horse and rider shot across the finish line, Jose thrust his fist in the air—and something made him open his hand. He closed it, and opened it again, like a magician who had just set a pigeon loose. Later, he would say, "I blew a kiss to God."

Funny Cide won the Preakness by nine and three-quarters lengths, the second-biggest margin of victory in the 128-year history of the race. He had run a mile and three-sixteenths in just 1:55.61.

Once again, the Sackatoga Stable owners and their wives went crazy in their box seats. But this time, they knew how to find the winner's circle. Together, they wove through the crowds to the track circle in a kind of victorious conga line. They danced through the aisles, with their hands over their heads, so no one would get lost. They chanted "Funny Cide!" If anyone needed a reference point, there was Gus in his canary-yellow pants and yellow-and-black-checked sport coat.

They started singing. First, they sang the Sackets High fight song, in honor of the Sackets High Patriots.

Then they sang a Frank Sinatra number, though wildly off-key. "Start spreading the news . . ."

It was one thing to win the Kentucky Derby. It was quite another to win the second leg of the Triple Crown with such a performance. Funny Cide now had a legitimate shot at the Triple Crown. And with the Triple Crown came an enormous financial bonus: Visa had offered five million dollars to any horse that could complete the sweep.

In the winner's circle, Bob Costas held a microphone in front of Gus Williams.

"Any chance you'd use some of that five million for a fashion consultant?"

With his dominant showing in the Preakness, Funny Cide instantaneously grew from a quaint success story into a sensation. Not only was the horse taller—now he had stature. Even Barclay was moved by an uncharacteristic feeling of triumph.

"He's a gift from God," Barclay said.

A t Barn Six, Barclay and Robin looked at the mail piled up: there were hundreds of letters addressed simply to "Funny Cide." Somehow, the post office had known where to deliver them. They tore open an envelope, at random. A girl from Arizona was writing to ask if she could be backup jockey to Jose. "I'm only sixty pounds and I'm a good rider," she wrote. "If you don't like me, you can send me back."

Funny Cide was becoming the darling of the horse-racing public—and of eBay. People couldn't get enough of him, or of his trinkets, and Internet auctioneers realized that, now that the horse was contending for the Triple Crown, anything associated with him would appreciate in value. The smattering of pins and buttons that had sprung up after the Derby now became a deluge. Posters that had been given for free at Churchill Downs were going for twenty dollars—and up.

It dawned on the Sackatoga owners that their gelding had ancillary potential. He would never stand at stud for six-figure fees, but he was a valuable animal nonetheless, and Jack set about trying to protect their interests. He formed Funny Cide Ventures to handle licensing of merchandise. He had a Web site created, with a Funny Cide store that sold Funny Cide T-shirts ($20), caps ($20), pins ($6), and buttons ($3).

Local brewpub owners in Sackets Harbor, Steve and Errol Flynn, made a brilliant proposal. What about Funny Cide beer? It was a perfect notion: the horse was a commoner, and his owners were regular beer-drinking people, not champagne-sippers.

If Funny Cide was the people's horse, there was one group of people who particularly claimed him as their own: New Yorkers. The kinship they felt with the horse was palpable, and in truth he seemed to share many of their qualities. He was an outsider who exuded grit and fought against long odds. He was a New York–bred whose home barn was Belmont Park, where a grandstand seat cost two dollars. His groom, Zach Quintana, was an immigrant who made $250 a week. His trainer was based in New York, nine of his ten owners were New Yorkers, and his jockey lived in New York.

Everywhere they went in New York, Funny Cide and the Sackatoga owners were treated as the local boys who'd made good. They were invited to meet the mayor of New York City, Michael Bloomberg, at his official residence, Gracie Mansion. Jose threw out the first pitch at a New York Yankees game, to roars.

The Garden City Hotel provided Jose with a limo and a suite

for his family, and they threw him a huge party. By then, the Funny Cide bumper stickers had come in, and so had the Funny Cide pins, and Dave Mahan was pinning everybody he knew. On the night of Jose's party, Dave set out to make the drive to Long Island in his car, which was plastered with Funny Cide stickers and memorabilia. On his way there, he got caught in traffic on the Long Island Expressway. He sat there, bumper to bumper, when all of a sudden the guy in the car behind him blew his horn. Dave glanced in the rearview mirror, and figured he had probably cut the guy off. The guy blew his horn again. Dave thought, *Buddy, get over it, I didn't hit you*, and glared at the guy through his sunglasses.

Next, the driver began maneuvering through traffic trying to pull up next to him. Dave figured he was in for a fight—this guy seemed awfully ticked off. He stared straight ahead as the guy drew alongside him, and tried not to look, but now the horn was blasting, so Dave glanced out of the corner of his eye.

The guy rolled down the window and screamed, "Funny Cide! Funny Cide! I know you! You're Funny Cide! I'm going to bet on him!"

Dave died laughing. He had figured he was about to get killed, and it turned out the guy was just a big fan of his horse.

The anticipation for a Triple Crown steadily ratcheted. Belmont granted 1,200 applications for press credentials. In any other season, the entire press corps for the race numbered only 750. Suddenly, everyone—including Katie Couric—wanted to talk to the owners of Funny Cide. One evening, J.P. was chatting away when he heard himself say, "I was talking to Tom Brokaw this morning . . ." He stopped in mid-sentence.

"Can you believe I just said that?" he asked.

The press descended on Sackets Harbor to do a story about the improbable horse with the unlikely owners. The reporters who came to town thought they'd find the residents picking straw from their teeth and hair. One writer said to the local schoolboard chairwoman, "Have you ever heard of my paper, the *Baltimore Sun*?" She smiled and nodded politely, but what she wanted to say was, "Have you ever heard of H. L. Mencken?"

The highway sign just outside of the village now had additional graffito on it. It read:

ENTERING HISTORIC SACKETS HARBOR
FUNNY CIDE RULES
ON TO BELMONT.

A couple of weeks before the race, the NYRA persuaded the Sackatoga owners to have a press conference in Manhattan, after which they filmed an "I Love New York" television commercial. They booked a famous steak house called Gallagher's. Knowlton arrived and met Tim Smith on the sidewalk. "Are you ready for this?" Smith asked. Knowlton nodded, and looked around. There was a horde of media, about a hundred spectators—and a line of New York police on horseback.

Nearby, Jose Santos studied the mount of one of the officers.

He reached up and patted the horse on the nose.

B ut with the anticipation came an irrational exuberance. Only eleven horses had ever completed the Triple Crown sweep— and none in twenty-five years.

Why was it such an obstacle? Distance. The Belmont Stakes posed a challenge of a mile and a half, a race of unprecedented length for most three-year-olds, and an especially grueling one for horses that had already run in the first two legs of the Triple Crown. The Belmont, held on June 7, would be Funny Cide's third big race in five weeks, and his longest.

To horses accustomed to crossing the line after a mile and a quarter or less, the Belmont must have seemed endless, and for the vast majority of them, it *was* too far. There was a reason why so many favorites failed and why the winners tended to be long shots who paid off at 30–1 or even 70–1.

A Triple Crown horse had to have enormous strength and stamina, and yet be tractable enough to pace itself, bide time and wait. No wonder Triple Crown winners were indisputable superstars. There was nothing modest about Secretariat, Seattle Slew, or Affirmed.

The *Washington Post*'s Andy Beyer said of the Triple Crown, "If a committee of experts tried to design the definitive test of American racehorses, it could not have devised one more effective." Oddly enough, however, the trio of races evolved accidentally. Sir Barton was the first horse to complete the sweep, in 1919, but there was no such thing yet as the formal Triple Crown. The term wouldn't be coined until the 1930s, when it was dubbed by a *Daily Racing Form* writer named Charles Hatton. It wouldn't be truly popularized until Whirlaway achieved it in 1941. And there wasn't even an actual trophy until 1950. Then, in 1987, Visa put a premium on the series by attaching the massive financial bonus to it.

The money hung there in the air, like a specter. It changed everything. Funny Cide's lifetime earnings through the Preakness Stakes amounted to less than two million dollars. Now he would be running for three times that in a single race. It was impossible for some of his owners not to savor the idea, and to contemplate the difference it could make in their lives.

But Dave Mahan was becoming intensely superstitious, and to him the money was like a jinx. To him, it was bad luck even to talk about it.

Dave's brother, Jimmy, called him right after the Preakness and said, "Do you know how much money you can win?"

"Yeah. I have an idea of how much it could be."

"No, really. You know how much money you're running for?"

"Yeah, I know how much money we're running for."

"How much is yours?"

"None of it is mine."

"What do you mean?"

"We didn't get it yet. We got to go run for it."

"Yeah, but *if* you win, how much is yours?"

"Jimmy, I don't know."

"I'll figure it out."

"*No*," Dave practically shouted. "Don't even think about figuring it out. I don't want to have any idea. It's not about that. If we win the race, I might start thinking about how much I just won—when I'm walking to the winner's circle. Not until then."

But their preoccupation with the money grew, and so did the press's and the public's. Visa sponsored a luncheon for the horse owners at the 21 Club in Manhattan, and the centerpiece of each table was a large prop check for five million dollars—blowups made out of cardboard, with nobody's name on them yet. The owners had finished lunch and were lounging around the table drinking coffee when someone from Visa said, "Can you guys sign the checks for us?" They wanted the prop checks as souvenirs.

A couple of the Sackets guys took out their pens and started signing.

"What are you doing?" Dave said. "You can't sign that. You want to jinx us?"

"Oh, come on," someone said.

"Hey, as far I'm concerned, you're counting your money," Dave said. "I'm not going to sign a five-million-dollar check before someone hands it to me and says, 'That's yours.' "

No one was more cautious in his thinking about the Belmont than that famous pessimist Barclay Tagg. Barclay did his best not to be preoccupied by the bonus, or to hope for too much. The fact was, Barclay was fed up with all the hoopla and publicity, which he felt was finally beginning to tell on Funny Cide's temperament, despite all his efforts and precautions. Photographers swarmed around the barn at all hours, twenty and thirty of them at a time. In the week before the Belmont, Leroy Neiman was supposed to paint the horse, and he set up his easel for the appointment. But Barclay pulled a no-show.

"He can come back after the race, and I'll tie Funny Cide to a tree," Barclay said. "He can paint him for a month if he wants to."

Barclay became increasingly laconic with the press. He showed up with Robin for the post-position draw just fifteen minutes before the ceremony started, wearing the same thing he always wore: pressed jeans, boots, and a baseball cap. He drank coffee until he was called, when he went to the dais and drew number four, and then left without a word. He had a thousand things in his mind— but he wasn't saying any of them aloud.

By now, Barclay's barn was guarded by two NYRA security officers, who stood watch over Funny Cide round the clock, while a third officer was stationed outside the barn gate. The only people Barclay allowed near Funny Cide now were Robin, his hotwalker, Raunie Hart, and the groom, Zach Quintana. They kept the horse entertained by letting him play in the pen, and they fed him treats. He liked bananas, watermelon, and peppermints.

Barclay wasn't being contrary, or overprotective. He and Robin could see the mounting tension in Funny Cide. The horse was getting bigger and more full of himself, and increasingly nervous and difficult to handle. He nipped at his shank, and he bit at the halter when Robin tried to fasten it. Sometimes he'd nip and toss his head for fifteen minutes before he would settle down, as if to say, "Okay, put the halter on me, I'm ready for my walk now."

To get the press off his back and keep them away from the horse, Barclay tricked them again, this time about what time Funny Cide would breeze. He told the press the horse would work out the next morning at nine A.M.—but instead, Funny Cide was the first horse on the track at five-thirty. Barclay wasn't going to risk more flashbulbs and a potential accident. The horse might buck, rear, lunge sideways. Anything could happen.

That morning, Robin literally couldn't hold Funny Cide back. He breezed five furlongs in a blazing fifty-seven and four-fifths seconds. It was nearly two seconds faster than any other horse that day, and faster than either Robin or Barclay wanted.

Robin could tell the horse was moving too fast in the first eighth of a mile. She grabbed hold of the reins and said, "You're going too quick." She felt something grab back, hard. The horse might as well have spoken to her, and what he said was, "I'm going to go even faster if you don't give me my head."

Robin gave him a little rein. He slowed down. The horse had

his own mind and knew what he wanted, and she had no choice but to go along with it. She could feel him saying, "I know what I'm doing—let me go." If you fought Funny, you lost.

He had become a challenging horse, and even an egotistical one. Funny Cide cantered past a group of photographers, who began clicking away. Funny immediately straightened up and pointed his ears, as if to say, "Get a good shot."

"Barclay, did you see that?" Robin asked.

"Yes," he said.

Horses knew the difference between winning and losing, Robin believed. She had known horses to literally be upset when they lost. She'd had one filly, Tampico, who would take hours to cool down if she lost a race. She'd pace and pace, agitated. If she won, she was content and cool within a half hour.

Funny eyeballed everything, and he seemed to know that the attention was for him personally. He would poke his head out of the stall and swing it back and forth, looking for his audience. His hot-walker, Raunie Hart, got the feeling that Funny Cide was saying, "Where's my fan club?" Also, he pointedly ignored the other horses. It was as though he knew he was the star.

But it was obvious that while the attention pleased Funny Cide, it also enervated him. He was increasingly skittish and mood-sensitive. On the morning before the Belmont, Robin took Funny Cide out to jog. He made it once around the track, but when Barclay reached out to lead him past the gap so he could do a second lap, Funny rebelled. He started high-stepping, and he accelerated. He dragged both Barclay and his pony clear past the grandstand before they calmed him down.

For the last twenty-four hours before the race, Barclay barred absolutely everyone from the barn—including even the Sackatoga owners. When another of his owners, Cot Campbell, wanted to come to the barn to visit his own horse, Barclay said, "I'm sorry, Mr. Campbell, but no one's coming into the barn from Friday noon, on."

Campbell said, "Well, I got news for you. I'm coming to see my horse."

Barclay said, "You can come if you want, but security is not going to let you in, and I'm not going to show him to you. No one gets in my barn unless they're employed by me."

Barn Six was now under total lockdown, Barclay informed the press, so they needn't bother standing around outside. "I'm going to have guards posted all night, and if you don't have a license that says you're employed by Barclay Tagg, you're not getting in." The ban wouldn't be lifted until Sunday, and then they could all come back. "I'm not going to church, so you can come Sunday and criticize me or whatever you want to do."

By now Barclay's reputation with the press was that he was sour. That was fine with him. If you wanted a circus horse, you went to the circus. Funny Cide wasn't a circus horse, he was a racehorse. "They're temperamental, geared up, very, very fit, they're confined, and they're very self-destructive," Barclay said.

But the press couldn't understand why Barclay continued to radiate pessimism. What if the horse somehow won? Would he finally celebrate then? Barclay refused to bite. He said, "There won't be any victory party after the race if he wins. I'll just come back here and see if he's eaten his mash."

Someone asked him what his battle strategy was.

"I don't like battle strategy," he said. "That's for war. It's a race."

If Barclay was grim, it was because he knew what few others were willing to admit: the horse had the odds against him, and this time, they were probably too long. Funny Cide was racing against the powerful weight of history. Since 1978, eight horses had won the first two legs of the Triple Crown—and all of them had failed in the Belmont.

Also, Funny Cide would be running against a strong field of horses that were more rested than he was. Empire Maker and Ten Most Wanted had both returned to the track, and they hadn't run since the Derby. They'd had five weeks off, and it had showed in their workouts. While Funny Cide had behaved skittishly, Empire Maker was powerful and relaxed. Bobby Frankel, Empire Maker's trainer, made it clear that he thought he had the superior horse, despite the Derby loss. He suggested that he had given away the Derby to Funny Cide by preparing his own horse too cautiously and overconfidently. He flatly predicted that Empire Maker would rectify the mistake in the Belmont. "If he beats me this time, he's a great horse," Frankel said.

Funny Cide was under constant stress, and so were his trainers. Barclay just wanted to keep the horse peaceful and quiet—but the world wouldn't let him.

The Sackatoga traveling party had grown to more than three hundred, a long, rollicking, chanting, semi-inebriated parade of people in Funny Cide T-shirts and caps, a floating party so large that it filled four buses.

At nine A.M. on Belmont day, they gathered in the lobby of the Sheraton Hotel on Long Island, mingling with a wedding party. Included in their group were reporters from several papers who'd asked to ride the bus, as well as the pastor of the Sackatoga owners, the Reverend Doug Comstock of St. Andrews Catholic Church in Sackets Harbor. Comstock joked around that he was present to safeguard their faith.

"Why shouldn't he be here?" J.P. cracked. "He only works one day a week."

Gus Williams lounged in the lobby drinking a beer, while others loaded the coolers with beer and Bloody Mary mix. Finally, it was time to pile onto the buses. "Let's go get the money!" Gus shouted. They trooped aboard.

"No, we're not superstitious," J.P. joked. "Just perpetually frugal."

Someone called to Father Comstock, "Hey, Father! We need more holy water!"

But at his barn, Barclay did not share the good cheer of the Sackatoga owners. That morning, he had risen and thrown back the curtains, and discovered that the weather was threatening. By nine A.M., it was raining heavily, a constant downpour under a sky as solid as a slab of slate. At Belmont, water stood on the track. The soft loam had become so soupy that it could have been poured into a bowl.

The rain didn't let up. All morning and into the afternoon, it continued to fall from an oppressive sky. Nevertheless, the clubhouse and the grandstand steadily filled with people. As post time approached, 101,864 had filled the seats, including Senators Charles Schumer and Hillary Clinton; director Gary Ross, who had just finished writing and directing the film *Seabiscuit;* Steven Spielberg; actress Sigourney Weaver; and a wide cross section of the city of New York.

Ladies stepped daintily through the mud in patent-leather pumps and cringed under their wide-brimmed hats trimmed with ribbon roses. Men covered their Hugo Boss suits with plastic garbage bags. All of them clutched soaked copies of the *Racing Form.*

In the parking lot, Belmont Park peace officer Andrea Vaz directed a massive string of cars. A lady pulled up in a sedan and stuck her head out into the rain. She wore a large button that said FUNNY CIDE.

"What do I have to do to park here?" the woman asked.

"Give up the pin," Vaz said.

The woman surrendered the pin. Vaz stuck it in the side of her hat and waved the woman into a spot.

In the seclusion of Barclay and Robin's closely guarded barn, the atmosphere was that of nervous apprehension and yet boredom, as the bad weather was making a long day even longer. Zach Quintana and Raunie Hart stared at the relentless downpour through a window, their chins in their hands, while Barclay and Robin stayed out of sight in their ramshackle inner office, anxieties gnawing at them. Could they have done anything differently to prepare Funny Cide for the Belmont? Maybe, maybe not. Each time they tried to gallop him, all he wanted to do was run off. Had the grind gotten to him?

Funny Cide, meanwhile, alternately shook his head back and forth impatiently, or leaned against the wall of his stall, as if he was bored, too. "The horse is smart," Zach observed. "He's known since last night that he's going to race."

Jose Santos tried to tell himself, and his family, that he was confident of victory. "Okay, kids," he said with bravado. "We're going to go watch Daddy make history." But this time, his feelings didn't match his words. He, too, gazed at the rain apprehensively.

Up in the clubhouse hospitality area, Penny Chenery, the owner of Secretariat, came by to say hello to the Sackatoga Stable owners and wish them good luck. She sat for a while and visited. The owners pulled their chairs into a circle and asked her about her own experience going for the Triple Crown. "Did you get nervous?" Dave asked.

"The thing that I worried about was disappointing all those people," she said. It summed up how they all felt, as they gazed around at the packed clubhouse and grandstand.

At last, it was time to go to the paddock, and still the weather hadn't relented. The sky was a solid wall of gray. Jose had to admit that Funny Cide was going to have a tough race. *He'll be okay,* Jose tried to tell himself.

Robin walked with the horse and Jose to the track for the post parade, and then removed Funny Cide's shank. Jose and Funny Cide made their entrance onto the track. As they appeared before the clubhouse, they were engulfed by a thunderous roar. Jose had never heard anything so deep and sustained from a horse-racing audience. As he jogged the horse, the sound continued to flow over and around them.

One by one, the horses began to load. Jose nudged Funny Cide toward the starting gate, and the noise ebbed. Now it seemed to Jose that the park had become almost eerily silent.

Robin returned to the paddock and looked around for Barclay, but she couldn't find him in the crush of people. She climbed up to the box that was reserved for them, but Barclay wasn't there, either. She was in an upper deck, high above the finish line, and to get down to the track again, she would have to fight the enormous crowds. Robin thought, *This isn't good. I don't like being up here, if I can't get down.*

The starting bell sounded. Now the Belmont crowd exploded in an even greater roar as the horses broke from the gate. Immediately, Robin could tell that Funny Cide was struggling. She watched him as he slogged through the slippery mud and she knew they weren't going to win the race.

Funny Cide, Empire Maker, and Scrimshaw ran three abreast until they reached the first turn—and then the roar grew when Funny Cide took the lead. Empire Maker eased back, and sat a length behind.

Barclay watched from another seat in the clubhouse, rueful. When the horses were just a few strides around the turn, he already knew what was going to happen. Funny Cide should have been running from behind and saving his energy. Instead, the horse was surging forward and fighting his jockey, just as he had fought Robin all week.

Aboard Empire Maker, Jerry Bailey could see that Funny Cide was "rank," meaning too eager to run. A horse that was rank usually wound up exhausted. "He was pulling on Jose, and my horse was really relaxed," Bailey observed later. "That's the key to a mile-and-a-half race. If a horse pulls on you the whole way, he'll have nothing left when he turns for home."

The field was moving at a moderate pace, but Funny Cide was wearing himself out. He ran the first half-mile in 48.70 seconds, and six furlongs in 1:13.51. Jose continued to try vainly to hold the horse back. With a half-mile still to run, the jockey sawed at the reins.

Now Empire Maker came up alongside them.

Jose finally asked Funny to run, but the horse didn't have anything left. It was over at the quarter pole. Between the slop, and the battle of wills, and the long Triple Crown season, Funny Cide was too weary.

Empire Maker passed him. Now so did Ten Most Wanted.

"Come on, Funny Cide!" Pete Phillips hollered, hopelessly.

By the last five-eighths of a mile, Jose knew they were in trouble. Funny Cide's hooves seemed to slip in the mud each time Jose urged him to run. The race was lost.

Empire Maker, the bay colt, reached the finish line a winner by less than a length over Ten Most Wanted. Frankel's horse had finally lived up to his breeding and his promise, and he had given Frankel his first victory in a Triple Crown race in a dozen attempts.

Funny crossed the wire, beaten by five and a quarter lengths. Still, he gamely finished in third place. His frantic gallop slowed. His hoofprints filled up with muddy brown water. The race had upheld its reputation as the most unpredictable and grueling of the three events.

In the clubhouse, Pete Phillips put his head in his hands and cried.

As Jose turned the horse and walked him back toward the clubhouse, he felt a moment's small, mean wish that Empire Maker had lost. But no sooner had he thought that than another thought chased it away. *God forgive me.* The best horse had won, and Jose didn't ever want to wish otherwise—the best horse should always win.

And then something strange happened. Jose heard a confusing

mass of sounds as he walked the horse. An ovation was spreading around the oval park. At first, Jose assumed it was for Empire Maker, but he couldn't see the winner. *We came so far, to get so close,* he thought. Then he realized that the applause was for Funny Cide. A hundred thousand people were on their feet. They screamed, and clapped, and pounded the balustrades for Funny Cide. Jose was stunned—the horse had lost the race. Jose had never experienced such a thing.

Robin struggled through the crowds and finally reached the ground level. She made her way to the track. In the clubhouse hallway, she could hear the continuous applause from the spectators, and she, too, thought it must be Empire Maker coming back to the winner's circle. She burst outside, and saw that it was Funny Cide that the New Yorkers were applauding. As Robin took the horse by the shank and led him from the track, the ovation continued, a deep, prolonged noise of affection.

Jose dismounted. Now Barclay appeared alongside them, ironfaced. "What happened?" he asked.

"He didn't handle the track."

Jose was surrounded by reporters and cameras. "He ran a good race, he dug, he tried," Jose said to a TV announcer, breathlessly. Asked if he could have done anything different, Jose said, "I'd have kept away Mother Nature."

In the box seats, the Sackatoga Stable owners struggled to accept what had just happened. Jack tried to be philosophical: in racing, they were supposed to lose more than they won. They had beaten the odds and won more than anyone could've dreamed. Funny Cide had made them feel like winners, not just for a day or two but for life.

J. P. Constance's only regret was that he had planned to surprise Karen with a gift. "I was going to buy my wife a kitchen," he said.

Dave Mahan felt awful. He strode through the emptying clubhouse, the hallways dirty as sin, looking for the owners' hospitality suite. When he finally walked into the suite, a party of his family and friends were there, sixty or seventy people cheering and clapping him on the back, screaming, "Funny Cide, Funny Cide!" and high-fiving him.

"I'm a caterer," Dave said. "I stuff chickens for a living. But right now I'm still the owner of a Kentucky Derby and Preakness winner, and they can never take that away from me."

Night came, and real darkness settled over what had been day-long semi-darkness. Brown water puddled in the dirt track, and in the gravel around the barns, and in the potholes of Man o' War Avenue, the road that ran past Barn Six. In the hour since Funny had crossed the wire, Robin and Barclay hadn't had time to absorb the defeat. There was too much to do; they had to talk to the press, and to the owners, and to Jose, and to their families, who had come to town for the race. First and foremost, they had to get the horse back to his barn and see that he was all right.

Reporters grilled Barclay on what had gone wrong. "I don't know what happened. He won't talk to me," Barclay said. "Maybe he didn't like the mud, or it wasn't the right race." One writer asked him if he was disappointed. "I've had bigger disappointments," Barclay said, honestly. "But this was a five-million-dollar disappointment."

Elsewhere, Bobby Frankel was celebrating his first victory in a Triple Crown race. "I had confidence in my horse all week," he said. But he also admitted, "I was a little worried. I thought maybe Destiny wanted that horse to win."

As the grooms washed Funny down, Robin herself combed the water from his neck. "All right, boy," she said, stroking him. "All right." She didn't want him to sense any disappointment in her voice, because she knew that he would feel it. She stayed with him for a few minutes, until she made sure that his ears were up. He was beaten, she noted, but not defeated.

Then she went into the office, and sat down, and began to sob. She wasn't crying for herself. She cried because the horse had tried so hard to do what he simply couldn't do.

Barclay came into the barn office and sat down heavily in his chair. "I feel terrible," he confessed to Robin. He felt terrible for the people who had been behind them, and who had cheered the horse so fervently. He had wanted to please them all. He wanted to please the world.

It continued to rain. The trainers talked about how hard the horse had tried. They couldn't be disappointed in him. He had gotten to all three Triple Crown races, and he'd won two of them and finished third in another. He had done that much—and that was a lot. Empire Maker had been bred to be a champion, and he might become one of the greatest sires. But Funny had beaten him, and beaten him in the biggest race in the world.

Jose Santos and his family made their way back to their apartment at the Garden City Hotel. Jose Junior was heartbroken. He took out his betting ticket, tore it into tiny pieces, and began to cry. Jose put his arm around his son. "Don't worry," he said. "There are going to be other opportunities."

That night, the Sackatoga owners returned to the Sheraton, where they had reserved a private room and brought down their favorite band from Saratoga (Blue Hand Luke) for a huge Triple Crown celebration. Together, they decided to hold the party anyway. They refused to dwell on a single lost race—they preferred instead to celebrate their unexpected success. As the band got under way and the owners danced and drank and toasted one another, a local reporter wandered into the room and was surprised to find them in a jubilant mood. "For a minute, I thought I'd wandered into a victory party," he said.

The next morning, Barclay and Robin returned to the barn. It was another day of chores, and the routine was reassuring. The animals were exercised, and they got their baths. They stood steaming in the gravel pit, water and soap streaming from them, and then they returned to their stalls and waited patiently for Barclay to bring them their feed buckets.

Just because you lost the Triple Crown and five million dollars didn't mean the horses stopped eating.

9.

Afterward

So he was a New York–bred. What does that mean? Eleanor
Roosevelt was a New York–bred.

—NICK ZITO

Funny Cide was a joyous acci-
dent. He was also the result of the crossing of various paths from
Ocala to Saratoga, of fortunate introductions, acquaintanceships,
handshakes, and word of mouth. But mainly, he was proof that a
cheap damn horse could run with pure class.

What makes a great horse? As Funny Cide demonstrated, it's a
question of more than just breeding, of a few strands of inherited
equine nucleotides—and it's a good thing, because otherwise,
thoroughbred racing would be a pretty boring sport. A champion
racehorse remains one of nature's fine precision instruments, and
an eternal mystery.

It will be left to the turf writers and the handicappers to determine Funny Cide's exact place in racing history, but he will be remembered as one of the most surprising horses of the half-century, and one of the most beloved. Certainly, he was adored by his owners and handlers, who came to regard him in almost anthropomorphic terms, as a creature of gentle amiability and yet deep and inexplicable competitive spirit.

Once, someone asked Barclay if he thought Funny was a great horse. "He's been great to me," Barclay said.

Other animals might be faster, but few showed the will and heart to sustain such speed in the interest of winning a contest. Arguably, no other animal that season raced as hard and as passionately as Funny Cide. And he had been willing to do it for a peppermint, or a stroke on the face, to please his handlers.

Everyone could relate to Funny Cide. Who hasn't felt like a cheap horse running in superior company at some point in their lives? Maybe that was why he so captivated audiences. The Belmont telecast on NBC was not just the highest-rated sports show of the week; it was the highest-rated show of any kind. Weddings stopped. At the Smith and Wollensky steak house in Manhattan, the dishwashers and busboys came out of the kitchen to watch the race.

There was that term Dave Mahan used in betting, "stepping out." It meant to leave caution behind, to see an opportunity for a smart wager and to stake something on it. With Funny Cide, they had all stepped out. Perhaps that was why they were such popular winners, why even non-race fans reacted so strongly to Funny Cide's victories. Like the horse, they were ordinary—hardworking people who had gone to work every day for thirty years, done their jobs, and raised their kids. Not too many people had ridden in a limousine, but everyone had ridden on a school bus. They were what gambling was supposed to be all about: little guys trying to get lucky.

People took immense satisfaction in what Funny Cide had achieved both on and off the track. The *Washington Post* remarked, "Since the Belmont Stakes, the entire industry has been infused with optimism. It senses that horse-racing is on the upswing and that it must capitalize on this opportunity. Even though Funny Cide missed sweeping the Triple Crown, he may have helped accomplish something even more remarkable."

"Precious few owners win big races," *Sports Illustrated* noted. "Far fewer make people care."

Some of the things that happened after the Belmont:

No one got rich. The Sackets Harbor crew each got a check for $40,000, their cut of Funny Cide's winnings from his Triple Crown campaign. They all returned home to the village and resumed their workaday lives on Hounsfield Street. Bonnie and Gwen splurged on makeovers.

Funny Cide raced twice more in 2003, but didn't win. After the Belmont, Barclay gave Funny Cide a lengthy rest, believing that the Triple Crown campaign had taxed him badly. He was proved right when, in August, Funny Cide finished a tired third again in a race at Monmouth Park, the Haskell, and spiked a fever afterward. Funny Cide was supposed to run in the signal race of the Saratoga season, the Travers Stakes, but the day before the race, after the $5,000 entry fee had been paid, Barclay checked the horse's throat after his morning gallop, found the mucus was back, and scratched him. Then in October, off an eighty-three-day layoff, Funny Cide raced in the $4 million Breeders' Cup Classic at Santa Anita. It was his first race against older horses, and the racing community applauded him for competing in its showcase event, but the temperature at race time hovered around 100 degrees, he finished ninth, and after the race Barclay vowed never again to race Funny Cide in hot weather.

For the next few months, he nursed him carefully, and it paid off. On January 10, 2004, Funny Cide returned to the races as a four-year-old and won seven-furlong allowance race at Gulfstream Park by five lengths. He literally left the rest of the field in the dust. You couldn't wipe the grin off Jack Knowlton's face. Even Barclay smiled.

And the awards came:

In October, Sackatoga Stable was honored by the National Turf Writers Association at a dinner in Pasadena, California, with the Mr. Fitz Award, exemplifying the spirit of racing. Previous winners included Allen Jerkins, Pat Day, and Laffit Pincay, Jr.

In January, it was the Big Sport of Turfdom Award from the Turf Publicists of America. Sackatoga Stable won for extraordinary achievements in thoroughbred racing coupled with a positive relationship with the media and cooperation with those who sought to promote the sport. Previous winners included some of the biggest owners, trainers, and jockeys in horse racing.

And then on January 26, 2004, came the biggest one of all. Funny Cide accomplished another upset: He revenged himself on Empire Maker by beating him out for the Eclipse Award as the nation's best three-year-old male in 2003, given by the National Thoroughbred Racing Association, the *Daily Racing Form,* and the National Turf Writers Association. Barclay Tagg wasn't surprised. "He showed up all year, stayed nice and sound, and had a charismatic value even I couldn't comprehend." Even Bobby Frankel conceded that Funny Cide was a deserving winner. "In my mind and in my heart, I knew he'd win it," Frankel said. "I think he deserved it. You can have only one winner."

Off the track:

Funny Cide Beer came out. The Sackets guys liked to joke that if the horse had won the Triple Crown, there would have been Funny Cide Champagne. But beer was good enough for them. It was a quality beer, too—as long as you didn't try to drink it in the morning.

The first time J.P. tried it, he said, "It would probably taste better if I hadn't just brushed my teeth."

Jose Santos finally convinced his son, Jose Junior, to recover from the boy's agonizing disappointment over the Triple Crown. Jose had been riding for twenty-seven years, and he'd had plenty of disappointments in his life, but Funny Cide was not one of them, he told the boy. "That horse gave me a beautiful feeling," he said.

Jose Junior began showing signs of wanting to become a jockey. Rita said, "I spent half my life watching my father, and then my brother, and my husband, and now I know, somewhere along the way, I'll be watching my son."

That summer after the Belmont, the boy turned nine. When Jose asked him what he wanted for his birthday, he announced, "I want to go to Sackets Harbor." Jose and Rita were baffled. It turned out that the Sackatoga owners had regaled the boy with tales of the village, describing the vast silvery lake and its shadowy shores, until he yearned to see it. Jose and Rita called J.P. and reported that their son wanted to come for his birthday.

Harold and Stephanie Cring threw a Hounsfield Street surprise party for Jose Junior on the back lawn, with all of the Sackets owners in attendance. Mark Phillips provided the boat, and the family spent part of the day on the lake, fishing. Jose Junior caught his first fish, a perch. Mark had the fish mounted and sent to Jose Junior as a birthday present.

Tony Everard continued to train horses at New Episode in his gentle, whimsical way. Yearlings wandered the pastures with egrets, while in the pens, Tony worked with the latest problem cases by jumping them. Tony believed he could usually straighten out a horse, no matter how much of a desperado, by jumping him. When horses jumped over barricades and fences for two or three weeks, they forgot all their shenanigans and were happy. "Takes their mind off their bad habits," he said.

When Tony wasn't training, he browsed through the pasture full of yearlings, looking for the next good runner. He and Liz were often asked if they regretted having sold Funny Cide to the Sackatoga Stable.

"Think I sell him if I know he can win the Derby?" Everard said. "I'd be daft."

"Who knows George Bush is going to be president when he's in the second grade?" Liz said.

Funny Cide's sire, Distorted Humor, once so poorly regarded by breeders, became the leading freshman sire of the season. Not only was he was represented by Funny Cide, but also by WinStar's Grade 1 stakes winner, Awesome Humor; a Grade 2 winner, Humorous Lady; and an Australian-bred stakes winner, Rinky Dink. The odd stranger, indeed.

Later that June, Dave Mahan and Jack Knowlton, accompanied by their wives, went back to Churchill Downs to receive the Kentucky Derby trophy. The track officials provided their transportation from the backstretch to the winner's circle for the ceremony: a yellow school bus. They circled the track in the bus, grinning like fools. They also climbed to the top of the two stepladders and fastened a plaque proclaiming Funny Cide the 2003 Derby winner alongside those of all previous winners.

B arclay and Robin, after weeks of living out of their suitcases, finally found a home. They received a 10 percent commission on Funny Cide's winnings, and while it still wasn't enough for Barclay to retire on, it was a huge windfall for them. One afternoon, they sat around the barn and discussed what to buy.

"Maybe we should buy a horse," Robin said.

But Barclay said, "We train horses. We're around them every day. We need to buy something different."

"What's better than a horse?"

"Think about it," he said. "It sounds great. It gets you all excited. But think of all the things that can go wrong. Bucked shins, bowed tendons. We don't need to buy a horse."

"Then what?" Robin said.

"We should buy a house."

And that's what they did. They found what they were looking for in Floral Park, just a mile from Belmont Park, a small but beautiful brick-and-clapboard Victorian with gleaming wood floors and a back garden. What made it perfect was that it already had a built-in glass case in the living room. Funny Cide's trophies were the first things they unpacked. They put them in the case before they even got curtains up.

B arclay continued to do everything the hard way, because he didn't know how to do anything the easy way. He didn't *trust* the easy way. The only way he knew was good horsemanship.

The Sackatoga owners continued to stand firmly behind Barclay. They were convinced that had he been in any other hands, the horse would have remained at the back of the barn and never won the Derby or the Preakness. It took small, conscientious handlers like Barclay and Robin to give Funny Cide the attention he needed, to nurse him through bucked shins and his curious respiratory condition, to personally check his feet and tendons and breathing each morning and evening.

Jack, Dave, Gus, and the rest of the Sackatoga Stable owners enjoyed the gorgeous summer racing season in Saratoga as much as ever, only this time with box seats and coveted party invitations. With some of Funny Cide's winnings, in March they had bought a new horse from Tony Everard, a beautiful two-year-old colt they named Saratoga Episode, who produced Sakatoga Stable's first win at Saratoga in August. They kept searching hopefully for another winner—even though they all knew that they had experienced the biggest long shot of their racing lives by winning the Kentucky Derby with Funny Cide.

It was Dave Mahan who summed up just how they all felt about Funny Cide. When Dave and Nadine finally began the long drive from New York back to Connecticut after the Belmont, he decided to use the downtime in the car to return some phone calls from the press. All of the questions were the same: "How do you feel," and, "How has this changed you?"

"Well, it hasn't," Dave answered.

In the car seat next to him, Nadine shot him a weird look. After a while, Dave hung up and said, "What?"

"You're wrong," she said.

"What are you talking about?"

"You're saying you haven't changed," she said. "But you've changed a lot."

Dave thought, *Uh-oh, here it comes.* Had he turned into a jerk, and gotten a swollen head? Was he not paying enough attention to his wife?

"How have I changed?"

"You're a whole lot happier than you used to be."

Dave thought about that. "You're right," he said. "I have changed. I am happier. I think I'm going to be happier for the rest of my life."

They would always have that moment on May 3, 2003, when their horse crossed the wire in the Kentucky Derby, a moment of disbelief and exultation as Funny Cide streaked past the twin spires and Jose Santos punched a fist in the air, and Barclay Tagg and Robin Smullen clutched at each other in the clubhouse.

In that moment, a thought occurred to Jackson Knowlton, ex–high school athlete extraordinaire, businessman and tireless problem-solver, responsible citizen, but also lover of cocktails, laughter, and racing, and chance-taker on the sly.

Look at this, Jack thought. *Doesn't this beat money?*

Acknowledgments

The authors would first and foremost like to thank Esther Newberg of ICM for her belief in this story, and for persuading others to believe, too. Also, we are indebted to Neil Nyren of Putnam, who was a caring and careful editor. Stuart Calderwood's thoroughness and extra time saved the manuscript from many errors. The people at the New York Racing Association and the National Thoroughbred Racing Association were unfailingly helpful and enthusiastic, as were countless other friends around the sport, such as Allen Jerkens, who offered their time and suggestions with no reward other than the sheer fun of the thing.